The New-York Times.

VOL. XXI....NO. 6357. NEW-YORK, TUESDAY, OCTOBER 10, 1871. PRICE FOUR CENTS.

A CITY IN RUINS.

The Terrible Devastation of Chicago.

Three Square Miles in the Heart of the City Burned

Twelve Thousand Buildings Destroyed—Loss $50,000,000

Every Public Building, Hotel, Bank and Newspaper Swept.

Appeals to Other Cities and a Noble Response.

Frightful Details of the Disaster from Our Own Reporters.

The Devastation of Chicago—Map of the Burned District as Far as Heard From.

THE THIEVES CONVICTED

Complete Exposition of the Ring Accounts.

Official Report of the Joint Com-

"All the News That's Fit to Print."

The New York Times.

VOL. L...NO. 15,926. NEW YORK, WEDNESDAY, JANUARY 23, 1901.—SIXTEEN PAGES. ONE CENT

THE WEATHER. Fair; wind northeasterly, becoming southerly.

QUEEN VICTORIA DEAD AT OSBORNE

Passed Away Quietly at 6:30 o'Clock Last Evening.

SCENE AT THE BEDSIDE

QUEEN BADE THEM FAREWELL

AMERICAN TRIBUTES TO QUEEN VICTORIA

President McKinley Cables Condolences to the New King.

WASHINGTON FLAGS LOWERED

...imes.

PRICE FOUR CENTS

EUROPEAN NEWS.

The Insult to Our Cruisers by Portugal.

The American Minister at Lisbon Demands Satisfaction.

Dismissal of the Commander of Fort Belan Requested.

Further Advance in Five-Twenties.

FINANCIAL AND COMMERCIAL.

"All the News That's Fit to Print."

The New York Times.

THE WEATHER.

VOL. LVIII...NO. 18,654. NEW YORK, TUESDAY, SEPTEMBER 7, 1909.—EIGHTEEN PAGES. ONE CENT

GAYNOR, UNPLEDGED, CONSENTS TO RUN

HARRIMAN SUFFERS RELAPSE.

LONDON APPLAUDS PEARY'S EXPLOIT

Instant Acceptance of His Report a Contrast to Skepticism Toward Dr. Cook.

HAD AWAITED HIS VERDICT

In order not to miss The New York Times of to-morrow, in which will be printed exclusively Lieut. Peary's own story of his discovery of the North Pole, order a copy from your newsdealer early to-day.

COOK GLAD PEARY REACHED THE POLE

Unmoved When, Wreathed with Flowers at Banquet, He Hears the News.

HOPE NOW FOR OTHERS

PEARY DISCOVERS THE NORTH POLE AFTER EIGHT TRIALS IN 23 YEARS

Notifies The New York Times That He Reached It on April 6, 1909.

HE WIRES FROM LABRADOR

Returning on the Roosevelt, Which He Reports to Bridgman is Safe.

IS NEARING NEWFOUNDLAND

McMILLAN SENDS WORD

SEVEN VAIN EXPEDITIONS

PEARY REPORTS TO THE TIMES

ANNOUNCES HIS DISCOVERY OF THE POLE AND WILL SEND A FULL AND EXCLUSIVE ACCOUNT TO-DAY.

Indian Harbor, Labrador, via Cape Ray, N.F., Sept. 6.

The New York Times, New York:

I have the pole, April sixth. Expect arrive Chateau Bay September seventh. Secure control wire for me there and arrange expedite transmission big story.

PEARY.

PEARY'S MESSAGE TO HIS WIFE.

CONFIRMED BY FELLOW-VOYAGERS.

The New York Times.

THE WEATHER.

NEW YORK, FRIDAY, OCTOBER 18, 1907.—EIGHTEEN PAGES. ONE CENT

AMERICAN HOTEL FOR BERLIN.

CONRIED AND BOYD AT ODDS IN STOCKS

PROFIT FIGURES WIDE APART

FIRST WIRELESS PRESS MESSAGE ACROSS THE ATLANTIC

Signalizing the Opening of the Marconi Service to the Public, and Conveying a Message of Congratulation from Privy Councillor Baron Avebury, Formerly Sir John Lubbock.

THE WESTERN UNION TELEGRAPH COMPANY.

London Via Marconi Wireless Glace Bay N S Oct 17th, Times, New York.

This message marks opening transatlantic wireless handed Marconi company for transmission Ireland Breton limited 50 words only send one many messages received Times signalizes event quite trust introduction wireless more closely unite people states Great Britain who seem form one Nation though under two governments and whose interests are really identical.

AVEBURY.

WIRELESS JOINS TWO WORLDS

Marconi Transatlantic Service Opened with a Dispatch to The New York Times.

MESSAGES FROM EMINENT MEN

Prime Minister Clemenceau, the Duke of Argyll, Lord Avebury and Others Send Greetings.

10,000 WORDS THE FIRST DAY

Marconi in Personal Supervision at Glace Bay and Greatly Pleased with the Results.

SIR HIRAM MAXIM'S TRIBUTE

MARCONI CONGRATULATES THE NEW YORK TIMES

FROM THE PRIME MINISTER OF FRANCE.

MISS VANDERBILT MUST TAKE CHANCES

H. P. WHITNEY ARRESTED?

DEUTSCHLAND STUCK CLOSE TO HER PIER

ROCKEFELLER TOO SAVING.

...SLAIN ...YOUTH ...COUNTRY

"All the News That's Fit to Print."

The New York Times.

EXTRA 5:30 A. M.

VOL. LXIV...NO. 20,923. NEW YORK, SATURDAY, MAY 8, 1915.—TWENTY-FOUR PAGES. ONE CENT

LUSITANIA SUNK BY A SUBMARINE, PROBABLY 1,260 DEAD; TWICE TORPEDOED OFF IRISH COAST; SINKS IN 15 MINUTES; CAPT. TURNER SAVED, FROHMAN AND VANDERBILT MISSING; WASHINGTON BELIEVES THAT A GRAVE CRISIS IS AT HAND

SHOCKS THE PRESIDENT

Washington Deeply Stirred by the Loss of American Lives.

BULLETINS AT WHITE HOUSE

HINTS OF CONGRESS CALL

CAPITAL FULL OF RUMORS

SOME DEAD TAKEN ASHORE

Several Hundred Survivors at Queenstown and Kinsale.

STEWARD TELLS OF DISASTER

One Torpedo Crashes Into the Doomed Liner's Bow, Another Into the Engine Room.

SHIP LISTS OVER TO PORT

Makes It Impossible to Lower Many Boats, So Hundreds Must Have Gone Down.

ATTACKED IN BROAD DAY

Only 650 Were Saved, Few Cabin Passengers

"All the News That's Fit to Print."

The New York Times.

THE WEATHER

VOL. LXVIII...NO. 22,296. NEW YORK, MONDAY, NOVEMBER 11, 1918. TWENTY-FOUR PAGES. TWO CENTS

ARMISTICE SIGNED, END OF THE WAR! BERLIN SEIZED BY REVOLUTIONISTS; NEW CHANCELLOR BEGS FOR ORDER; OUSTED KAISER FLEES TO HOLLAND

SON FLEES WITH EX-KAISER

Hindenburg Also Believed to be Among Those in His Party

Kaiser Fought Hindenburg's Call for Abdication; Failed to Get Army's Support in Keeping Throne

BERLIN TROOPS JOIN REVOLT

Reds Shell Building in Which Officers Vainly

Socialist Chancellor Appeals to All Germans To Help Him Save Fatherland from Anarchy

WAR ENDS AT 6 O'CLOCK THIS MORNING

MUST EXERT ALL OUR POWER

To Bring a "Government That Is Running Amuck to Terms."

WANTS LIBERAL CREDITS

A TUMULTUOUS GREETING

HISTORY
OF THE WORLD
For Young Readers

CONSULTANTS:

Louis V. Nannini, Ed.D.
Supervising Principal
Middle Island Central District
Middle Island, New York

Richard Dawe, M.A.
Chairman, History Department
Setauket Schools
East Setauket, New York

John J. Forester, Ph.D.
Lecturer in Education
New York University

Margot L. Wolf
Design and Production

HISTORY OF THE WORLD

For Young Readers

Written by Paul J. Gelinas, M.A., M.Sc., Ed.D.,
Supervising Principal, Union Free Schools, District 2,
Suffolk County, Long Island, New York

Assisted by Robert Scharff, M.A.

GROSSET & DUNLAP • Publishers • NEW YORK

Foreword

The story this book tells is a strange and thrilling story. It is also a true story. And more than that, it is "the story of stories"—*Every other story that has ever been told is a part of this one.* For this is the story of man on his planet.

It starts in the danger-haunted forests and sun-scorched plains where naked, grunting men fought for life with their bare hands. It continues with man's first great discoveries—the spoken word, the stone tool, fire. These lifted man above the animals. The story continues with inventions—the refining of metal, the written word, the planting of crops, the wheel. These made men civilized. Invention follows invention—men become more and more civilized.

As you read the story of man the inventor, you will notice a curious fact: *Inventions come faster and faster.* It took Stone Age men hundreds of thousands of years to think of a few little improvements in their stone tools. Yet in the last twenty-five years, men have invented atomic-energy reactors, space ships, medicines of almost miraculous power, microscopes that let men see the very building-blocks of their own living flesh, television circuits which send colored pictures thousands of miles in a few thousandths of a second . . . .

Why is this? Why does our knowledge grow so fast now, when only a thousand years ago it grew so slowly? Have our brains become bigger and more powerful? No, the answer is something entirely different: *Knowledge helps us get more knowledge.* By knowing what men have done in the past, and how they did it, we can think more deeply and clearly and cleverly. What has happened is that men have learned more and more about men of the past; men have written down their ideas and deeds for men of the future.

In other words, men have learned to think about history. Man the historian has come to the aid of man the inventor. That is why this book and the story it tells are so very important.

Donald Barr, Headmaster
The Dalton School, New York, N.Y.

Library of Congress Catalog Card Number: 65-20032

Contents

PICTURE CREDITS

Key to picture position: t—top; c—center; b—bottom; l—left; r—right. Combinations: br—bottom right, etc.

Acropolis Museum, Athens: 130 bl.
American Museum of Natural History: 12, 13, 22-23 t, 25, 27, 51, 282, 284 tl.
American President Line: 255, 273 r.
American Telephone & Telegraph Co.: 354.
Association of American Railroads: 348, 349.
Austrian Consulate: 203, 227.
Bettmann Archives: 169 l, 195, 232, 323 b, 324, 325 t, 358.
Boston Museum of Fine Arts: 131 r.
British Information Service: 251 r, 357.
BOAC: 39 t, 250.
Brown Brothers: 76, 213, 319.
Rafaello Busoni: 37, 39 r, 68, 107, 111, 129, 156 l, 164-65 t, 186, 188 tl, 204, 205, 206 b, 291, 297 r, 298 l, 328, 329, 342, 343, 356.
Curtiss-Wright Corp.: 352.
Royal Danish Ministry for Foreign Affairs, Press Dept.: 281.
Robert Doremus: 26 r, 32, 33, 59, 94, 95, 100, 106, 110, 114, 115, 124-25, 127, 128, 134, 149, 151, 152, 160-61, 178, 179, 189, 198, 215, 216, 233, 235, 241, 265 r, 267 br, 275 t, 277, 280, 309, 317, 318, 341 tr, 344-45, 366, 367, 368 l, 369, 370.
Florida State News Bureau: 295.
Ford Motor Co.: 350 cl, 351 cr.
French Government Tourist Office: 181 t, 224.
Ewing Galloway: 56, 132, 283.
General Motors: 350 bl, 351 br.
German Tourist Information Office: 181 r, 183 r, 218, 221, 225, 226.
Grace Line: 284 cl, 285 r.
Greece, Royal Consulate and National Tourist Organization: 105, 112 l, 113 r, 116, 117, 118 tr, 130 br, 131 t.
John Hull: 66-67, 72, 73, 84, 85, 87, 89, 97 r, 148, 160 1, 168 1, 180, 238, 239.
Indian Government Tourist Office: 254, 255, 256 l, 257.
International Harvester Co.: 337.
Israeli Office of Information: 91.
Italian Line: 272, 273 t.
Italian State Tourist Office: 163, 168 t, 219, 229.
Jamestown, Virginia, C. of C.: 296, 297 t, 314.
Jamestown Foundation: 302, 303, 304.
Jewish Theological Seminary of America: 90.
Matthew Kalmenoff: 18, 20, 22 l.
Library of Congress: 308, 316, 325 r, 326, 354, 362, 363, 364.
C. T. Loo: 263 tl.
Massachusetts Dept. of Commerce: 298 t, 299, 323 r, 324.
Harry H. McChesney: 28, 54, 78, 97 t, 102, 138, 175, 176, 202, 212, 222, 248, 258, 265 bl, 270, 292.
Metropolitan Museum of Art: 30, 34, 35, 36, 38, 41, 42, 43, 44, 45, 46, 47, 74, 112 b, 113 t, 118 l, 119, 120, 121, 135, 141, 142, 143, 167 t, 171, 182 t, 183 b, 207, 208, 209, 210, 211, 220, 231, 261 r, 262, 263 tr, 263 r, 300, 301 r, 320.
Mexican Government Tourist Office: 283 r, 289 l, 290.
National Aeronautics and Space Administration: 381.
National Park Service: 313.
New Mexico State Tourist Bureau: 286 tl, 287.
New York Public Library Picture Collection: 40, 140 t, 153, 167 r, 169 r, 174 l, 188 bl, 190, 197, 206 l, 228, 230, 246 b, 268, 275 r, 298, 321, 368 t.
Pan-American World Airways: 166, 174 t, 282, 284 b, 285 t.
Pepperell Mfg. Co.: 339 r.
Plymouth Plantation: 312.
Santa Fe Railway: 286 b.
Smithsonian Institution: 301 b, 339 t, 341 cr.
Spanish National Tourist Office: 217.
Standard Oil Co. of N. J.: 81, 260, 261 t, 264.
Studebaker Corporation: 351 tr.
Darrell Sweet: 194, 267 tr, 268, 274, 278, 279.
Swiss National Tourist Office: 191.
TWA: 31, 53, 145, 156 t, 157, 165 r, 187.
United Nations: 255 t, 256 t, 376.
U. S. Army Signal Corps: 375, 377.
U. S. Navy: 374.
University Museum of Chicago, Oriental Institute: 57 tr, 61, 71, 75, 99.
University Museum of Philadelphia: 62, 64, 65.
Virginia State C. of C.: 315.
Leonard Vosburgh: 14, 15, 16, 17, 19, 21, 25, 49, 57 b, 63, 236, 237, 243, 244, 245, 246 r, 297, 305, 341 br, 350 tl, 359.
Western Union Telegraph Co.: 353.
Wide World: 373, 378.
Margot L. Wolf: 356.

THE YOUNG EARTH AND EARLY MAN

5 billion years ago Formation of the Earth.

600 million years ago Appearance of Life (Age of Hidden Life).

210 million years ago Beginning of Age of Reptiles.

60 million years ago Appearance of Mammals.

1 million years ago Beginning of Glacial Age (First Glacier).

OLD STONE AGE

about 500,000 years ago Java Man, Peking Man. (Second Glacier)

Third Glacier

about 120,000 years ago Neanderthal Man.

Fourth Glacier

about 75,000 years ago Cro-Magnon Man.

about 10,000 years ago Post-Glacial Age.

NEW STONE AGE

about 7,000 years ago

BRONZE AGE

about 3,700 years ago Egyptian-Mesopotamian, Cretan-Greek Civilizations.

A Stone's Throw in Time

HISTORY is often called a journey into the past. Generally, if we decide to make a long trip, we seek the advice of a travel agency. Our travel agent helps plan the journey and makes our reservations on trains, ships, and airplanes, as well as at hotels. But the travel agent cannot help when we wish to travel backward in time to the days of our earliest ancestors. There are no trains, ships, airplanes, or even magic carpets, to take us into the past. We have only our imaginations and books to carry us back into history.

Let us put our imaginations to work. Suppose that we have been lost for many days in a great forest—hundreds of miles from the nearest town. We have no supplies. What do we need to keep alive? Food and water? Yes, first and fore-

Over one hundred million years ago, long before man appeared on earth, giant sauropods roamed the forests and marshes. This was the "Age of Reptiles," and the brontosauruses shown above were important representatives of the ancestors of our reptiles of today.

most. Shelter? Yes, someplace where we will be dry and warm, yet protected from the broiling sun, rain, snow, icy winds, storms, blizzards, and bad weather. Certainly, we must have food, drink, and shelter to go on living.

If there are no fruits, berries, nuts, or vegetables growing in the forest, we may have to hunt wild animals. But we cannot hunt without weapons. And to build a roof over our heads, a shelter, or a hut, we also need tools. In order to stay alive, we should have weapons and tools, as well as food, drink, and shelter.

But we are lost in a forest. We are without supplies, and there are no stores where we can buy anything. There are only grass, bushes, trees, hills, streams, and wild animals. What will we do? *How* will we stay alive?

What did the earliest peoples on this earth do? Let us use our imaginations to travel back hundreds of thousands of years ago to find out.

THE CAVE DWELLERS

Life was hard and dangerous for early men. They were often at the mercy of wild animals. And they knew little about the world around them.

As they roamed through the woods and fields in search of food, they found berries, roots, nuts, seeds, and twigs. With the help of sticks and stones, they killed small animals and birds. Sometimes they were lucky enough to find wild honey in the hollow of a tree and perhaps a few eggs in the deserted nest of a bird.

Because this daily search for food kept them always on the move, our ancestors had no permanent homes. To be safe from wild animals, they often slept in trees, or sought shelter inside a cave, or under a rocky ledge. They also built temporary shelters of branches and leaves when a cave or ledge could not be found.

While man's first weapons were wooden clubs and stones, he soon learned that spears were also very useful. These were made of long, thin branches with sharp points. Later, he discovered that he could cut the points with sharp stones. Then he learned that certain stones, when chipped, had very sharp edges. Such a sharp-edged stone, which we now call a flint, made a fine tool for cutting or scraping. Still later, man found a way of attaching a handle to a sharp-

Neanderthal man, about 120,000 years ago.

Java man, about 500,000 years ago.

While the oldest types of man, the Java and Neanderthal, do not look like men of today, Cro-Magnon man was much more "modern" in his appearance. (Our pictures are reconstructions from the skulls and bones of early man.)

Cro-Magnon man, about 75,000 years ago.

edged stone. This made an ax, which could be used to cut down trees and clear a path through the woods and forests.

Then after many, many years, man found that he could shoot arrows with the aid of a wooden bow. Indeed, with bow and arrow, our early ancestors could hunt much more skillfully than those who used hand-thrown stones or spears as weapons. Because their tools and weapons were made of stones, this early period is known as the Stone Age, and its people are called Stone Age people.

No one knows exactly when the Stone Age began. However, it lasted hundreds of thousands of years. And even today, certain Stone Age customs still exist in some parts of

It was quite an achievement when man first dared to "steal fire from the gods" (caused perhaps by a volcano or lightning), but he had to keep the fire burning, since he did not know how to make it himself.

the world. For example, members of some Australian tribes still cling to ancient customs. They dress as their forefathers dressed. They live on berries, nuts, and wild honey. And they still make use of stone tools and weapons.

During most of the time that early man was learning to use stone weapons and tools, the northern half of the earth was covered with great sheets of ice, called glaciers. The earth was much colder then than it is now—even in the summer the weather was worse than in our coldest winters.

So it is not surprising that the most important discovery of Stone Age men was the use of fire. Scientists believe that men began to use fire to warm themselves and to cook their

Early men in front of their cave, making stone tools.

One of the first implements used by primitive man may have been the jawbone of an animal.

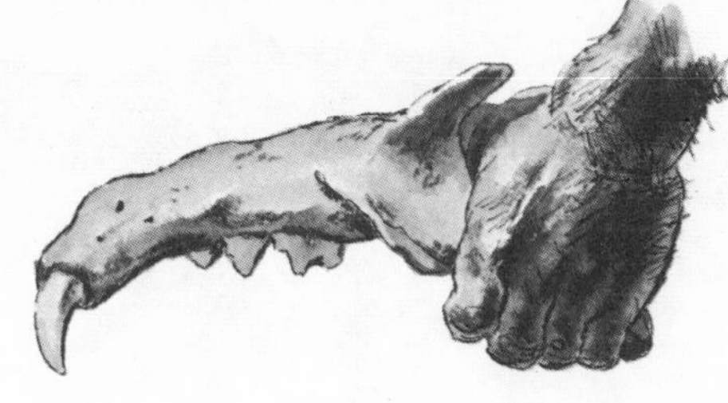

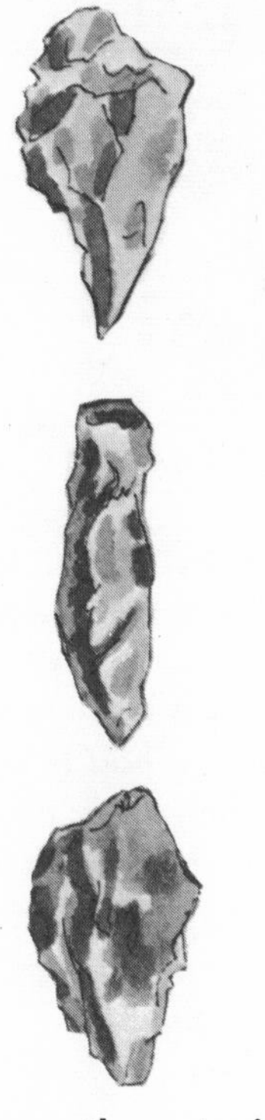

Above are three typical Stone Age tools.

food about half a million years ago. No doubt lightning started a forest fire and the Stone Age men learned they could keep warm by standing near the blaze. Then they carried some burning branches home and kept the fire going by throwing on more wood. Guards had to be posted all night to keep the fire burning, because no one knew how to start a fire again once it had gone out. Tens of thousands of years may have rolled by before some brighter-than-ordinary Stone Age man or woman learned how to start a fire—by rubbing two sticks together, or by using the sparks caused by striking certain kinds of stones together.

After the earth began to warm up about 25,000 or so years ago, the great glaciers began to melt. The people did not have to work so hard just to keep warm, so they found time to make better and better stone weapons and tools. They also learned new ways to use them.

A STONE AGE FAMILY

Before resuming our imaginary trip through the Stone Age, let us pause near the mouth of a large cave and look in. We see a man and woman sitting there. Their children,

The inside of a Cro-Magnon cave. Life was "far advanced" compared to that of Neanderthal man, but still very primitive.

two boys and a girl, are playing one of their favorite games —maybe a sort of checkers. The father is chipping pieces of stone from a large rock, and shaping them into instruments that will later be useful as knives and scrapers.

When he stands up, we notice that his heavy, powerful body is hairy. His head and neck are not held erect from his shoulders, but are bent forward. His forehead slants back. His eyebrows are thick and bushy. His nose is broad, with wide nostrils. His jaw is heavy, and his chin slants inward. His legs are bent outward below the knees, so that he does not walk quite upright. But this crookedness of limb helps him to move with more speed while searching for food for his family. Most of his time is spent in hunting food for them. And, of course, for himself.

The mother is equally busy. She scrapes a bearskin that will soon be made into warm clothing for her children. The two boys, helped by their little sister, are now piling up pieces of wood near the mouth of the cave—where a fire will burn all night to scare animals away.

As each is busy at his appointed task, there is little time for conversation. These people have not yet learned to talk easily among themselves. Finally, the mother finishes scraping the bearskin and starts to prepare a meal.

The boys, delighted, beckon to their sister. Together, they rush forward. Each grasps a long stick, upon which they will cook the chunks of meat the mother now offers them.

Then the father strikes his flint. Soon a fire is ready, and the long sticks are held over the flames. In this way, the meat is broiled or barbecued, Stone Age style. And when it is ready to eat, the parents and children lose no time in enjoying their delicious supper.

With the coming of darkness, the three children, very tired, are soon fast asleep in their corner of the cave. Mother and father, crouched before the fire, are ever on the alert for their most dangerous enemy—the huge bear who once inhabited this very cave. But thanks to the fire and to the shelter that protects them, they feel quite safe.

As we continue our journey through the Stone Age, thousands of years speed by. In appearance, the people begin to look slightly different. They stand taller, and their legs are straighter. Their heads are set more firmly on their shoulders. Their cheekbones are high, somewhat like those of the American Indian. And by about 8,000 years ago the Stone Age people came to look like today's men and women.

Their lives are neither as hard nor as dangerous as those of their ancestors. As the years have passed, they have

Scraping the skin of an animal to prepare clothing was a cumbersome job for the late Stone Age man.

Today we strike a match to make fire; primitive man had to strike two stones together, or use a firesaw or a firedrill, but making his own fire, instead of having to take it from one constantly burning, was a great step forward.

grown wiser, acquired knowledge, and learned to improve their crude tools and weapons. They have learned to communicate with each other; to build better shelters. They have found it easier to obtain food, and have even reached the stage of making certain rules, in order to keep peace among families, neighbors, and friends.

The Stone Age people of this particular era live closer together. Instead of wandering, they tend to remain in the same area. Often they have two homes. They live in caves during the wintertime. And in summer, they occupy huts located in clearings in the forest. We notice many changes in their way of life. For instance, they choose to live in huts because they are cooler in the summer. And, in cold weather, they return to their caves for warmth.

Also, instead of searching for food by himself, the head of the family now has several companions. Hunting has become more highly organized. At various times, groups of men and their families, especially the sons, get together in large groups to plan their hunting drives.

As we look in on such a gathering, a young man dashes into camp. Waving his arms excitedly, he reports that a herd of wild horses is grazing on the other side of the hill. Now, all the men and boys set to work. They spend hours

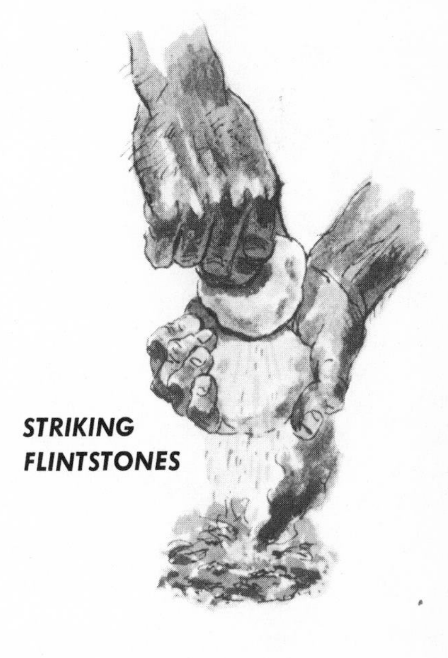

Fire was a powerful weapon against the wild animals who might have been previous "tenants" in the cave man's "house."

in preparation, meanwhile keeping a close watch on the herd of wild horses.

Finally they creep up on the grazing animals—each group of men having been given special tasks to perform. Even the direction of the wind is important; for these wild creatures must not smell danger, or be warned of the hunters' approach. At last, with a mighty roar and the beating of many clubs upon the ground, the hunters rush forward. The wild horses lurch and stampede; they cry out in terror, and hastily gallop away.

In spite of the fires, built especially to keep the herd in line, some horses manage to escape. But others are trapped, and cannot get away in time. The hunters let fly with their stone-tipped spears. Like a downpour of rain, the arrows fall upon the terrified animals. And now the hunters have meat for several meals; and skins for many articles of clothing.

But not all the men in the camp have taken part in the hunt. One in particular devotes much of his day to chipping flint, making spear points and carving tools, knives, and scrapers. His reputation for useful flints is well-known to all his neighbors. Others bring him their stones for chipping. In return for his labors, they give him food; and now they have promised to build a hut for him.

After man learned how to improve the grinding and polishing of flint, his tools became better. And there was a greater need for this stone, which actually is a very hard mineral. This valuable stone is extracted from the earth. And since certain men spent all their time digging for flint, we might describe their work as one of the world's first mining operations. Deer horns and pieces of bone were used as shovels. And like the early toolmaker, who was provided with food and lodging in exchange for his labors, these miners also received similar rewards.

Many of the Stone Age men were artists, craftsmen, architects, and engineers. They often made unusual designs on wood, or decorated the handles of their weapons with life-like figures. From bone, ivory, and soapstone, they carved small statues of the animals they hunted. But the best workmanship of all was seen in their cave paintings. On the walls, ceilings, and at the rear of their cave dwellings, these talented artists drew remarkable pictures of reindeer, horses, bulls, and other animals.

The cave artist was a most important man in the tribe. When he learned that a hunt was about to take place, he mixed four colors: red, white, yellow, and black. Then he lit a hollow-stone lamp filled with fat, and entered the cave he intended to decorate. On the wall, he would paint a reindeer, and a mammoth (one of the earliest ancestors of the elephant family). Then, he would draw a red arrow through the heart of each animal. These creatures were believed to be at the mercy of the hunters once their pictures appeared on the wall.

The painter may have been given food and lodging in payment for his work, just as the toolmakers and miners were rewarded for their labor. People were beginning to be paid for doing the sort of jobs for which they were best suited.

Drawings on the wall of a Cro-Magnon cave.

The digging stick was one of the first farm implements.

THE FIRST FARMS

Continuing our travels through the long-ago Stone Age, we also notice the next great forward step in man's progress. He became a farmer. Often, the people lived in areas where patches of corn, wild wheat, and barley grew. Early man had found that these grains were good to eat.

The women used flint-bladed knives to cut the stalks. Then, with the help of the children, they pounded the stalks with sticks until the kernels were separated. How these people discovered that grain seeds could be planted, we can only guess. Perhaps the farmers and their families just scattered them here and there, on the ground, near their camps, and hoped they would sprout.

To cultivate the plots of land where they wished to grow the grain, early Stone Age farmers generally stirred the ground with a digging stick. They also used a hoe made from either shell or stone. Later, someone thought of making a stone-tipped plow with which to turn over the soil.

When the people raised their own crops, they had to pay close attention to the seasons of the year, and to the length

This is a photograph of a replica of a Neolithic (New Stone Age) village about 2700 B.C.

of nights and days. Possibly they set up stones to mark the changing position of the sun. And as a result of perhaps such practices, and their study of the sun's movements, they found a way to make a calendar.

Herds of wild sheep, hogs, goats, and horses also enjoyed wheat and barley. Thus they were attracted to these patches of cultivated grain. Of course, the Stone Age people killed animals in self-defense, as well as for food. And it was a long time before they learned to tame and care for their animals, to use them for herding and hunting, and as guardians, in some instances.

Possibly the first animal to be tamed, or domesticated, was the dog. We do not know how this came about, but perhaps it happened like this: a wild puppy dog wandered away from his mother and roamed through the forest until he came to a cave where people lived. The children of the cave played with him and fed him. Then came their plea, "May we keep him? He's lost and has no home."

Thus, long ago, the dog became man's companion and faithful friend; for the ancestor of our modern dog lived side by side with his master early in the Stone Age. He shared the cave man's dangers, watched over his few possessions, became fond of his family, and was always the faithful companion, ready to fight and die for his friends.

The Stone Age hunters, accompanied by their dogs, followed herds of wild cattle. And, as time passed, quite a number of these animals grew accustomed to the ways of their masters, and became relatively tame. So they were helpful and useful.

Teams of oxen worked in the fields. The horse, donkey, and camel were used as beasts of burden. And it was soon discovered that the milk of cows were good for infants.

In due time, people also learned how to shear sheep and weave the fleecy wool into warm coverings. Families settled down with their own patch of land and their own livestock. They no longer had to go wandering through the forests in search of food. They could thus stay closer together and get to know each other. Where the land was productive and men could farm and raise crops, small villages began to appear. Since many of the people planned to stay settled for a long time, permanent homes of wood, stone, mud, or grass were built.

Life became somewhat easier for those who decided to stay on the land because all the settlers learned to work together and to co-operate. With more spare time, and less fear of wild beasts, the Stone Age farmers began to concentrate on handicrafts and self-improvement.

They made polished stone axes and sickle blades. The women ground certain stones into beads and pretty ornaments. They molded clay into bowls, drinking cups, and other useful items.

The Stone Age farmer also had time to think about Nature. And he probably wondered who or what made the sun and the moon rise and set; who sent the rain, the snow, and the winds. And why. He may have even wondered how the world itself came to be. When the lightning flashed and

Some groups of New Stone Age men settled in villages like the one shown in our picture. This model of a Swiss lake dwelling is in the American Museum of Natural History.

the thunder roared, he was probably scared of this unknown *something* that seemed to dart right out of the sky and head straight toward him. When the rain fell gently on his crops, and when the warm sun made them grow, perhaps he gave thanks to whoever had sent them—to the beings he called gods and goddesses.

At a later date, he would build monuments and shrines where he and his family, his friends, and neighbors might worship these kindly deities who watched over them from afar.

THE RIDDLE OF STONEHENGE

In the southwestern part of England, Stonehenge, one of the greatest mysteries of early man still baffles those who try to explain it. No one knows why these huge stone markers —some arranged in rows, some in circles—were erected.

One circle contains thirty stones, fourteen feet high, seven feet wide, and a little more than three feet thick. Within this circle is grouped another ring of smaller stones. There are others in the shape of horseshoes. And in the center of this strange collection there is a sort of altar.

At right, an artist's conception of how Stonehenge might once have looked, and below, some of the things found at the site.

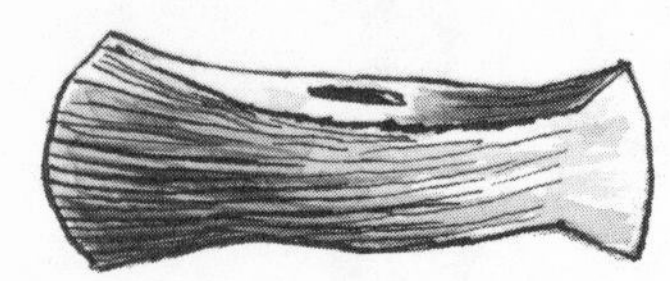

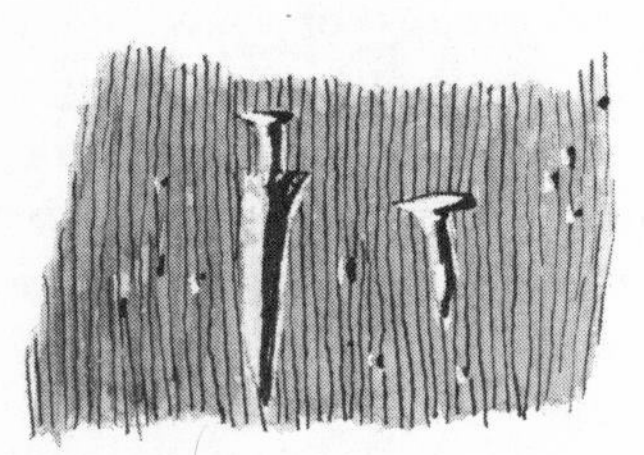

For how many years did the inhabitants of ancient Britain labor to erect this unusual temple—perhaps in honor of one of their favorite gods? Who were their gods? Nobody knows. Many have sought the answer to this puzzling question down through the centuries. But the riddle of Stonehenge still remains unsolved.

It is suggested that these stones may have served as a temple for sun-worshipers. And recently there has been an attempt to prove that they may indicate the movements of sun and moon and their relationship to other celestial bodies.

THE BEGINNINGS OF CIVILIZATION

There are two helpful ways to study the past. The first is to read the records written down by people who lived at the time. The second is to study the tools, weapons, buildings, art, and other objects left behind by early peoples.

Real history began with written records. If no *written* records can be found, the period is called prehistoric. This simply means before history was written down as it happened.

Our imaginary trip through the Stone Age took place in prehistoric times. All that we know of these ancient people who used stone weapons and tools comes from finding the objects that they used in their daily lives and guessing how they used them.

From now on our imaginary journey through the past will take place in historic times. We will know more exactly when things happened because suddenly, about 5,000 years ago, men began to become civilized. They began to live together in cities. They began to use metals instead of stones for tools. And, most important, they learned how to write!

In many parts of the world, civilization sprang up. Independent of each other, because people had not learned to travel great distances and be able to return home, these different civilizations grew in Egypt, in the Fertile Crescent of the Middle East, in the Indus Valley of what is now Pakistan, in the Hwang Ho Valley of China, on the Aegean Islands in the Mediterranean, and, somewhat later, among the Andes Mountains of South America and the lowlands of Mexico and Honduras.

The ruins of Stonehenge in England attract many visitors, who stand in awe in front of these reminders of man's early past — giant stones whose purpose we can only guess at.

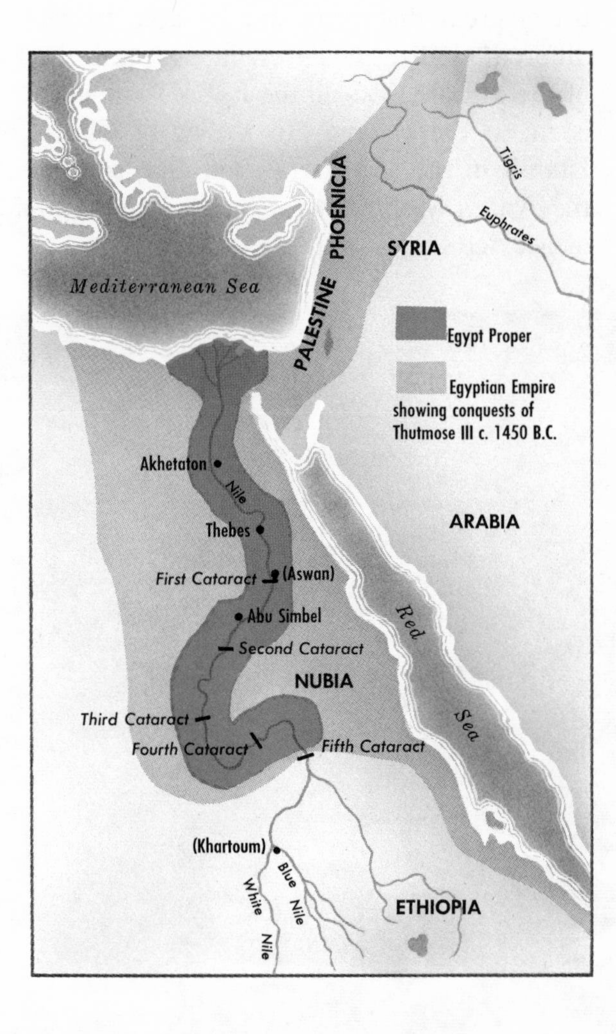
Mediterranean Sea
PALESTINE
PHOENICIA
SYRIA
Tigris
Euphrates
Egypt Proper
Egyptian Empire
showing conquests of
Thutmose III c. 1450 B.C.
Akhetaton
Nile
Thebes
ARABIA
(Aswan)
First Cataract
Abu Simbel
Second Cataract
Red
Sea
NUBIA
Third Cataract
Fourth Cataract
Fifth Cataract
(Khartoum)
Blue Nile
White Nile
ETHIOPIA

circa 3300 B.C. Kingdom of Upper and Lower Egypt.

circa 2900-2700 B.C. King Menes united Upper and Lower Egypt.

2700-2200 B.C. Old Kingdom (Capital: Memphis). Art and architecture thrive. Age of the Pyramids.

2100-1788 B.C. Middle Kingdom (Capital: Thebes). Classical age of Egyptian literature.

1788-1580 B.C. The Hyksos, invaders from the East, brought horse and chariot. Period of Hyksos rule.

1580-1350 B.C. Establishment of New Kingdom under succession of dynasties.

1447 B.C. Death of Thutmosis III, Empire Builder.

1375-1358 B.C. Rule of Amenhotep IV (Ikhnaton), worshiper of "One God."

1292-1225 B.C. Ramses II, Builder of monuments.

1200-1090 B.C. Ramses III (1198-1167) defeated "People of the Sea." Ramses IV-XII (1167-1090), a series of weak rulers.

945-661 B.C. Succession of foreign dynasties (Ethiopian, Libyan) and period of Assyrian domination (Ashurbanipal sacked Thebes in 661.)

663-525 B.C. Pharaohs from the city of Sais revived Egyptian rule.

525-404 B.C. Persians under Cambyses conquered and ruled Egypt.

332 B.C. Alexander the Great annexed Egypt to his empire.

323-305 B.C. Ptolemy I Soter became governor of Egypt (323) and then king (305), founding Ptolemaic line, which lasted almost 300 years.

47-30 B.C. Cleopatra VII, last ruler of the House of Ptolemy. Killed herself rather than accept imprisonment by the Roman, Octavian.

30 B.C. Egypt became a Roman province for more than 300 years.

A.D. 624 Arabs conquered Egypt, making it a Moslem nation.

The Land of the Nile

When the first Stone Age tribes wandered into the fertile valley of the River Nile, they must have thought it a delightful spot. For, while much of this ancient kingdom was dry and barren, and sandstorms whipped the nearby desert, the climate of the sheltered valley appealed to the weary travelers. There was enough food and water for the men, women, children, and animals. No one would be forced to go hungry, nor would they have to seek shelter in caves. And so these adventurous Stone Age people decided to make their home in Egypt.

Here, in this pleasant northeast corner of the great African continent, they would settle down to hunt, fish, farm, build, and live contentedly for the rest of their days. And so would their children, their grandchildren, their great-grandchildren, and all their future descendants.

Not long after the first settlers of Egypt came, no rain fell for quite a while. The trees began to wither; the grass became brittle and dry; and even the mighty Nile dwindled. Indeed, the people who lived in the valley feared that it might disappear for ever. Would the sun-scorched crops fail? Would there be a terrible famine, they wondered? Would everyone, including the animals, die of hunger and thirst?

But, even as they wondered, the river began to rise—higher and higher. And soon the rushing waters, dark with slime and mud, filled the almost-empty mouth of the Nile, and spilled over into the surrounding countryside.

From the finds in early Egyptian tombs we can get quite a good impression of what life in those days must have been like. This is a model of a riverboat, found in a grave in Thebes.

At left, the court of Pharaoh Rameses II in the ruins of the temple of Luxor. Below, the same temple seen from the Nile — Egypt's "highway to history" — with native sail-boats passing slowly by.

Many of the villagers fled before the raging flood. Panic-stricken families abandoned their homes and all their belongings. Yet, others bravely withstood the deluge. And, when the waters went down, they patiently helped each other repair the damage.

After the Nile returned to its normal level, the plants, the crops, the trees, and the grass, were stronger and healthier than ever before. And henceforth, as if to make certain that all growing things had enough to drink, the floods came back each year. Grateful farmers hastened to the temples to thank their gods for sending them an abundant harvest.

During the dry season, of course, when no rain fell, the land became parched and thirsty—except in a few low-lying places where pools of flood water remained. In these shady nooks, the ground always stayed fertile and green. But the higher ground turned brown because it was exposed to the direct rays of the sun.

Finally, the farmers learned to dig ditches and canals that extended from the banks of the river to their fields, and thus kept the crops watered and nourished, even during very dry spells. But, in order to cultivate and make better use of all their acres, the farmers also had to find a way of bringing moisture to the higher areas. At first they probably carried water in pails, or buckets, made of animal skin. But this was extremely hard work, and took more time than they were able to spare.

Then, one day, some bright handyman-about-the-delta built what he called a *shadoof,* or water-raising device, consisting of a long pole upon which a container of water, suspended by a rope, might be raised and lowered by hand. With the aid of this invention, the user dipped an empty vessel into the river. As soon as it was filled to the brim, he raised it, and swung the pole around so that the pail emptied its contents into the nearest ditch or canal. Thus propelled by a group of *shadoofs,* water could reach all levels, even the highest. And this remarkable do-it-yourself sprinkler system was undoubtedly one of the earliest methods of irrigation.

THE GIFT OF THE NILE

Let us now take a make-believe stroll through a small Egyptian village—in the summer month of June, centuries before the birth of Christ. We notice that everyone has gathered near the river to await the rising of the waters. They wish for a plentiful supply of moisture, good crops, and a fruitful harvest. And every day, with the aid of a huge dipstick, the waters of the Nile are measured. Then, at last, to the delight of the villagers, an official announces: "The waters are rising! Soon our mighty river will overflow its banks. Our lands will thirst no longer!"

The good news spreads rapidly. Delighted grownups speak of their crops, and of all their hopes and dreams. The

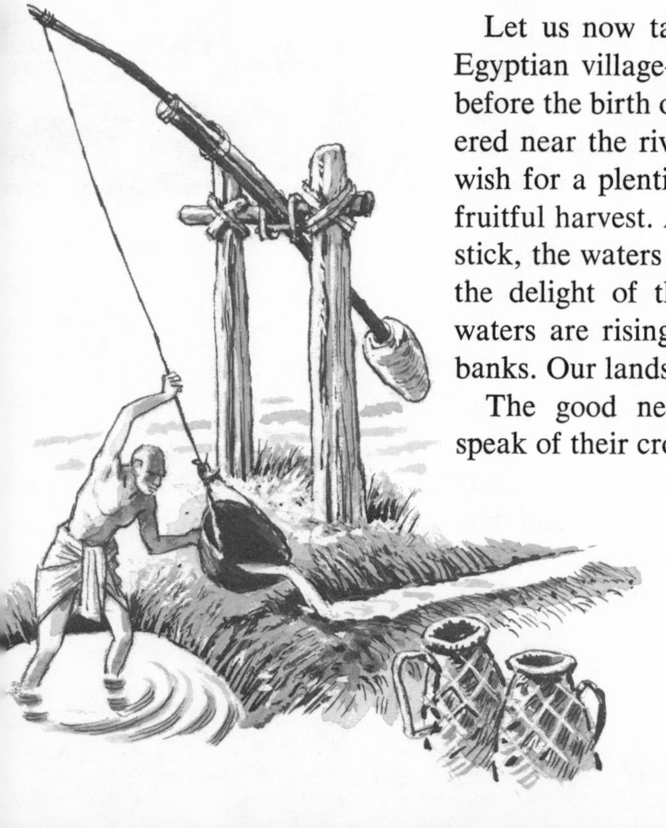

The shadoof, an ancient Egyptian irrigation device, is still used today.

children express their pleasure in much the same way as today's young people express theirs. They sing, and dance, and play games, and clap their hands, and make lots and lots of noise; while their parents journey to the temple to give thanks to their gods and goddesses.

Now, all who dwell in the fertile valley of the Nile, and all who live near its muddy delta, must travel to higher ground until the welcome floods have drenched their crops.

Then the feasting begins; and there are bullfights, wrestling matches, and all kinds of ancient sports. There is dancing—and gaiety and laughter, too—for this is a happy time of year. The merrymaking continues until a messenger returns to the high ground with the latest tidings. Villagers, priests, wise men, and members of the royal court prepare to offer renewed thanks to the gods. Once again, they proceed to the temple.

The Nile has at last reached its highest point. The irrigation ditches and canals will soon be filled to overflowing. Thus the sunburned plains and the parched high ground will also receive their supply of life-giving water. The chief priest reverently raises a bundle of grain toward the sky; while the people pay homage to Osiris, their hero-god who, having once died, is said to have been restored to life in order to serve them as Judge of the Dead, King of the Underworld, and god of their lands.

And, were we to prolong our imaginary trip for a few more months, we would, of course, see the River Nile, looking normal once again, when its waters had receded.

We would also see the farmers planting barley, wheat, cotton, and flax—and all the other crops so necessary to people everywhere, whether they be ancient Egyptians, who lived many centuries ago, or modern men living in the twentieth century.

Later, at harvesttime, the new wheat crop is cut and stacked. Oxen tread the stalks and strip the coverings from

Drawings on the wall of a tomb show that wrestling was an old Egyptian sport.

the seeds. Then, armed with shovels, a group of workers step forward to separate the husks from the kernels and the chaff from the wheat. Gradually, we see that the husks are stripped and discarded, while the seeds of grain fall back to the ground. The process is repeated until only the seeds remain. The crops have again been harvested. Another year has passed.

The Nile has been generous to those who live and work in the valley. And all citizens respect it as a hard taskmaster. For it has compelled those who live along its banks to co-operate as good neighbors should; to help each other in every way possible.

In the course of time, one man, whom the people chose as their ruler, became more powerful than all the other officials. It was he who made the laws—and saw that they were enforced.

But, as head of state, the king was much too busy to farm,

build, become a trader, a merchant, or a shopkeeper. In other words, he was dependent upon his subjects for his job, his daily bread, his fine robes and, of course, his magnificent estates.

So his subjects, as the people were called, had to give him a certain share of all the crops they raised, or the various useful items they produced. These were probably the first "taxes" ever paid by a people to the head of a government. However, taxes were not paid in money because coins and currency, as we now know them, had not yet come into being.

The models of a granary on page 34, of the slaughterhouse at left, and of the cow and calf below are all about 4,000 years old and were found in graves in Thebes.

THE PHARAOH, HALF-MAN AND HALF-GOD

Since the early Egyptians believed that the monarch was also one of their gods who had been sent to live on earth as their supreme ruler, they accepted him without question.

Thus he had little difficulty in enforcing his will and commanding their respect. From the time of King Akhenaton's reign, whenever they spoke of their king, they invariably spoke of him as their Pharaoh, which means "great house." And when the Pharaoh, or ruler died, his eldest son inherited this title.

Of course, there were other very important persons besides the Pharaohs. There were the priests who advised them; and who, in fact, shared the authority of their ruler.

There were also the generals of the armies, judges, and tax-collectors. And, for their assistance, the ruler rewarded these aides and followers with huge tracts of land. So, they became wealthy and prosperous.

The farmers, laborers, and craftsmen unhesitatingly obeyed the landowners as their immediate superiors. And while they toiled, watchmen, or overseers, stood by to make sure that the workers in the fields, and in the shops, gave their masters an honest day's work.

The Egyptians worshiped several gods and godesses. In addition to Osiris, they also believed in sun, moon, star, and animal gods and built many temples in their honor. And while they could not see their favorite gods in person, they often visited the temples and brought offerings of fruit, vegetables, and handicrafts, which they laid at the feet of their idols.

The ancient Egyptians were a most devout people. They

These burial jars were used to hold the internal organs of the mummified body.

also believed in another life after death, and for this reason, embalmed (that is, treated with sweet-smelling oils and spices to prevent decay) the bodies of their departed relatives and friends. As soon as the person passed from this life, the next-of-kin arranged for the funeral. After preparation for burial, the body, or mummy, was swathed in yards and yards of specially prepared linen, and placed in a mountain tomb with various personal effects—perhaps certain toilet articles and, in the case of children, favorite toys—to keep them happy in the next world. Desert tribes and plainsmen were naturally entombed at ground level, protected from grave robbers and wild animals beneath the mounds of rock or stone.

The interior of Tutankhamen's tomb revealed treasures of incredible riches. Three coffins were found, one within the other, and the third (superimposed here over the picture of the tomb's interior) was of solid gold. The embalmed body of the young Pharaoh was preserved in it.

THE AGE OF THE PYRAMIDS

Gradually, the burial mounds were made larger and larger. And, of course, rich people built higher mounds than the poor. Until finally, great pyramids marked the last resting places of kings, nobles, and their relatives.

One of the oldest pyramids still in existence was erected

When a nobleman died models of musicians were buried with him, to "keep him from getting bored during his long travels in the other world."

about 2700 years before Christ, in honor of a Pharaoh named Zoser. Forty-two stone steps lead upward to a height of 190 feet—like a great staircase rising into the heavens. This may be the oldest man-made structure in existence—designed, it is said, by one of King Zoser's high priests who was also a gifted architect.

A century after Zoser ruled the Egyptians, King Cheops, who is also known as Khufu, commanded his architects to build the Great Pyramid of El Gizeh near Cairo, one of the largest monuments in the world. Thousands of men are said to have taken twenty years to complete this enormous structure wherein the king, with all his earthly treasures, was buried long ago. The huge stones had to be ferried across the Nile, and then raised about 500 feet above the ground.

No one has yet been able to determine how these resourceful Egyptians ever finished such a difficult job with the few tools available to them in those ancient times.

Egypt, where the ancient and modern ages meet. Arabs pause in front of the Great Pyramid of Khufu (the sphinx is on the left in the picture) and watch an airplane overhead.

But their engineers and architects built so well that, even today, the interior of the Great Pyramid is in fairly good condition. However, nearly all of the treasures have been stolen.

For 500 years after the burial of Cheops, each succeeding king built his own pyramid or tomb. Here lay the deceased members of royal families and the mummies of those lesser mortals who had served the rulers in the days of their glory.

The cavernous interiors were lavishly decorated, and the walls were covered with picture-writing that recounted the story of the dead Pharaoh's life. It was only when these tombs and temples were opened by scientists (many years later) that much of the history of an ancient Egyptian civilization was revealed to the rest of the world.

Even today, bordering the desert for miles, we come upon centuries-old tombs and shrines, and images of gods and Pharaohs carved in stone.

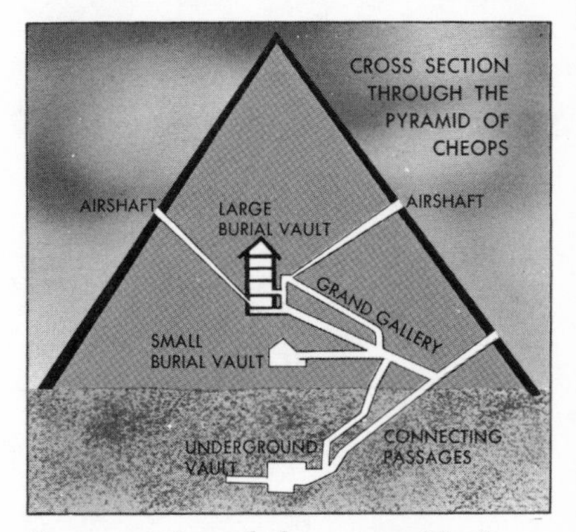

Cross section of the pyramid of Cheops.

Tomb drawings of a burial. Above right, the coffin is transported down the Nile in the special "boat of the dead," followed by many other boats, among them a boat of weeping women (above).

FROM ALPHABET TO ZODIAC

These industrious and inventive people left not only the great pyramids and temples, but also many other things which we of later civilizations have inherited.

For example, they devised a special way of measuring land—the forerunner of our present-day system of surveying. This method of recording boundaries was invaluable. It let everyone know scientifically (for the ancient Egyptians were also pretty good mathematicians) exactly where they and their land stood before and after the yearly floods.

Egyptians also learned to mark the passing of time by observing the movements of the sun, moon, and stars. Moreover, those who lived in the Nile Valley had to keep an account of the number of days between floodtimes. This led to the development of a calendar.

Based upon the movement of the sun, moon, and stars, the Egyptians divided their year into twelve months, allowing thirty days for each month. Then at the end of each year, they added five extra feast-days, for a total of 365 days. But in order to develop even this ancient ancestor of our modern calendar, they had to have some idea of the length of time it took the planet earth to orbit the sun. Nowadays, the length of the solar year, as it is called, is 365 days, 5 hours, 48 minutes, 45.51 seconds.

Another of their inventions was the shadow-clock, a form of sundial, on which the shadow cast by the sun told them

The valuable Stele of Neu-waf and his family (18th dynasty). Now in the Metropolitan Museum in New York.

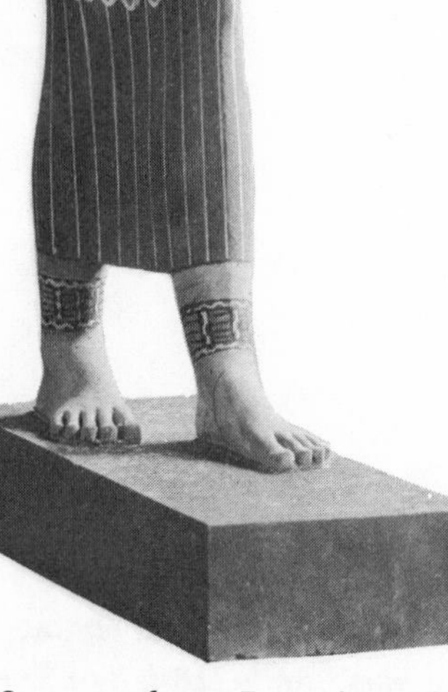

Statue of an Egyptian girl bearing a basket of meats.

the time of day. This device consisted of a piece of wood with a crosspiece at one end. There was a scale on the long arm, marked off for the hours. The day was divided into two halves of six parts each. In the early morning, the crosspiece was set toward the east, and its shadow fell along the long arm. As the sun rose higher in the sky, the shadow grew shorter. The location of the shadow on the scale indicated the hour of the day until noon, when the shadow vanished. After noon, the crosspiece was placed toward the west, and the hours from midday were indicated by a shadow on the long arm.

The ancient Egyptians also introduced us to various types of writing. At first, with chisels, they carved word-pictures and symbols on stone tablets. These records of their history and civilization are known as hieroglyphics. Later, they developed a more convenient method of writing on scrolls of papyrus (paper, to us!). Try to imagine *yourself,* chisel in hand, balancing a stone tablet on your lap while you finish your homework or dash off a little thank-you note to Grandma.

Of course, only the simplest facts could be written down in this manner. However, certain of the ancient Egyptian signs gradually developed into a kind of primitive alphabet. And after papyrus (which is made from a plant found near the banks of the Nile) came into use, the alphabet must have been easier to write and teach. Indeed, these Egyptian ABC's may have inspired the Phoenicians, from whom our own alphabet derives, to replace the more difficult word-pictures or hieroglyphics with sounds and symbols.

In the other Egyptian methods of writing, the signs no longer resemble the pictures from which they evolved. Rapid strokes with a pen on the soft surface of papyrus led to briefer signs. And we must also thank the Egyptians for showing us how to make ink.

Black ink consisted of vegetable gum mixed with water

and colored with lampblack. Red ink contained the same mixture, colored with iron oxide, instead of lampblack. Pens were first made by splitting the long stems of the papyrus plant. Layers of this reedlike plant were then soaked, pounded, scraped, and pressed into thin sheets. Sheets of papyrus measured ten to fifteen inches, and were joined together in rolls from ten to 200 feet in length.

Since these sheets were awkward to handle, the resourceful Egyptian, when reading, rolled his papyrus up on a stick, and unrolled a little at a time. Finally, when he had finished reading his "book," he rolled it up on another stick.

Since only a few of the ancient Egyptians knew how to write, there were trained experts to help them. Known as scribes, these men were very important and greatly respected in the community. The tools of a professional scribe consisted of two reed pens and a case; two small jars of water; and a palette with two little wells in which he could easily mix his black and red ink. This writer's tool kit could be carried over the shoulder or by hand. So, pens, jars, and palettes were usually tied together for convenience.

The literature of ancient Egypt was made up of religious and non-religious texts. And, as their civilization progressed, many folk tales and collections of proverbs were also set down in writing. One popular Egyptian story is similar to that of our well-loved Cinderella.

It seems that a beautiful Egyptian girl named Rhodopis was bathing in the Nile. Suddenly, an eagle swooped down and carried off one of the slippers she had left on shore; the bird flew at least 500 miles to the ruler's palace; and dropped the slipper into his lap.

King Mycerinus interpreted this as a message from the gods. Later, he dreamed that the slipper belonged to the most desirable maiden in all Egypt. After searching the highways and byways, he found the owner of the magic slipper, a damsel more radiant than he had ever imagined.

Statuette of Ptah-Sokar-Osiris, an important Egyptian god.

They were married, of course. And, as Queen of Egypt, she brought the King such joy and happiness, that he built in her honor the third pyramid of El Gizeh, near Cairo.

The Egyptians learned many new things that had not hitherto been known. Imhotep, who was the first architect of the pyramids, was also an astronomer, inventor of the calendar, and perhaps one of the first practicing physicians in history.

His medical skill must have inspired the confidence of his patients, for he was literally worshiped during his lifetime. And over 2,000 years after his death, he was still looked upon as a god. Historians call Imhotep one of the most gifted men of antiquity.

Because the ancient Egyptians were keenly interested in a life-after-death and were also a very superstitious people, they were apt to consult fortune tellers. Furthermore, they sometimes found it difficult to choose among the magic of their priests, sorcerers, and soothsayers, and the medicine of their doctors. Documents on which are inscribed the symptoms of various diseases and details of treatments and cures were found in many of the tombs. These records indicate that the Egyptian knowledge of surgery, based on scientific data, was advanced.

The god Horus, part man, part bird, spearing an antelope. The carving of the antelope is on the pedestal.

THE SPLENDOR OF THE ANCIENTS

On our imaginary trip through ancient Egypt, we also find that the people loved beauty. This feeling is reflected in the homes of the rich. The houses of nobles, priests, and landowners were usually sun-dried brick, or wooden structures, surrounded by high-walled gardens.

But most Egyptians had less furniture in their homes than we commonly have in ours–low divans, carved tables of unique design, decorative chairs, and footstools. Straw mats and handwoven rugs were their early version of our modern

Above, a reproduction of the wall of a tomb from about 1450 B.C. showing boatmen gathering papyrus, and below, the funerary model of a weaving shop.

An ancient Egyptian "vanity." The circular space in the middle was used by the elegant lady to prepare her cosmetics.

floor coverings. And both inside and out, their walls were richly colored. Saucers of oil, with floating wicks, provided light after dark; and small, high-set windows, draped with homespun cloth, shielded the occupants from the heat and glare of the sun.

The upper-class Egyptians were invariably clad in flowing robes and sandals made of papyrus. Even the less-privileged citizens wore some kind of loose tunic, or covering. The garb of their kings, or Pharaohs, was similar but, of course, was much more richly embroidered and sashed.

And naturally, even then, the ladies spent a lot of time improving upon Nature—with extra special coloring for hair, eyes, cheeks, lips, fingers, and toes.

Statue of a scribe reading a papyrus from about 1400 B.C.

Because of the climate, youngsters wore almost nothing until the age of three or four. Then they were dressed in pint-size versions of their elders' attire. They were taught to respect their elders at all times; and to honor and obey their parents—their mothers, in particular. For women, in that ancient land, were held in the highest regard, and wielded a great deal of power in the home.

Both sexes were fond of jewelry and personal adornment: necklaces, bracelets, rings for ears and fingers, and colorful beads. The men used bronze razors, cut their hair very short, and wore wigs made of sheep's wool. The women also affected this form of headdress.

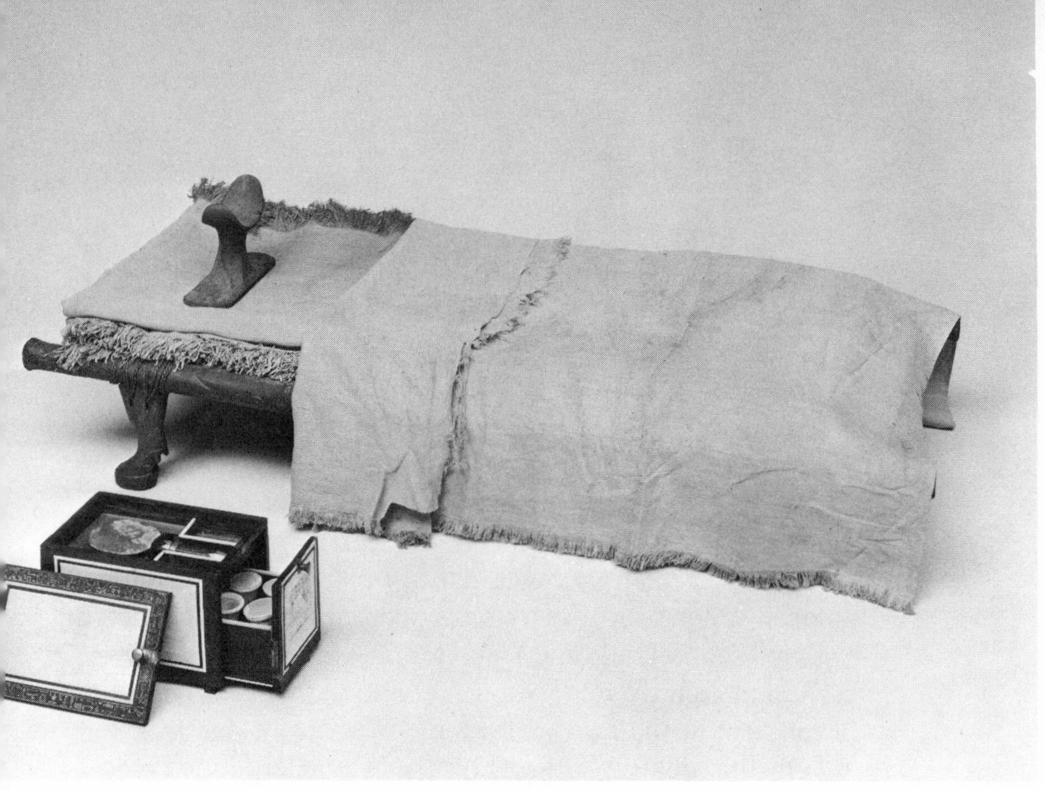

Egyptian furniture: a bed with linen and a toilet chest with mirror and ointment jars. On top of the bed is the head-rest, which looks less comfortable than our pillows of today.

OUTSIDE THE HIGH-WALLED GARDENS

Although the poorer children had little or no schooling, the more fortunate boys and girls were taught by the priests. They were instructed in the arts of writing, reading, and drawing. As they progressed in their studies, they were taught history, the language and literature of Egypt, bookkeeping, and mathematics. The more scholarly pupils advanced to higher subjects, such as religion and astronomy.

However, many of the young people came of working-class families. And many were humble peasants–farmers and laborers living in sparsely furnished thatch-roofed mud huts. These people worked from dawn to dark. And when the tax man came around to collect a share of their crops, they probably complained (as loudly as we do) of the high cost of living. For, even though money had yet to be invented, the income tax bureau did a thriving business in cotton, wheat, and barley, or whatever was acceptable to their king, to whom the taxes were paid.

And, as the young enjoy games of all kinds, so did Egyptian boys and girls play with homemade balls, dolls, hoops, and other toys.

And most Egyptian boys liked nothing better than a hunting or fishing trip with dad.

We would also see many pet animals, cats in particular, if we were to explore some of the typical Egyptian homes. We would learn that cats were believed to be sacred. Often, they were given elaborate burial ceremonies. And grasshoppers were kept in cages made of plaited rushes; monkeys picked grapes at harvesttime; gazelles were popular in many a household; and some families even kept *pet crocodiles*—though we don't suppose these weird, crawly reptiles ever slept at the foot of Junior's bed.

On this ticklish subject, by the way, Herodotus, who is known as "the father of history," said, many centuries ago: "If you wish to catch a crocodile, bait a hook with a large chunk of meat. Then let your line drift out to the middle of the river, while you remain on the bank holding a live, squealing pig or sheep. Upon hearing these cries, the crocodile will seize the meat and swallow it. Then, pull in your line with all your might. And as soon as the crocodile is within reach, plaster his eyes with mud—and the rest of the job is easy."

Easy, that is, if you possess a squealing pig or sheep, plenty of strength, and enough courage to throw mud in the crocodile's eyes before he decides that *he* is the fisherman—and *you* are the bait!

And now, on our imaginary tour, let us go sightseeing in Thebes, capital city of ancient Egypt. In the colorful bazaars, we meet some of the traders.

A fisherman offers part of his catch for a pair of sandals. Many merchants accept bags of grain in exchange for other useful goods. A few are even willing to let you pay them off in oxen.

Then, just around the corner, we notice a barber placidly at work in the shade of a palm tree—shaving the head of a small boy.

And nearby, busy potters spin their wheels, humming contentedly as they transform great lumps of clay into vases, jars, and bowls.

The words of the Pharaoh return to our mind as we explore the street of carpenters: "Let the people build and make beautiful our Egypt!" Here, we see men cutting wood, planing, and smoothing boards, shaping them with great skill to make objects of beauty and utility. We stop to admire the handiwork of the cabinetmakers, the leathercraftsmen, the weavers, and the glassblowers.

Years fly by. And we suddenly find ourselves wandering (in our imagination) through other fascinating cities of the Middle East. We learn that the people who once lived in these areas built up a thriving trade with the neighboring Egyptians.

Early Egyptian glassmakers at work.

And, in the course of time, the traveling Egyptian merchants and traders returned home with wood, ostrich feathers, ivory, gold, spices, gems, rugs, perfumes, oils, and other goods. In return for these wares, they exchanged leather, pottery, linen and cotton, carved wood, bronze tools, and weapons, jewelry, various grains, and even toys.

"SPEED DEMONS" ON THE NILE!

We discover that these gifted people are thought to have been among the first people in the world to use wind as a means of powering a boat. For it seems that while men in most other parts of the world were still riding logs, the Egyptians were using sailboats. Indeed, archaeologists have found clear pictures of sailing vessels—and even a few models of ships with sails—in the tombs of some of the Egyptian Pharaohs; neatly arranged so that the spirits of the departed would be sure of transportation in the land of their afterlife. These models of ancient vessels give us a good picture of the type of craft used by the early Egyptians. And eager to reach our next port-of-call, we resume our trip through ancient lands.

More than 3,000 years before the Christian Era, the Egyptians were dealing in wheat and cattle along the River Nile and across the Red Sea. They used lightweight boats made of plaited or braided reeds because wood was not abundant in their desert land. To keep the curved ends of their vessels from drooping into the water, they also tied a rope from bow to the stern. And from one single-pole, water-tight mast, they hung a sail.

These boats were built to sail ahead of the wind. But as soon as the wind blew crosswise, the sail was lowered and paddles moved the craft forward.

As they acquired more knowledge and skill, the Egyptians —in order to make their merchant-ships seaworthy—fitted

The photograph on the opposite page shows the ruins of the Temple of Karnak. The temples were not only houses of worship, but were also used as observatories to study the sun and stars.

It looks like a stage set, but it is really a restaurant in modern Egypt, half an hour's drive from the center of Cairo, the capital, with an ancient pyramid as a backdrop.

them with wooden planks imported from Phoenicia, a thriving land on the eastern shores of the Mediterranean. They also carried out other improvements. Eventually, they produced an extremely useful vessel.

Nowadays, of course, we look upon these funny little boats as quaint. Yet, in ancient times, they were probably hailed as "the speed demons" of the Nile.

THE FALL OF "THE GREAT HOUSE"

Centuries passed. One Pharaoh after another ruled the kingdom of Egypt. Serene in the knowledge that the valley of the Nile was difficult to invade, they built up a great civilization. As their power increased, so did their greed. They reached out and helped themselves to so many nearby countries that they became a mighty empire.

But, as we soon discover in history, empires rise and fall. And conquerors eventually are themselves conquered. So, about 3,700 years ago, the Egyptian armies were defeated by the Hyksos—a wandering group of conquerors who had developed new weapons made of bronze and who used horses and chariots to terrify their enemies. After about 160 years the Egyptians learned to make their own bronze weapons and how to use horses in battle, so they again won their independence. Then, about 3,100 years ago, with the coming of the Iron Age, Egyptian armies again began to be defeated by invaders who used even stronger new weapons made of iron. Unfortunately for the Egyptians, the Valley of the Nile had no iron deposits, so the Egyptians no longer could compete with their neighbors. Egypt was repeatedly invaded and never again regained its lost empire.

The Jews

586-538 B.C. Jews ruled by Babylonians.

538-332 B.C. Period of Persian rule. Temple in Jerusalem rebuilt. Nehemiah (445-433) restored walls of the city.

332-198 B.C. Jews ruled by Alexander the Great (332-323), and then by the Ptolemies of Egypt.

168-163 B.C. Jews under Judas Maccabeus rose up against Antiochus IV (Epiphanes) who had declared Judaism illegal.

63 B.C.-A.D. 395 Palestine ruled by Romans. Herod the Great (37-4 B.C.), King of Judea, rebuilt temple of Jerusalem. Jesus of Nazareth born between 6-4 B.C.

Phoenicia

circa 1500-1447 B.C. Most of Phoenicia conquered by Thutmosis III of Egypt.

circa 1200-1000 B.C. Important Phoenician cities became independent kingdoms.

circa 1000-774 B.C. Hiram I provided Phoenician craftsmen for Solomon's building projects and also a Red Sea fleet.

774-625 B.C. Assyrian rule. Phoenician cities paid tribute.

625-586 B.C. Short period of complete independence for Phoenicia.

586-538 B.C. Chaldean period. Tyre besieged for thirteen years (585-573).

538-332 B.C. Persian rule. Country divided into four kingdoms: Sidon, Tyre, Arwad, Byblos.

332-323 B.C. Alexander the Great conquered Tyre and gained control of other Phoenician cities.

286-197 B.C. Phoenicia ruled by Egypt.

64 B.C. Pompey created the province of Syria, which included Phoenicia.

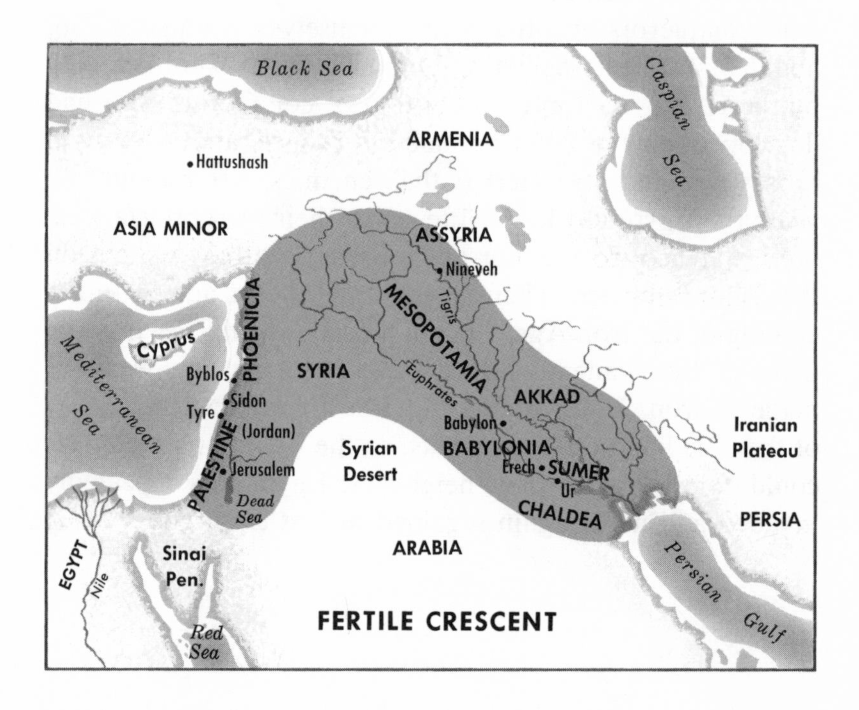

CHAPTER 3

The People Who Made Mountains

THE BIBLE tells us that the first man and woman lived in the Garden of Eden, where they daily enjoyed the fruits of this earthly Paradise, the fragrant flowers, and the beautiful sunshine. They had no worries or problems, for the earth was generous. They always knew where their next meal was coming from. And their days and nights were carefree.

Some people believe that this legendary garden was to be found in the rich valley that lay between the Tigris and Euphrates rivers.

But, whether or not the Garden of Eden actually existed, it is known that many centuries before the era of recorded history, and long before Christ was born, the land between these Asian rivers undoubtedly cradled a part of the early human race.

Perhaps, in those far-off days, hunters and herdsmen

A photograph of the river Tigris today. The boat in the foreground is a gufa, a craft in use since ancient times.

chanced to wander into this fertile region, liked what they saw, and decided to settle down.

As in the valley of the Nile, the climate was pleasant. There was food and shelter for all, including the animals.

Both rivers teemed with fish. And, as the ancient Egyptians had established themselves along the Nile's banks and in its fruitful valley, so other tribes chose to do likewise in their own newly found land where the waters of the Euphrates and the Tigris unite and flow as one mighty river to empty into the Persian Gulf.

THE FERTILE CRESCENT

Then, the annual floods came, and the waters rose higher and higher. It was the story of the Nile repeated. Many of the early settlers took fright, gathered their families and their few belongings together, and left forever. But even as in ancient Egypt, some courageous pioneers decided to stay. And when at last the waters subsided, they planted their crops and the earth, moist and fertile, supplied their every need. No longer homeless wanderers in search of food and lodging, the farmers tilled their soil and planted their seeds. The builders erected reservoirs in which to store water for use during the dry seasons.

And, as we have already seen in Egypt, they also built canals and ditches so that their farmlands, fields, and gardens would never die of thirst.

This valuable piece of earth, shaped rather like a half-moon, lies with its back arched against high mountains to the north. And to the south, it faces a sea of sand. For this reason, it was sometimes called the Fertile Crescent. However, to the Greeks, this ancient territory was more familiarly known as Mesopotamia, which means "between rivers."

Today, it forms part of the modern kingdom of Iraq.

But unfortunately, the earth no longer yields abundant crops. And the sands of the nearby Syrian Desert blow hot and dry across these once-bountiful lands.

This is an ancient statue of a typical Sumerian; notice his flounced skirt.

THE CITY-STATES OF SUMER

Many groups of peoples contributed to the growth and development of Mesopotamia. The earliest were the Sumerians, whose civilization flourished at about the same time as

The Sumerian soldiers in their chariots were feared by their many enemies.

that of ancient Egypt—about 5,000 to 6,000 years ago. Just as, in ancient Egypt, the fertile valleys of the Nile were rich and prosperous, so in Mesopotamia well-established cities were to be found in the regions bordering the Euphrates.

The Sumerians lived in independent city-states. Each boasted its own special gods, and a ruler who also served as the chief priest. Often, these priest-kings would engage in bitter fights among themselves. As a result of this strife, the city-states of old Mesopotamia lived in constant fear of attack.

Geographically, the Sumerian peoples were less protected than the early Egyptian settlers. Thus, their territory, whose valuable acres were much coveted by greedy outsiders, was frequently invaded by hostile tribes; for the valleys of the Tigris and Euphrates were more accessible than the lands of the Nile.

Ruthlessly, these murderous hordes would attack in the dead of night, and seize everything they could lay their hands on.

One tribe would swoop down and conquer another tribe. For several centuries, they were at constant war with each other. Roving bands of marauding mountaineers, in search of food and shelter, would clash with wanderers from the desert.

Thus, the story of old Mesopotamia is one of constant wars and invasions; of endless struggles, and of desperate, power-hungry conquerors determined to vanquish all who dared to oppose them.

On our imaginary tour through one of these ancient strongholds, we discover that it is surrounded by a vast brick wall built especially for the protection of the city and to safeguard all of its inhabitants. We pass unchallenged through a well-patrolled gate—for one of the advantages of imaginary journeying is that a person may come and go as he pleases—and wend our way down narrow, dusty streets past

The often windowless houses kept the heat out during the day, and the flat roofs were used for sleeping in the cool nights.

the houses and workshops and past the bazaars of the merchants and traders. We see craftsmen busily wielding their primitive tools. We hear the strange cries of sharp traders in the busy marketplace, and the protests of bargain-hunters.

Because there is a scarcity of lumber and stone in these parts, we discover that the early Sumerian builders used bricks—made from a sun-dried mixture of molded clay and straw, or grass.

This ancient do-it-yourself type of brickmaking usually took place after the seasonal floods, when the waters of the river returned to their accustomed level, and the clay was still moist. The Mesopotamians referred to this period as "the month of bricks."

The Sumerians built flat-topped houses, made of brick-plastered-with-mud. And their furniture was not unlike that of the early Egyptians.

Sumerian fisherman (from a mosaic panel of 4,500 years ago).

Although no one knows for sure, it is believed that some unknown Sumerian genius discovered the greatest invention in the history of transportation—the wheel. At least carvings in the city of Sumer show that carts with wheels were being used there 5,500 years ago. No other civilization shows evidence of such an early use of the wheel. And the Indian civilizations of the Americas never did discover its use.

ANCIENT SKYSCRAPERS

Continuing our stroll down the broad highway of the past, we finally reach one of the great showplaces of a Sumerian city. Here, a guard detains us; but only long enough to bid us welcome to the royal domain. We pass through a cool, shaded courtyard and enter a beautiful park.

The palace of the priest-king and his noblemen scribes, officials, musicians, and singers is truly magnificent—almost a city in itself. There are storehouses for grain, tools, and weapons; treasure chambers; and immense workshops for the royal potters, leatherworkers, spinners, weavers, jewelers, and craftsmen, appointed to serve the monarch until he decrees otherwise.

In the center of the park, we come upon the shrine, or temple, of the Sumerian gods. In height, it towers over all the other buildings in the city, as New York's Empire State Building seems to soar above every skyscraper in sight. Indeed, this massive Sumerian temple stands like a mountain in the heart of the town. An oddly enough we learn that this splendid edifice was raised so that the wishes of all the settlers might be gratified whether they came from the hills, the mountains, or the plains—but most of all, because the gods of the people required a home worthy of their exalted presence, even though no one ever *saw* them.

The temple, we notice, stands up on a raised platform many stories high. We approach it by a ramp which, in turn, leads to a circular staircase. The great tower, known as the *ziggurat,* or holy mountain, rises high above the platform, almost nudging the sky. And the favorite god of the Sumerians, according to popular belief, lives here. Here, too, he is showered with gifts, which are brought to the shrine by processions of priests. And we are amazed to discover that they enter the private chamber through an arched doorway. However, these early Sumerian craftsmen are expert design-

The Tower of Babel of the Bible was, most likely, one of the ancient ziggurats, a model of which is shown above. Below, aerial view of the ziggurat after being excavated in Ur.

Wrestling and boxing were both of religious significance in ancient Mesopotamia. This is an ancient stone carving showing two boxers squaring off for a bout.

ers, we soon learn. In fact, they were among the first people in history to build arches.

From the tops of these towers the priests studied the stars. We are told that, among other things, they observed a pattern of heavenly bodies which has come to be known as "the zodiac."

Like their Egyptian neighbors, they believed that the sun and the stars were gods, controlled by a chief god who could see into the future, foretell coming events, and direct the stars in their courses.

And so the priests (whose gods are considered to be immortal and endowed with rare powers) believed that they themselves, through their knowledge of astrology, were similarly gifted. This ancient belief, we are told, is still held by certain peoples.

But we must resist the urge to stargaze. And so, descending to sea level, we mingle again with the humble toilers in the valley below.

Some of the farmers are busy in their fields; other workers await the orders of their overseer, or boss. And as we make our way toward the outskirts of the kingdom, we come upon a group of shepherds tending their flocks

Soon, we realize, it will be harvesttime again. And again the people will bring their thank-offerings to the temple. The priests, in ceremonial procession, will retrace their steps to the shrine. And all the gods–but especially their chief god –will be honored.

BOOKS OF BRICK!

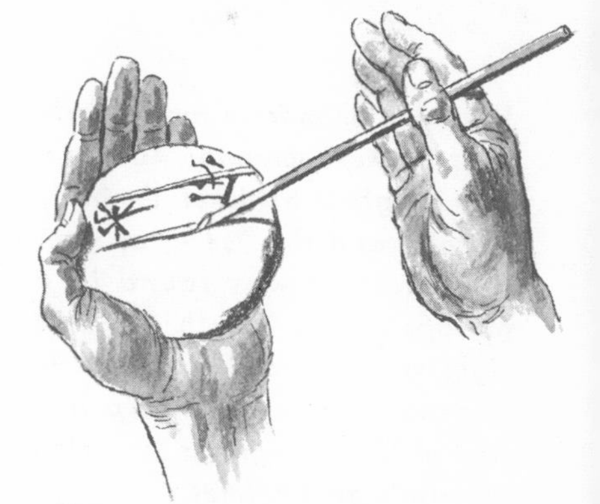

The scribes, or official writers of the Sumerians used a reed stylus, or slender needlelike ancestor of the modern pen to record events on tablets of moist clay. Their system of writing–which consists of wedge-shaped signs and symbols–bears little resemblance to ours.

Furthermore, (no matter what penmanship method we use) ours is just *writing*. But this Sumerian penmanship has a most impressive name, cuneiform, which derives from the Latin word, *cuneus,* meaning "wedge." And even as we wonder how these ancient writing tablets could survive the wear and tear of passing centuries, we are reminded that they were baked in the sun and were thus preserved.

Above, two "pages" from a "book" of brick — a Mesopotamian clay tablet — and underneath, how the stylus was used to "write" on the tablet.

The earliest writing of the Sumerians and other ancient peoples, as their knowledge increased, has become known as picture-writing.

Nearly all that modern man has learned of Mesopotamia and the surrounding regions was recorded on clay tablets, or "brick books," that were found many years after the zealous scribes had passed from the scene.

Some of these books record the comings-and-goings of kings and generals. Others tell of love and lovers, of poets and peasants, of war and peace; of how Sumerian pugilists, or boxers, taped their fists before entering the arena.

We linger a while longer. For it is whispered that we are about to hear a most fabulous tale of a *Mock King-for-a-Day*.

And then, entranced, we are held spellbound. But, alas, only for a few brief minutes. Because the mock king, who reigns in glory for so short a time, must lose his head in the end.

But another mock monarch, Enlil-Bani, who is actually a poor gardener, is soon chosen to succeed the young, handsome fellow who has just forfeited his head. And fortunately, the gardener has better luck. There is music. There are dancing girls and much feasting. Yet, in the perfumed courtyard, a hangman's noose awaits the victim.

Valuable finds from man's early past in Mesopotamia: Above, a ram caught in a thicket; the body is gold, and the fleece, of shell and lapis (it was found in a Mesopotamian "death pit"). At right, a Sumerian lyre, an early ancestor of the modern harp, and and at the far right, a Sumerian warrior's gold helmet.

Meanwhile, poor, doomed Enlil-Bani, (for he knows that his hours are numbered) gazes sadly about him. Seated upon the throne, he dreads that awful moment when, in tribute to the new year, he must surrender his crown, and also his life, as demanded by Fate.

Then, just as his "reign" is about to end in tragedy, one of the true king's messengers brings news of the ruler's sudden passing.

"The king is dead!" he announces sadly. "Long live the king!" the crowd roars. Courtiers press forward, bowing and scraping. But not in mock adoration, now! For a humble gardener has become their royal highness. And Enlil-Bani not only manages to keep his head on his shoulders, but faithfully reigns over his loyal subjects for more than twenty-four years.

This may only be Mesopotamian folklore, of course. But at least Enlil-Bani, according to this ancient legend, lived happily ever after.

THE FIRST STOREKEEPERS

Another powerful group of people, the Babylonians, under a strong leader named Hammurabi, overthrew the Sumerians some 2,000 years before the Christian Era. But this foreign monarch neither enslaved these worthy people, nor did he destroy their civilization. Instead, it became a part of his kingdom, Babylonia, the principal city of which was known as Babylon.

This clay pot from Ur in Mesopotamia is over 5,000 years old.

King Hammurabi was a man of foresight and wisdom who encouraged his people, now citizens of one great nation made up of city-states, to trade with each other.

Up and down the Euphrates they paddled their funny little boats woven of reeds and grasses. Some of these vessels were circular and not unlike oversized saucers in appearance. These craft were handled by one or more persons equipped with an oar. And each boat also could carry a couple of donkeys!

Upon arrival at Babylon, the cargo was sold, the boat was broken up, and the wood and skins of which it was made exchanged for other goods obtained in the city's markets and loaded onto the donkeys for the return trip.

Later, we discover that these ancient mariner-builders greatly improved upon their original handiwork. Traders were then able to travel greater distances. Indeed, they sailed down the Persian Gulf, and eventually reached the country we now call India.

They also sailed to ports in Egypt and to exotic Mediterranean islands and towns. Here, they established friendly relations. And in time, they built up a flourishing market for Babylonian metal-work, tapestries and rugs, grain, certain fruits, pottery, and leather goods.

In exchange for these objects, the traveling merchants brought home the wood, stone, and other wares much needed by their own craftsmen. They also brought silks, ivory, animal skins, gem stones, spices, and gums.

A number of historians regard the ancient Babylonians as the world's first storekeepers. For it seems that they actually sold the goods made by their own people, as well as items brought back from other lands. And unlike the methods used in other shops and bazaars where the barter principle was customary, nuggets of gold, silver, and other metal were accepted as a media of exchange.

Certain shrewd merchants also took the precaution of marking the metals that came into their hands, after having weighed them, to make sure they were not cheated. Then the metals were used again as a means of buying other goods. In this way, dealers and traders were spared the bother of re-weighing the same pieces whenever they changed hands.

Soon, these marked pieces were taken at their "face value" and without question. Later, silver became a most useful trading metal, according to weight and size. Each piece had a name. One was called a *shekel;* another a *mina.* And mathematical-minded Babylonian traders finally decided that it took sixty *shekels* to make one *mina.* So we now discover that coins and currency are also pretty ancient.

Furthermore, the merchants in Babylon devised a system of weights and measures. For liquids, they had been using an earthenware jar of a certain size, the property of their king.

And, in time, this royal water-vessel became their standard measure for liquids. This presumably was the forerunner of our gallon, quart, pint, and half-pint measures. In many areas of Europe, and on other continents, of course, they use different terms. But the principle remains the same.

The weight of solids, we note, was determined by a system of pounds and ounces. And as we know, these standards are still widely used throughout the world.

The length of cloth, land, and other commodities was

A frieze of bulls on a temple wall. The bull was a sacred idol of the Babylonians.

originally measured in feet. But not any old feet! The most important foot in the realm was that of the king. Thus, his majesty's foot became the standard length for measuring.

However, we doubt if the merchants and traders rushed across town to the palace to check up on their ruler's foot every time this measuring problem cropped up. Twelve inches made one foot, we are not surprised to hear; though surely even kings' feet vary in size. And a yard consisted of three feet. But let us figure no further, or we shall become quite confused. Suffice it to say, *our* weights and measures obviously go back a long way! And then, as now, a uniform standard of weights and measures was a boon to everybody.

In conducting their business affairs, Babylonian storekeepers and traders also required arithmetic. So they developed tables for adding and subtracting, for multiplication and division; and a system of counting by twelves and tens. Their dozen, which we have inherited, was in fact another Babylonian first. And, of course, all the merchants kept a record, or an account of what they had bought or sold, and their profit and loss.

The use of clay writing tablets in business led to yet another familiar custom. When a man wrote a letter, or a receipt, he wished to affix his mark, or signature, so that that the recipient would know to whom he must send an acknowledgment.

Seals were used for this purpose. These were made of bone, stone, or clay; and shaped like a finger. Each seal bore a carved picture, perhaps of an animal, a god, or some favorite object. Then the seal was pressed into the moistened clay tablet and became the person's signature.

And, now that we think of it, the Seal of the United States of America is imprinted on all our paper currency. It also appears on many other official documents. So, in quite a number of respects, the ancient Babylonians were really very modern.

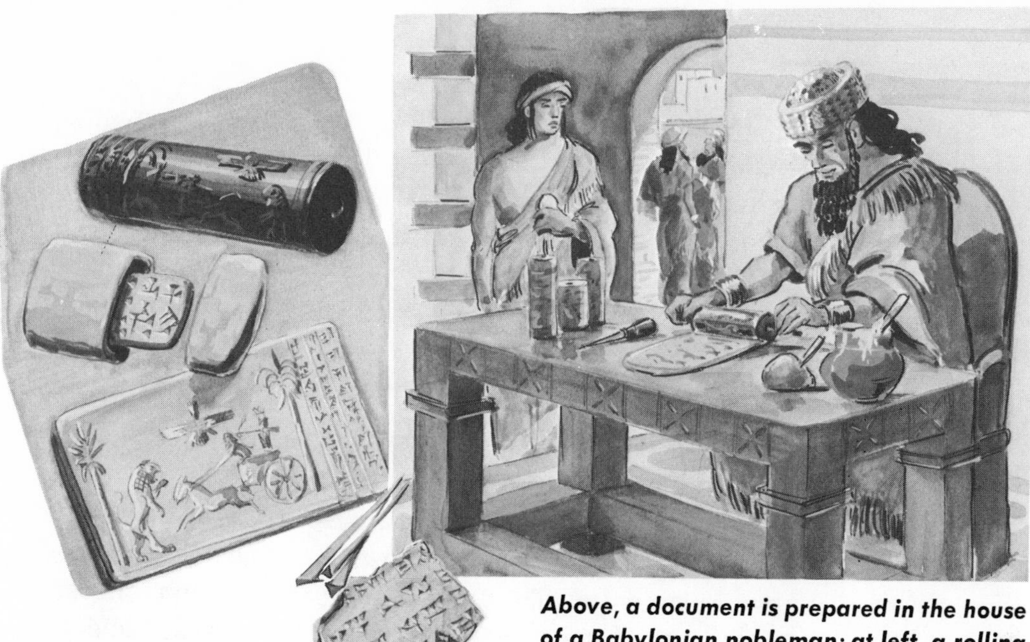

Above, a document is prepared in the house of a Babylonian nobleman; at left, a rolling seal and clay tablets.

Their priests, in much the same way as those of the Sumerians, studied the stars. However, they also made a map of the sky. And by watching the movements of the heavenly bodies, they learned to tell when an eclipse of the sun would occur.

The year was divided into twelve months, consisting of thirty days each. And every six years, one month was added.

The libraries of Babylon were well-stocked–with ancient "books" written on clay tablets upon which everything was recorded–from stirring tales of noble warriors and good and bad kings to the details of fruitful harvests, taxes, and unsuccessful lawsuits.

Babylonian schools provided each schoolchild with a ball of soft clay. After he had shaped and molded it into a tablet, he was ready to practice the cuneiform writing (with his stylus), of which we have previously heard. And we now hear that he had to memorize the more than 600 syllables that made up the Babylonian method of spelling!

Besides writing and spelling, the children were taught reading, religion, history, astrology, mapmaking, and the study of signs and omens. The boys were also taught to shoot with bows and arrows and to take part in other outdoor sports.

THE CODE OF HAMMURABI

Possibly the most enduring contribution of the ancient Babylonians to the moderns was a set of *written* laws.

Before Hammurabi came to power, each tribe made its own rules and regulations. Thus, a passerby who innocently broke one of the rules could be wrongly accused and punished for violating a law of which he was unaware.

The King considered this most unfair. And when he became ruler of Babylon, he instructed his advisers to make a study of the tribal rules and regulations, retaining the good ones and discarding the bad.

Under his guidance, the Hammurabi Code applied to all citizens, rich and poor alike. And everyone knew that these laws were carved on a stone pillar in the Temple of Babylon.

The King also decreed that "copies" of these laws be "written" on stone tablets and dispatched to every city in the land.

Many of these old laws and rules would be considered cruel by today's standards. For example, if one man broke another man's arm, his arm also had to be broken. If one person blinded another, he had to forfeit his own sight. But, of course, this ancient custom of demanding "an eye for an eye and a tooth for a tooth" no longer applies.

However, wrongdoers can never be allowed to go unpunished. Otherwise, in *any* society (ancient or modern), no peoples could ever feel secure. And the basic tenets of the Hammurabi Code are still valid.

On the opposite page is a photograph of the top of the six-foot stone on which the law code of Hammurabi was engraved. It shows Hammurabi receiving the laws from Shamash, god of justice.

Portrait-plaque of the Assyrian king, Tiglath-Pileser III, who conquered Israel.

Detail from a relief found in Kalah, Assyria, showing soldiers and officers during an attack.

Moreover, now, as then, all legal cases may be appealed in a higher court, and brought to retrial, if need be.

THE ASSYRIANS, "THE ROMANS OF ASIA"

A third group assumed control of Babylonia many centuries after the death of Hammurabi. Ultimately, this tribe of fierce warriors, the Assyrians, conquered all of Mesopotamia, Egypt, and a number of other lands. They destroyed the city of Babylon. And Nineveh became the seat of power and the capital of their mighty empire.

This ancient city on the Tigris was surrounded by a wall fifty feet thick, and 100 feet high. The Assyrian rulers lived here in great splendor, surrounded on all sides by mountain streams, huge limestone statues of bulls and lions (some with wings, others with men's heads), and slaves who labored night and day to gratify the whims of these despotic monarchs. Smarting under the whips of the overseers who drove them, these human chain gangs not only quarried the lime-

Detail from a panel on the famous black obelisk found in Kalah, showing the Jewish King Jehu paying homage to the Assyrian King Salmanasar.

stone, but were then forced to drag the enormous slabs for vast distances. Many died of exhaustion.

The Assyrian officials wore rich ceremonial robes. But, alas, the workers were ill-clad, ill-housed, and often hungry. Their king had dozens of servants, kept them busy waiting on him from dawn until midnight, and was greatly feared.

But their king, Ashurbanipal, performed one great accomplishment: He supervised the building of a library stocked with countless clay tablets. And, to this day, these famous "brick books"—one of which relates the Biblical stories of Creation and of the Flood—are still preserved.

Assyrian soldiers were proud of their savagery and boasted about it. They were bloodthirsty conquerors; and deprived the ancient Sumerians and Babylonians of their liberty, their culture, their homes and, in numerous cases, even their lives.

At the height of their glory (between 722 and 626 B.C.) they plundered, ravaged, and fought their way through the land between the rivers. They did little to inspire the oppressed peoples.

And we are neither surprised nor sorry to hear that, in 612 B.C., the great city of Nineveh was destroyed by yet another horde of invaders, the Chaldeans. Thus did the reign of the merciless Assyrian tyrants come to its inglorious end.

THE KINGDOM OF NEBUCHADNEZZAR

Under the leadership of King Nebuchadnezzar II, the Chaldeans assumed control of the Fertile Crescent.

The new ruler established headquarters at Babylon and proceeded at once with the task of rebuilding the former capital of this troubled land.

He caused the city to be enclosed by a wall of tremendous proportions, stoutly built to withstand the onslaughts of enemies and surrounded by a deep moat, or water-filled ditch.

Even so, Nebuchadnezzar was lonely in this palatial, fortress-like city. "Where is there a maid beautiful enough to be Queen of Babylon? Our Queen?" his subjects asked. The King sadly shook his head. Where, indeed? Then he sought the advice of his counselors. But no suitable wife could be found.

Yet, beyond the great brass gates that encircled his palace, Nebuchadnezzar knew that somewhere in the outer world there dwelled such a maiden.

For, alas, this bachelor monarch had seen no future wife, no priceless jewel, no queen of his dream, among the beauties of Babylon. But, in his wanderings, he finally found a radiant princess in a distant land of mountains and forests.

But his lovely bride soon grew tired of her adopted country. It was flat and uninteresting, she declared. She besought her husband to let her return to her own homeland before she pined away.

Because of his love for this beautiful damsel, Nebuchadnezzar said: "Name anything your heart desires—and you shall have it."

"I desire a hill," sighed the homesick Queen, "to remind me of Media, the far-off land where I was born, and where I lived contentedly."

"Your wish shall be granted," the King promised.

The winged lion, a guardian of the gate, from the palace of Ashur-nasirapal II (885-860 B.C.) at Kalhu, Assyria, the modern Nimrud.

A painting of the reconstruction of Babylon (604-561 B.C.) with the Ishtar gate in the foreground.

And so, to restore the happiness of his fair and fretful lady, Nebuchadnezzar ordered his slaves to construct a woodland retreat in the heart of the city of Babylon—on the roof of his palace, in fact. Planted with colorful flowers, and fragrant shrubs and trees, it at once became the Queen's favorite bower, for it reminded her of the home for which she still yearned.

An artist's conception of the Hanging Gardens of Babylon, once considered one of the seven wonders of the ancient world.

Today, this enchanted spot is remembered as the famous Hanging Gardens of Babylon, one of the seven wonders of the ancient world. Of course, the old city was destroyed centuries ago, and nothing remains of its former grandeur.

As time passed, the city grew more and more worldly and pleasure-seeking, its inhabitants more irresponsible. "Let us eat, drink, dance, sing, and enjoy life!" they chorused lustily.

Nebuchadnezzar was rich in worldly goods. He had everything a human being could wish for. But in spite of great power and wealth, the King was no longer a happy man. At last, imagining that he had suddenly been transformed into one of the beasts of the field, the unfortunate ruler lost his mind. He also lost his kingdom.

King Nebuchadnezzar was succeeded by a weakling. And the ancient Babylonians blindly pursued their reckless way of life, interested only in themselves and their worldly goods. They feasted and drank. And were not alarmed by the ominous saber-rattling of a Persian king named Cyrus, who was busily conquering their neighbors, right, left, and center.

Why should they worry about this foreigner, Cyrus? Babylon had walls strong enough to protect its citizens against such puny upstarts! "Let's drink to the downfall of Cyrus!" they shouted. "This Persian tyrant wouldn't dare to storm our great walled citadel!"

But Cyrus did dare. And so, more than 535 years before Christ was born, Mesopotamia, the beautiful land between the rivers, passed from glory into oblivion, by way of the Persian Empire.

Mesopotamia

circa 2850-2450 B.C. First dynasty of Ur.

circa 2450-2270 B.C. Akkadian Empire. Sumerian culture adopted with modifications. Progress in sculpture.

circa 2270-2145 B.C. Gutium people conquered Babylonia. Reign of Gudea (c. 2250) marked high point in Sumerian literature.

circa 2140-2030 B.C. Empire of Ur under Third Dynasty, extended from Ashshur to the Persian Gulf and from Susa to Lebanon. Period of thriving commerce.

circa 2030-1900 B.C. Decline of Sumerians; loss of national identity.

circa 1900-1600 B.C. First Dynasty of Babylon. Hammurabi conquered all Mesopotamia and issued his code of laws.

1600-1150 B.C. Kassites conquered Babylonia, and ruled it for 450 years.

900-729 B.C. Assyrian wars with Babylonia.

729-625 B.C. Babylonia became part of the Assyrian Empire.

625-538 B.C. Neo-Babylonian (Chaldean) Empire; under King Nebuchadnezzar, Babylon known as greatest city of ancient world.

Assyria

circa 2600-2000 B.C. City of Ashshur became part of Akkadian Empire.

circa 1830-1810 B.C. Babylonia ruled Assyria.

circa 1810 B.C. Shamshi-Adad regained independence for Assyria and extended its domain.

1341-1232 B.C. Assyria fought many wars and consolidated its position.

1116-1093 B.C. Assyria gained control of trade routes of Western Asia.

933-782 B.C. First Phase of Assyrian Empire. Use of new war equipment (battering-ram and siege engines) brought Tyre, Sidon, Jehu, and other areas under Assyrian rule.

745-625 B.C. Second Phase of Assyrian Empire. Submission of Israel (734). Damascus taken (732). Tiglath-pileser III became king of Babylon (under name of *Pul*).

689 B.C. Destruction of Babylon by Assyrians under Sennacherib.

681-625 B.C. Babylon rebuilt. King Ashurbanipal, patron of arts and letters. Library of cuneiform tablets established at Nineveh.

625-602 B.C. Nineveh destroyed by Cyaxares, King of Media. Assyria ceased to exist as a nation.

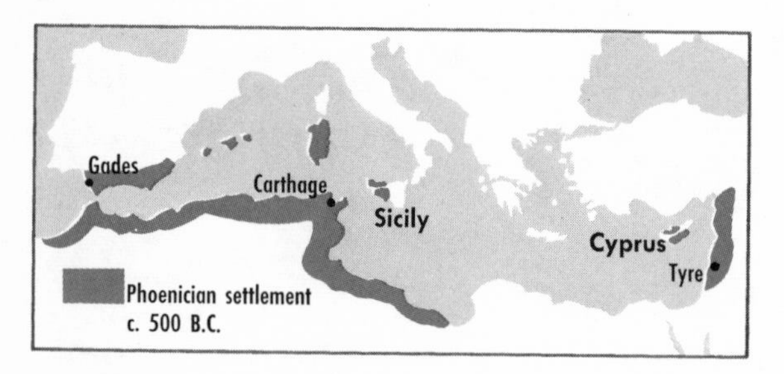

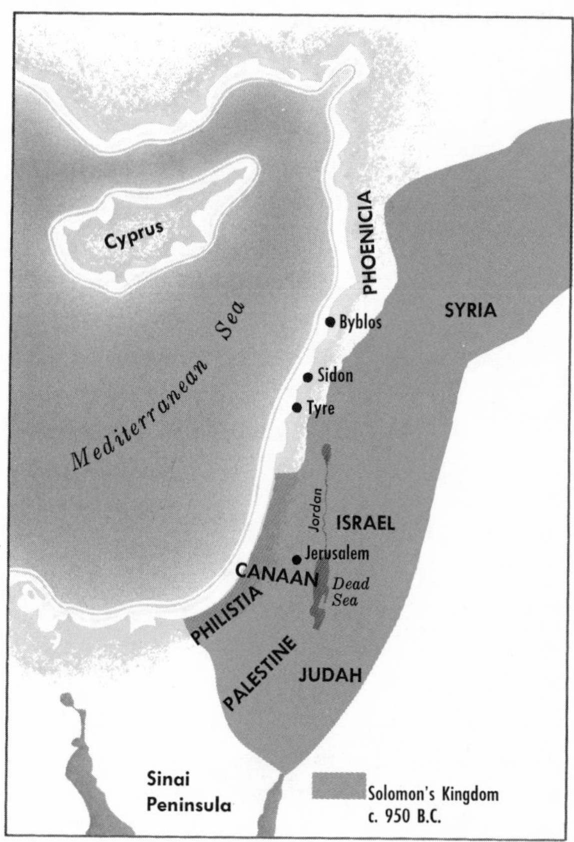

Worshipers, Traders, and Empire-builders

GREAT size does not always make a great person. Nor does great size make a great country. Many of the smallest nations of the world have contributed much to the growth and development of modern civilization. For example, history reminds us of the Hebrews and Phoenicians, two ancient peoples who bequeathed a priceless heritage of culture and tradition to all of us.

These peoples lived at the eastern end of the Mediterranean Sea in and around a land called Palestine. This land lay between the great civilizations of Mesopotamia and Egypt, but was not so rich in soil or other natural resources.

We owe much to the Hebrew scribes, for it was these farsighted men who recorded their history, after they mastered the art of writing. Indeed, the Hebrews, or Jews, not only gave us the Old Testament, but, in so doing, they told their own story of oppression, wandering, despair, and search for peace, which, at last, they were to find under the leadership of Moses.

And, of course, the early Phoenicians, as well as being great sailors and traders, who nowadays would undoubtedly succeed as big business tycoons, left us the alphabet.

THE LAND OF THE BIBLE

About 4,000 years ago, Abraham, the father of the Jews, led his people out of Mesopotamia to the land of Canaan, later called Palestine. He and his fellow-Hebrews were convinced that there was only one God. However, their Supreme Being was not merely a god of the sun, the moon, the river, the earth, or the mountains. He was *the* God of *all* things. His name was Jehovah. And they held, it was Jehovah who created the universe and everything in it.

When Abraham died, his son became the leader of the Hebrews. And eventually Jacob, a grandson of Abraham, inherited this formidable task. Jacob, who was also called "Israel," was the father of twelve sons.

One of these, Joseph, aroused the jealousy of his brothers because he was his father's favorite. So, while still a young man, they sold Joseph as a slave to a band of travelers bound for Egypt. Of course, the eleven wicked brothers had to explain Joseph's sudden disappearance, so they told their father that he had been slain by a wild animal.

Meanwhile, the Egyptian Pharaoh, was constantly disturbed by peculiar dreams. One night, after a vivid dream in which he saw seven very thin cows devour seven extremely plump cows—yet still appear underfed, in spite of their huge meal—he hastily summoned the court interpreters. Unfortunately, none could explain the meaning of their ruler's dream.

Then, one of his servants told him of a certain young

A picture of today's Land of the Bible. It could not have looked much different to Abraham, who had come from Mesopotamia with his followers and flock.

Hebrew slave, newly arrived in the land of the Nile, who might prove helpful.

Couriers were quickly sent forth. And soon, Joseph found himself in the presence of the king.

The young man listened attentively, considered for a few moments, and then, gave his opinion of the strange dream. "Your Majesty," he said, "it is the will of God that this land will have seven years of plenty followed by seven years of famine."

"Then we must make preparations," the Pharaoh replied, much impressed by Joseph's wise words. "But what can we do?"

"Let your chief minister arrange to collect one-fifth of Egypt's produce during each of the seven prosperous years.

Then make certain that the surplus grain is stored against leaner days. When the seven prosperous years are ended, and the time of famine comes upon the land, the chief minister will see that none of your citizens are deprived of a fair share of food."

The Pharaoh and his courtiers were greatly impressed by the wisdom of this young foreigner. "Since the God of your people has endowed you with the power of revelation," said he, "I now appoint *you* my chief minister."

During Egypt's period of prosperity, Joseph faithfully carried out his plan. And no one went hungry, even in the seven lean years which he had predicted.

But, alas, in the land of Canaan there was also a scarcity of food. And upon learning of the abundant crops in nearby Egypt, Joseph's brothers set out for the valley of the Nile.

In due course, they were led before Joseph. But at first, they did not recognize the kinsman whom they had cruelly sold into bondage. At length, they told him of the reason for their visit.

"We have come from far-off Canaan," they explained, prostrating themselves before the Pharaoh's chief minister.

"Who are these men?" Joseph asked.

"They hail from one of our neighboring lands, Excellency. They declare themselves to be the sons of Jacob, a Hebrew patriarch and father of twelve.

"The sons of Jacob?" Joseph repeated in amazement.

"Yes, Excellency. We are of the tribe descended from Abraham, who settled in Canaan, not far from the kingdom of Babylonia in the valley of the Euphrates."

"And one of your brothers was the favorite son of Jacob? Where is he now?" Joseph inquired.

"He was destroyed by wild animals."

"And were not these animals also his brothers?"

The visitors gasped; then, in their sudden fear, they dared to look upon the king's chief minister. But surely this great man was their brother! Now their guilty consciences reminded them of the wrong they had done him and panic seized them.

Did Joseph remember that his own flesh-and-blood had cast him out? Would he ever forgive them for this wicked deed? Would he order their imprisonment and immediate death at the hands of Egyptian soldiers?

Joseph did none of these things. He instructed attendants to see that his brothers were laden with food and gifts. Then he asked that all of them be granted permission to remain in Egypt. And the ruler, who was greatly indebted to Joseph, graciously assented, saying, "Surely, our rich Nile Valley can provide ample food for all who would live and work among us."

Joseph thereupon bade his brothers fetch their families and return to Egypt, where a stretch of land known as Goshen would be theirs. Here, he promised, the sons of Jacob and their families might dwell in contentment for the rest of their days.

THE TWELVE TRIBES OF ISRAEL

So, the Hebrews came to Egypt, and for many long years lived peacefully beside their Egyptian neighbors. Those who settled in the region about 1700 years before Christ's birth called themselves Israelites, because they were descended from Jacob of Israel. The years passed. Joseph and his eleven brothers eventually died. But all of their descendants remained in Egypt.

In time, the new Pharaoh (envious of the success of the Israelites in the land of his forefathers) came to the throne.

He pretended complete ignorance of Joseph and all that this inspired Hebrew had accomplished in behalf of the Egyptian peoples. Indeed, because he was envious of the Hebrews, the ruler soon began to look down upon them.

Well aware of their growing strength and influence, he

feared that they might some day unite with his enemies and destroy the Pharaohs. So, he resolved to make them his slaves and forthwith appointed unscrupulous overseers to supervise them and their work, which was endless.

By their sweat, toil, and often, by their blood, great monuments were built, and huge fortresses, pyramids, and temples erected. But despite the relentless cruelty of the Pharaoh, the Israelites remained a proud and united people.

The king, upon realizing that he could never break their spirit, decreed that all male infants born of Hebrew parents must be put to death. In this manner, he argued, the Israelites, as a race of human beings, would eventually be destroyed forever.

Models of granaries from about 2500 B.C. found in a tomb in Egypt. This is the type of building, mentioned in Genesis, in which Joseph had grain stored during his reign as viceroy of Egypt.

As we remember from our Bible history, however, a certain Hebrew mother who had recently given birth to a son was determined to save him at all costs. So, she placed her child in a receptacle made of bulrushes, and hid this floating cradle among the tall reeds which grew in abundance along the banks of the Nile.

Some time later, the Pharaoh's daughter, strolling near

Rekhmire, the vizier of Pharaoh Thutmosis III (about 1460 B.C.), had the walls of his tomb painted with scenes of his time. Thanks to him, we have the picture at right which gives an idea of the slave labor of the Israelites in Egypt. The biblical account of this period is in Exodus.

the river in the company of her maids-in-waiting, discovered the babe. She presumed that the infant was of a Hebrew family. Nonetheless, this daughter of "the great house" carried the small cargo to the palace, adopted the child as her own, and gave him the name Moses, which is said to mean "from the water."

Moses was reared as an Egyptian prince. But though he was surrounded by luxury and wealth, the boy was not happy. And his misery increased at the sight of overworked Hebrew slaves with scarcely a rag to their careworn, sun-blistered backs.

It was his earnest desire that these, his own people, be released from captivity. And in an effort to secure their liberty, Moses pleaded again and again with the Pharaoh; but to no avail.

Not long after the king had declined to free the Hebrew bondsmen, a series of disasters overtook the valley. The waters of the Nile became red and poisonous. There followed plagues of frogs, and lice, and flies. Cattle died. A great earthquake shook the land. The Egyptians, quivering

Statue of Moses, sculptured by the great Michelangelo.

with fear, appealed to their ruler. The Pharaoh, in turn, sent for Moses. Now it was the king himself who besought the aid of another.

"Ask your God to stop these terrible things," he begged. "And I will gladly let your people go."

But, alas, he failed to keep his promise. And the Israelites were treated even more cruelly. Then, a still more devastating blight descended. One night, the eldest son of every household in the land of Egypt was cut down; only the Israelite families were spared.

Again, the Pharaoh sent for Moses. "Take your Israelites, and all their goods and chattels and depart forever from my kingdom," he ordered. "For only then, I fear, will our misfortunes cease."

Moses, we learn to our great relief, immediately made ready to fulfill the monarch's request. Messengers were sent to the home of every Israelite. Far into the night, everyone prepared for the long journey eastward.

But, no sooner had the homeward-bound Israelites reached the edge of the desert, than the king changed his mind and bade his soldiers and henchmen mount their chariots and recapture the newly freed slaves without delay. The plagues were over, he announced. Work must be resumed.

Faltering in their tracks, the children of Israel, seemingly trapped, were bewildered. Ahead of them swirled the waters of the Red Sea. To their rear, the pursuing charioteers gathered speed. In their despair, the weary wayfarers began to complain bitterly.

"Is this why God delivered us from Egypt? That we might die of hunger and thirst in the wilderness? Would not life, even as slaves, in Egypt, be preferable to this living death?"

Distressed by the anguish of his people, Moses tried to soothe and comfort them as he would a lost child. "Have faith, my people," he urged. "Have faith. You will yet behold the glory of the Lord."

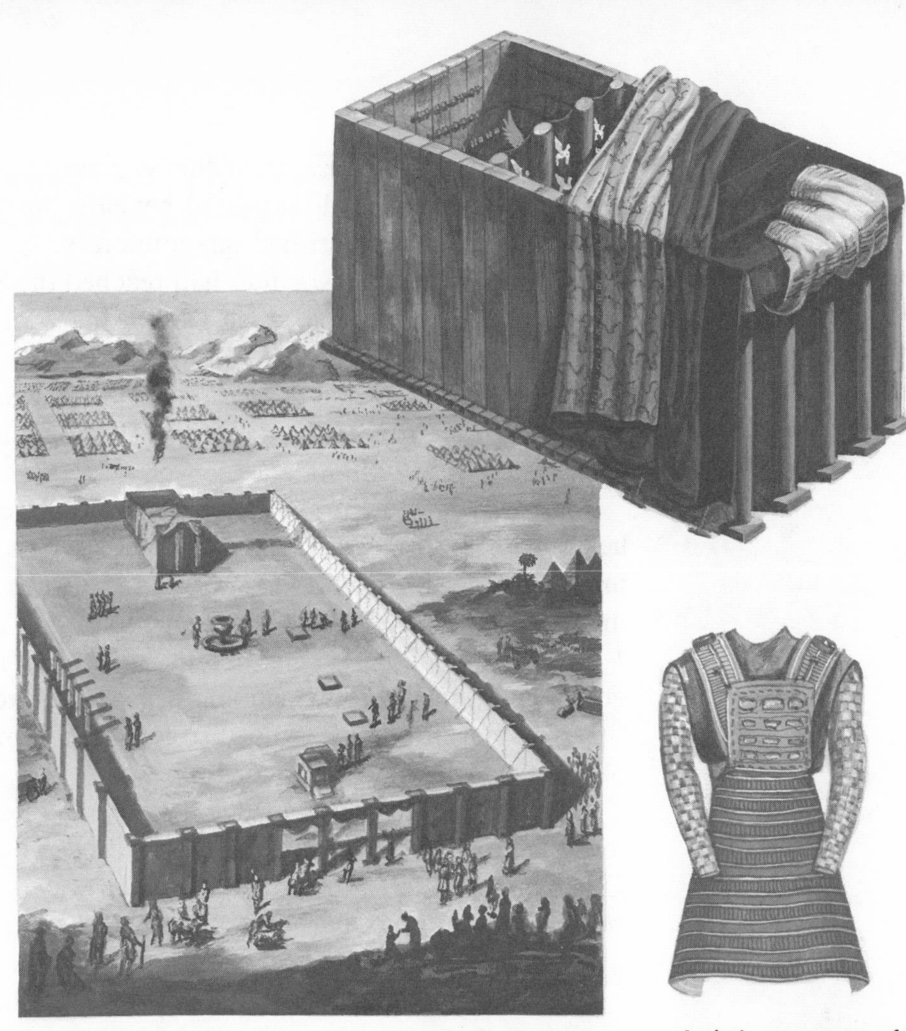

Artist's concepts of the Sanctuary, a close-up of the Tabernacle, and the garments worn by the high priest during the wanderings of the Israelites in the desert as described in the Bible.

We are told that God at that moment commanded Moses to lead the Israelites to the very shores of the Red Sea. As the thundering hoofs of Arabian steeds were heard in the distance, Moses was told to raise his rod above the seething waters.

An east wind suddenly raged with such violence that the waters miraculously parted. Thus did Moses, by the word of God, lead his people to freedom and safety.

When the Egyptians reached the water's brink and saw the path that led to the farthermost side of the Red Sea, they started across in pursuit of their victims. But the wind ceased to blow, and the angry waters soon engulfed them.

Their gleaming lances, their fine crested headgear, their splendid chariots—all disappeared beneath the waves. And all the king's forces perished ignominiously.

But, even when the Israelites had reached the Sinai Peninsula on the edge of the Arabian Desert, many of the followers of Moses were afraid and wished to turn back.

And when they came to the foot of Mount Sinai, Moses ascended to the top for he desired to be alone, to meditate, and to seek spiritual guidance.

For forty days, he prayed and invoked the guidance and help of God. And when at last he came down from the mountain top, Moses brought with him the Ten Commandments, a list of God's laws for the people.

But he found that in his absence they had fashioned a golden calf, and were worshiping it according to the Egyptian custom; the Jews had lived so long in Egypt that many of them had learned to honor false gods.

When his wrath had abated, Moses persuaded his people to return to their belief in one God, and gave them the Ten Commandments as a divine guide to their way of life. *"Thou shalt not kill. Thou shalt not steal. Thou shalt not bear false witness,"* he admonished them.

Then he spoke of God's other rules for the benefit of all mankind. And gave them renewed hope that the Promised Land would one day be theirs.

For forty years the Twelve Tribes of Israel roamed, like gypsies, far and wide, searching for a country in which at last they might settle. Ever dreaming of a land of milk and honey, they longed for peace and a resting place safe from those who would deny them their birthright—safe from those who would exploit and enslave them.

In our travels with the wandering tribes, we also learn that Moses, according to an ancient legend, viewed the Promised Land from a mountain peak, and thought it the most glorious spot he had ever laid eyes on. But unfortunately, he died before his dream became a reality.

At left, a relief from the eighth century B.C. shows a man using a sling, the weapon David killed Goliath with. Below, a relief from approximately the same time shows the blowing of the ram's horn; the biblical story of Joshua tells how the sound of the ram's horn destroyed the walls of Jericho.

Then a powerful military leader arose in their midst. The Hebrews conquered Canaan. And the Promised Land was divided among the Twelve Tribes of Israel.

At this time, the Hebrews had no kings. They were governed by judges, minor officials who had no palaces, no servants, and no personal finery.

Yet, in due time, they bethought themselves—since other great peoples are ruled by kings—the Jews must also find a monarch. A judge named Samuel agreed. And he chose Saul to be their king. After a brief ceremony, during which the first king was anointed with olive oil, modest headquarters were established. Gradually King Saul united the Twelve Tribes of Israel. At length, they became one nation.

The slayer of the giant Goliath, David, who played the harp and served as armor-bearer to Saul, succeeded him.

For more than seven years he reigned as King of the Tribe of Judah. About 1000 B.C., he became King of Israel. A mighty warrior, David conquered many nearby territories, captured the mountain fortress of Jerusalem, and founded

The clay tablet at right was found in Canaan and shows a musician playing a seven-stringed instrument very similar to the harp which David played for Saul, described in the Bible.

Model of the Temple of Solomon. This is how the building must have looked before it was destroyed by Nebuchadnezzar.

his capital there. He was a rich and powerful king. And during his reign, the people prospered.

Solomon, a son of David, followed his father to the throne in about 970 B.C. He was a wise man, and a highly-respected judge.

Solomon was very fond of luxury, it is said, and kept a lavish court. But, in spite of his love for worldly goods, he contributed much to the progress and growth of his country's trade.

He built the first temple in Jerusalem, a beautiful edifice, although noticeably smaller than Solomon's own palace. But during his reign, the people became restless and uneasy. They disapproved of his using forced labor. They also looked with great displeasure upon his wives, because they worshiped foreign gods. And taxes were much too high—almost unbearable, in fact, due to his extravagance.

Of course, he had many good qualities. And eventually, his son would have to take his place. The poor youth inherited all these old problems and worries that his father had been unable to cope with, in spite of his knowledge and wisdom.

THE TEN LOST TRIBES

Rehoboam succeeded Solomon. And when it became clear that the new king was going to be just as expensive as the old, the ten northern tribes revolted.

Led by Jeroboam I, they formed the northern Kingdom of Israel, and established its capital at the city of Samaria.

The southern kingdom was known as Judah; its capital was Jerusalem. But alas, the northern kingdom of Israel, though larger, more powerful, and richer than the south, was destroyed by the Assyrians about 720 years before Christ, and its homeless people were taken to Nineveh.

Judah remained independent until 586 B.C., but it finally was attacked by the Chaldeans, who, led by Nebuchadnez-

The famous synagogue at Capernaum, Israel, was built in the first century B.C.

zar, entered Jerusalem, destroyed it, and captured the Hebrews.

Among their prisoners were the three Holy Children of the royal House of Judah: Hananiah, Mishael, and Azariah.

Nebuchadnezzar made these three young men his special servants. He also gave them Babylonian names. Hananiah became Shadrach. Mishael received the name Meshach. And Azariah was called Abed-nego.

But even though they were hostages of the king, and forced to obey him, they did not forget their God.

They refused the monarch's food and drink as the sacred laws of Israel decreed. But perceiving that they were possessed of knowledge and wisdom, Nebuchadnezzar considered them more learned than all the sages in his kingdom. And, as they rose in his esteem, they incurred the wrath of jealous Babylonian leaders.

"These holy ones from Judah," they sneered, "defy your laws. They neither honor the king's gods, nor bow down before the golden idols which Your Majesty worships."

Nebuchadnezzar summoned his three special servants without further ado. "Honor *my* gods!" he thundered. "And if you do not obey me, I will cast you into a fiery furnace. Will *your* God save you then?"

Shadrach, Meshach and Abed-nego did not flinch. "If our God wills it, and deliver us from the flames, so be it. Otherwise, we are willing to perish rather than submit to your orders."

Speechless with rage, the king now bade his servants stoke the furnace to its greatest heat. Then he caused the three Hebrew captives to be hurled into the flames. The fire was so hot that body-servants standing nearby were burned to death. But Shadrach, Meshach, and Abed-nego, we learn, to our joy, remained unscathed.

The astonished king, scarcely able to believe his eyes, cried out their names, and commanded them to approach the royal presence.

Unharmed and smiling, the holy trio advanced toward him. And from that day forward, they were allowed to worship their God in peace. Furthermore, they attained the highest offices in the kingdom of Babylonia.

Later, the Persian ruler, Cyrus, released all Hebrew captives and sent them back whence they had come. But their nation had ceased to exist. And for centuries, they were destined to be without a king and without a country, until at last they came into their own, and established themselves in a twentieth-century Israel.

Here, today, rising generations of sturdy modern Hebrews, or Israelis, live, learn, work, and play—no longer beset by fear, hunger, and the constant threat of destruction.

"THE CARRIERS OF CIVILIZATION"

To the north of the land of the ancient Hebrews lived the Phoenicians. A people of herdsmen, navigators, and traders, they settled as colonists on a narrow strip of land along the eastern shores of the Mediterranean about the same time the Egyptians first were becoming civilized.

This palm-studded coast soon became known as Phoenicia, perhaps in honor of the wanderers, who had been named Phoenicians by the ancient Greeks.

The land was fertile, they discovered. But there were not enough acres to provide food for all who wished to settle there. However, these hard-working people, many of whom were sailors, turned to the water, wherein fish abounded. They built small fishing boats, and at first stayed close to shore. But the calm Mediterranean lured them into deeper channels. So, they made larger vessels in which they were able to travel greater distances to fish and trade in foreign seas off far shores—even beyond one of the famous Pillars of Hercules, which our modern geography books call Gibraltar. Some Phoenician sailors are believed to have sailed around Africa.

The Phoenician olive press was similar to the one used for grapes. Olives or grapes were put in a basket and pressed out. The juice flowed through a hole in the platform into jars.

Other travelers in the pre-Christian world were not so courageous as the Phoenicians. Indeed, we are not too surprised to hear that many a sailor thought twice before getting into deep waters, lest his boat be swallowed up by the sea-god, or tumble through the waves into nothingness.

But the Phoenicians were the most adventurous traders and sailors of their day. They traveled and traded in remote foreign lands. And some, it is said, even settled in Cornwall, in the southwestern corner of the nation we now call Britain.

Because of the growth of trade and commerce, which flourished for hundreds of years, the Phoenicians needed larger vessels. So, they devised the bireme galley, which is a craft equipped with two banks of oars; and also the trireme galley which, as the name implies, had three banks of oars.

Propelled by this extra power, they gained more speed without increasing the length of their boat. Phoenician seamen also learned to draw up charts as guides for their mariners. But, of course, they never lost sight of the North Star, which was, and still is, a guiding light of all who sail the seven seas.

The Phoenician coastline was noted for its fine harbors. Two of these were large and splendid ports, the ancient cities of Tyre and Sidon. The Phoenicians also colonized the city of Carthage in Africa, which became extremely prosperous as a result of their endeavors.

These enterprising merchants traded in many wares, from ivory and tin to gold, incense, precious jewels, silver, copper, wood, and grain. And all their transactions were duly recorded on papyrus by scribes using pen and ink.

This eventually led them to develop a new method of writing. For while they had no symbols themselves, they copied the Egyptian hieroglyphics (the acquaintance of which we have previously made), but they eliminated all unnecessary strokes and signs. They continued to refine and improve these until their new word-pictures alphabet numbered twenty-two letters. And from this ancient alphabet (after considerably more revision, and the passage of centuries) came our modern ABC's.

The busy Phoenicians also traveled over land. They piled their wares onto asses, and often onto camels, and traded not only in Babylonia, Canaan, Egypt, but even in distant India. How our modern shutterbugs would have relished the sight of great Phoenician caravans moving across desert and plain, laden with carved ivory, precious metals, cedars of Lebanon, and lengths of shimmering purple cloth.

They are said to have driven a very hard bargain. They are also presumed to have been way ahead of their customers when it came down to brass, or rather tin, tacks. But they couldn't nail down the *alphabet* and take it with them. So they left that to us.

Not all Phoenicians were sailors, fisherman, or traders, it seems. Some were skilled craftsmen, noted for their beauti-

The Phoenicians were excellent shipbuilders. Their cargo ships sailed to the islands of Britain for tin, to western Africa for spices, to Greece for wine and olives, and to nearby Egypt for linen and grain.

ful metal and glass wares. Indeed, their glass beads were so well-known and admired that sailors in many a Mediterranean port used them for trading purposes. Much of the costly purple raiment of monarchs and moguls owes its magnificent coloring to the murex, a shellfish of Phoenicia.

And when King Solomon built his magnificent temple in Jerusalem, he hired Phoenicians to carve the massive wooden columns that adorned the golden altar and the vast lavaboes in which the priests cleansed themselves before performing their sacred rites. These huge vessels which could hold thousands of gallons of water were embellished with raised figures of angels, animals, and flowers.

Our knowledge of the Phoenician culture derives from the word of others. They left no poetry and, other than the basis for our alphabet, made no significant contribution to the arts or sciences. Evidently they valued money above all else.

Even so, they were quick-witted, highly observant, and receptive to the ideas and customs of all with whom they had dealings. And this probably explains why we sometimes hear them spoken of as "the carriers of civilization."

"THE KING OF THE WORLD"

When Babylon and Assyria were building their fabulous empires in the land between the rivers, a king named Cyrus ascended to the throne in the mountain domain of Persia. The Persians had not yet developed a high degree of civilization.

They lived in the valleys cultivating their fields and tending their sheep. They had no large cities; only small villages. But King Cyrus soon conquered the neighboring tribes. And in time, they became an important part of his realm.

Under the leadership of this soldier-king, they learned

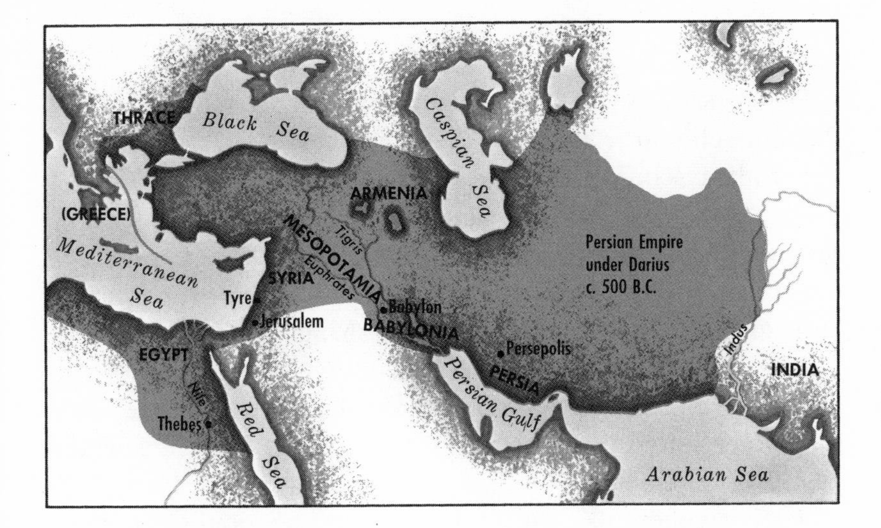

At left, a map of the Persian Empire of about 500 B.C. (the time of Darius); below, a Persian gold coin from the fifth century B.C. showing King Cyrus with bow and arrow.

1) to speak the truth, 2) to fight with bow and arrow, and 3) to ride well.

Then, Cyrus the Great, as he came to be known, organized a march on Babylon. And as we already know, he finally seized this fortress-city. But the conquered peoples were not enslaved or ill-treated. This most generous invader permitted them to freely worship their own gods and live at peace with one another.

Cyrus also liberated the Hebrews from captivity in Babylon, where Nebuchadnezzar had ordered them sent and restored them to their native land. After their release, the Hebrews became known as the Jews.

LED BY THE MAGI

In the practice of their faith, the Persians adhered to the teachings of an inspired wise man named Zoroaster. This spiritual leader may have lived during the time of Solomon, who, as we know, was also a man of great wisdom.

But Zoroaster traveled among his people, preaching and praising the good spirit of light—or Mazda.

Darkness was the bad spirit, said the founder of the Persian religion. And the priests who made sure that vigil lights always burned in the temples were called the Magi.

As a result of their close association with the good spirit, these keepers-of-the-sacred-flame were said to possess extraordinary powers. And, as we can rightly guess, the words "magic" and "magician" derive from Magi.

All these ancient races had their own special customs, religions, and rituals. For instance, the Persian noblemen wore long hair and beards, make-up, earrings, bracelets, and perfume.

Their womenfolk, except for beards, no doubt did the same. But in those days, ladies of all social ranks lived mostly in harems, and veils screened their faces from the public gaze.

Yet, whether rich or poor, everybody celebrated birthdays. Neighbors and friends were invited to take part in the festivities; if the family could afford it, a whole ox or camel was roasted for the occasion.

The most important guest was seated at the right hand of the host. (The right hand, as a rule, was the one that held a weapon.) Thus, when one Persian met another, it was customary for him to indicate that he was not concealing a dagger.

And those of us who love dogs will be glad to hear that these ancient people shared our affection for "man's best friend." When an individual died, his pet was brought to his side in the hope that evil spirits would at once depart. And dogs were never turned out of the house—but encouraged to sit or lie before the fire. Even a mad dog was well cared for. And if he could not be cured of his affliction, he was muzzled and leashed, but never mistreated. Those found guilty of abusing dogs were punished severely.

For recreation and as training for war, boys of the privileged classes were taught to ride. And Persian youths were

Above, the ruins of the Royal Palace of Darius at Persepolis (now in Iran); below, a detail from the pictured stairway depicting a tribute procession.

also superb marksmen, javelin-throwers, hunters, ballplayers, soldiers, athletes, and swimmers.

Ball-bat was a popular sport among the Persians. A combination of our polo, tennis, and volleyball, ball-bat was played by boys and men. The latter played ball-bat on horseback; the children played it on foot. It was also a favorite of spectators. Thousands of onlookers would line the playing-field to watch an important game.

The appearance of a band of musicians, playing a special march, would signal the start of the game. Then, the two teams, with as many as fifty players on each side, would face each other. Each player held a wooden bat, or paddle, in one hand and the reins of his horse in the other. The referee threw the ball between the two teams. The game was under way!

"Go and get it!" the crowd would yell. The player who caught the ball with his bat would hit it with all his strength so as to send it high over the heads of the opposition. The object of the game was simply not to let the ball touch the ground. The players kept the ball in the air by striking it with the bat, and scored a point whenever the opposing team did not return it, or failed to keep it in the air.

Cyrus was followed to the throne by his son, Cambyses.

And the son was succeeded by Darius. It was the latter who widened the boundaries of the Persian Empire until Egypt, Babylonia, Assyria, Phoenicia, and Palestine were included.

But the most significant achievements of this empire-builder did not take place on the battlefield. He constructed roads, established a postal system, built the greatest navy of his time, and introduced the practice of money-coinage.

He made use of messengers-on-horseback (indeed, the Persians were great horse-fanciers), and organized an effective means of communicating with his troops, whether in battle or serving as a sort of ancient National Guard.

The soldiers, messengers, and especially-appointed spies were therefore the eyes and ears of the ruler. And no citizen dared refuse to pay huge sums in taxes as demanded, lest an informer publicly denounce him as an enemy of the king, and a traitor.

It is said that King Darius once boasted that the mighty Persian Empire extended so far south that men were unable to live there, because of the heat, and so far north that they soon froze to death.

Be that as it may, however, rebellion eventually brought about the rise of Darius II, and the fall of his empire-building predecessor.

Crete

circa 4000 B.C. Bronze Age in Crete (pottery, other crafts).

circa 2300 B.C. Hieroglyphic writing.

circa 2000 B.C. Crete unified under Cnossus (Knossus) and Phaestus dynasties.

circa 1600 B.C. Height of Cretan civilization. Hieroglyphics replaced by linear script. Culture of Crete spread to Greece proper; this is the civilization portrayed in *Iliad* and *Odyssey*.

circa 1400-1100 B.C. Palaces of Cnossus and Phaestus destroyed by raiders. Decline of Cretan civilization. Dorians succeeded Achaeans as conquerors and introduced Iron Age.

The Early Greeks

circa 3000-2000 B.C. Greeks migrated southward from Balkans.

circa 1300-1184 B.C. Arcadians settled in central Peloponnese, and Achaeans occupied Mycenae. Achilles sacked Troy (1184).

circa 1100 B.C. Dorian invasion. Conquest of Megara, the Argolid, and Laconia.

circa 1000 B.C. Greeks migrated to Asia Minor. Three distinct groups emerged: Aeolians, Ionians, and Dorians.

circa 900-600 B.C. Government by aristocracy. Geometric style in painting of vases.

circa 650-500 B.C. Lyric poetry flourished. Geometric style in art replaced by Oriental style. The Milesian School of Philosophy: Thales, Anaximenes, and Anaximander.

Sparta (Peloponnes)

circa 736-716 B.C. First war with Messenians; Spartans defeated and enslaved them.

circa 650-630 B.C. Second Messenian War. Sparta crushed revolt led by Aristomenes. Sparta reorganized under rigid military discipline.

Athens

683 B.C. Hereditary kingship abolished, and limited to annual term of office.

594 B.C. Judicial and economic reforms of Solon.

circa 565 B.C. Peisistratus became famous as the conquering general against Megara at Salamis.

561-527 B.C. Peisistratus became tyrant, and sought to break down power of nobles.

539-500 B.C. Persian conquest of Ionia shifted artistic and intellectual progress to Greece proper.

490 B.C. Battle of Marathon; Persians defeated by Athenians.

480 B.C. Annihilation of Leonidas' Greek army by Persians

under Xerxes at Thermopylae. Greek fleet defeated Persians at Salamis.

circa 479-404 B.C. Height of Athenian power; notable artistic and cultural development. Pericles, Athenian statesman (457-429), dominated the age. Development of Greek drama: Aeschylus (525-456), Sophocles (495-405), Euripides (480-406). Building of Parthenon (447-432). Sculpture of Pheidias (500-431).

431-404 B.C. Peloponnesian War with Sparta and other Greek states led to Athenian defeat and decline.

Macedon

356-337 B.C. Rule of Philip II of Macedon; conquered all of Greece (except Sparta); succeeded by son, Alexander III (the Great).

334-333 B.C. Alexander crossed the Hellespont and defeated King Darius of Persia at Battle of Issus.

332-331 B.C. Expedition to Egypt; founding of Alexandria.

329-323 B.C. Alexander ordered Greek states to deify him as son of Zeus; they refused. Alexander's expedition to India. Alexander died at Babylon in 323; beginning of Greek cultural decline.

circa 400-323 B.C. Cultural life of Fourth century Greece dominated by great philosophers: Socrates (469-399), Plato (429-347), and Aristotle who taught Alexander (384-321). Sculpture of Praxiteles (385-320).

CHAPTER 5

Europe's First Civilization

AT THE EASTERN END of the the Mediterranean Sea between Asia and Europe, hundreds of green islands sprinkled in the warm, blue Aegean Sea provided the homeland for the next great civilization we shall visit. This Aegean, or Minoan, civilization gave Europe its first use of bronze, its first cities, and its first written history. From it sprang the great culture of ancient Greece to which we moderns owe so much—including the idea of democracy.

Along the shores of the Aegean Sea and on its islands the gods and goddesses, heroes and heroines of ancient mythology, supposedly loved and fought, worked and played. Our art and literature are filled with many references to these legendary beings and their deeds—Zeus, the king of the gods; Apollo, god of the sun; Pluto, god of Hades—the land of the dead; Athena, the goddess of wisdom; and Mount Olympus, where the gods and goddesses lived when they were not roaming the earth playing tricks on mankind.

The people of this ancient civilization loved to hear the songs that wandering minstrels sang about the ancient gods and heroes. Let's pause in our imaginary journey to listen to one of these singing poets. Strumming a stringed musical instrument called a lyre, he begins:

"Sing, O Goddess, the anger of Achilles, son of Peleus, that brought countless ills upon the Achaeans. Many a brave soul did it send hurrying down to Hades, and many a hero did it yield a prey to dogs and vultures, for so were the counsels of Zeus fulfilled from the day on which the son of Atreus, king of men, and great Achilles, first fell out with one another."

This is the beginning of the famous epic poem *The Iliad* that was composed thousands of years ago supposedly by the poet Homer. We say "supposedly" because no one knows for sure even whether Homer was a man or a myth. The story of *The Iliad* tells of a period of forty-nine days in a ten-year war between the Greeks and the Trojans. The Greeks were led in the war by King Agamemnon of Mycenae. They were trying to recover Helen, the beautiful wife of Agamemnon's brother, King Menelaus of Sparta. She had been stolen from Menelaus by Paris, the son of King Priam of Troy, a city on the eastern shore of the Aegean sea. In the story told by *The Iliad,* the greatest Greek warrior, Achilles, has angrily quit fighting because of a dispute with Agamemnon, and has gone to sulk in his tent. Without the mighty sword of Achilles to help them, the Greeks lose many men in the fighting. But when Achilles' dearest friend, Patroclus, is killed, he again takes up the fight and slays Hector, the greatest warrior of the Trojans.

If we had time to stay longer, we could no doubt get the wandering minstrel to sing us the other great epic attributed to Homer, *The Odyssey*. This poem tells the story of the

Above, the entrance to the palace of King Minos in Knossos; below, a fresco from the wall of one of the rooms in the palace, showing athletes in the favorite sport of the Minoans — bull-jumping.

Greek hero Odysseus "who travelled far and wide" while returning home from the Trojan War. The gods help and hinder Odysseus as he wanders by ship back and forth across the Aegean Sea. He and his men live among the Lotus-Eaters of Africa, blind the one-eyed Cyclops of Sicily, outwit the beautiful sorceress Circe, and have many other adventures before returning to their island home of Ithaca.

Still another of the many myths about the Aegean peoples tells of Theseus, the son of King Aegeus (for whom the Aegean Sea is named). It seems that every nine years King Aegeus of Athens is forced to send seven handsome young men and seven beautiful girls to King Minos of Crete, a large island at the southern edge of the Aegean Sea. Minos, in turn, sacrifices the Greek young people to the Minotaur, a monster that is half-man and half-bull and that lives in a labyrinth, or maze, beneath King Minos' palace. The myth goes on to tell how Theseus persuades his father to send him as one of the sacrificial youths in an effort to kill the Minotaur. Theseus falls in love with King Minos' daughter Ariadne, who in turn gives him a magic sword and a thread which he strings behind him as he goes into the labyrinth. Theseus kills the Minotaur, follows the thread back out of the labyrinth, and returns safely to Athens.

Until about a hundred years ago almost everyone thought of these myths and legends as being fairy tales that were no truer than those about Cinderella or about Snow White and the Seven Dwarfs. But one person believed otherwise: Heinrich Schliemann, an amateur archaeologist who had been fascinated by Greek mythology as a boy. When he grew up, Schliemann became a wealthy businessman, and he then set out to see if he could discover some of the places told about in *The Iliad, The Odyssey,* and the other myths.

The "Trojan Horse," which turned the tide of the legendary battle.

A fallen hero is put to rest. The city of Troy can be seen in the distance.

Digging on the Turkish shore of the Aegean Sea in the 1870's, Schliemann found the remains of an ancient city that he was convinced was Troy, and others became convinced, too, when he found a great treasure of gold jewelry in the ruins. Then, a few years later he found the ruins of the Greek city of Mycenae and another even larger treasure of gold and silver.

Excited by Schliemann's discoveries, other archaeologists began digging in the Aegean lands. They disclosed to an astonished world that an ancient civilization had indeed flourished on the shores and islands of the Aegean Sea at the same time the Egyptians were building along the Nile and that the Sumerians were creating cities in Mesopotamia.

Crete was the center of a far-flung naval empire because of its strategic location, almost equal distance from the mainlands of Europe, Asia, and Africa. This Aegean civilization reached its height from about 1600 to 1400 B.C. The palaces of the kings were huge buildings with many rooms and usually were several stories high. At Knossus, the largest of the many cities that once existed on Crete, archaeologists uncovered a magnificent palace that spread over six acres and was equipped with running water and toilets that flushed! (An accomplishment in sanitation not achieved again by a European civilization for another 3,500 years.) The people of the Aegean civilization knew how to manufacture copper and bronze objects, and they traded their products with peoples in Egypt, Italy, Sicily, Greece, and even distant Spain. Their art work reveals them to have been a gay, joyous, and nature-loving people who were fine artists and athletes. But, about 1400 B.C. the great palace at Knossos burned, and from then on the Aegean civilization became less important than that of nearby Greece.

Bounded on the north by Albania, Yugoslavia, and Bulgaria, the mainland of Greece extends southward to the Mediterranean, eastward to Turkey and the Aegean Sea, and westward to the Ionian Sea.

At least 3,500 years ago, wandering shepherds from northern grassland regions (in search of greener pastures for their flocks, and food and shelter for their families and themselves) sighted the fertile plains and valleys of Greece, and wandered no more. They built primitive houses of mud and brick, and soon discovered that they could raise wheat, barley, and vegetables in the valley; figs, olives, and grapes thrived on the lower mountain slopes. The nearby seas abounded in fish. There was ample food for all.

And, while these wanderers from the north were industriously planning their own civilization, merchants and traders from other flourishing lands to the east mingled with the early Greek settlers and taught them many new skills.

They learned to weave cloth, and to make beautiful vases and bowls. They built "modern" city dwellings, and they erected temples to their gods.

Eventually, these resourceful people learned the Phoenician alphabet, and adapted it to their own language. The Phoenicians also taught them how to build sturdy sailing craft, and how to encourage trade with other nations. And soon, Greek vessels, manned by adventurous young travelers, were sailing the Aegean, Mediterranean, and Black seas.

Returning voyagers told fabulous tales which naturally caused some of their countrymen to become restless. And, in this way, numerous Greek colonies were formed.

Thus, we stay-at-home tourists, riding backward through many cultures, many lands, and countless centuries, are not one bit surprised to meet, along the sunlit Mediterranean shores, and in out-of-the-way ports near the Black Sea, Greek sailors and merchants, busily exchanging olive oil, figs, wheat, and corn, for tin, copper, gold, and dazzling arrays of gaily colored cloth.

A pretty fair *trade,* it seems to us.

Each of the early tribes from the north, we discover, settled in a different part of Greece. And while all inhabitants shared the same language, followed the same customs, and worshiped the same gods, they were not under one government.

Mountains, interspersed with small rivers and streams, divided the country into valleys, and thus separated the various groups. But in time, these settlers in these outlying villages joined with their neighbors and formed their own communities, or city-states. Consequently, as had been the case in ancient Mesopotamia, these fiercely independent peoples of Greece often clashed with one another.

There were a number of city-states in Greece. And two of these were destined to become known far and wide. One was Sparta; the other was Athens.

THE SPARTAN LIFE

Let us first pay a make-believe visit to the city-state of old Sparta.

Upon arrival, we find that ancient Sparta is a plains city,

surrounded by hostile neighbors. Ever vigilant, and always ready to repel the onslaughts of foes, Sparta boasts no protective walls, no buttress against invading hordes; indeed, nothing but stouthearted citizens.

And, when we ask a youth why the territory is wide open, so to speak, we are assured that every citizen is a brick in the wall of Sparta. Thus, when we read or hear of "Spartan behavior," we form a mental picture of tremendous courage and the willingness to die rather than give in.

We also learn that Sparta has two kings–one to keep an eye on the other to see that neither grows too big for his crown, or otherwise abuses his royal privileges. These rulers are advised by a committee of five, and a council of elder statesmen who formulate the laws.

The inhabitants of Sparta, we find, comprise three groups: The Helots, or slave-laborers, farm the land under strict discipline, and are obliged to pay taxes (in the form of produce) to the state. Furthermore, they must raise sufficient food for all the peoples of Sparta.

The second group is made up of Aegeans, the traders and craftsmen who are friendly neighbors permitted to reside in Sparta as free men–but without political influence or a voice in national policy-making.

The third and smallest group of Spartans are career-

All training in a Spartan boys' camp was geared to train the young pupils to be dauntless fighters.

The painted detail above, which depicts a Trojan battle scene, is from the ancient Greek vase shown below.

soldiers. These young men enter the army when they are eighteen and, unless they are killed in action, are required to serve until they reach the age of sixty.

And, since every Spartan warrior belongs to the state, all are rigidly supervised. Male infants are carefully examined at birth; those found delicate, or unfit, are forthwith rejected and left to die—no weakling can ever hope to serve the Spartan cause.

The period of training, it seems, begins at home where the boy, until he reaches the age of seven, is taught by his mother that he must always be brave. For a Spartan must be ready to lay down his life for his country, and must never surrender to its enemies.

The Spartan mother then hands her son his large battle-shield, and sends him forth to continue his training under stern military men who instruct him in the arts of war and self-defense. They teach him also to remain steadfast and never to complain or show signs of emotion, no matter how great the provocation.

We note, therefore, that it is the mother's duty to see that the youth grows up strong, obedient, submissive, and prepared, if need be, to sacrifice his life for Sparta.

Indeed, we learn of one noble mother, with five sons at war, who upon hearing that all had been slain in combat, is said to have cried out: "I am not concerned with the loss of my sons! Did Sparta win?"

As for the Spartan diet: Their fish, meat, black soup, figs, wine, cheese, and bread sound fairly palatable. Then again, the verdict of a guest, who once tried their black soup, leaves considerable room for doubt.

"Now I know why these Spartans are unafraid of death,"

Painting on an ancient Greek dish shows a soldier exercising.

this dissatisfied customer declared, as he refused a second helping, some 2,400 years ago.

At the age of eighteen, all soldiers are legally bound to find a wife. But even after marriage, the new bridegrooms must continue to eat in barracks with their fellow-conscripts. *And* provide their own food!

After dinner, however, they are permitted to return to their homes, but without light so that they would grow accustomed to marching in total darkness.

The above photograph confirms that the women of modern Greece have not forgotten their traditions. The detail below showing Greek women working wool on a loom is from a vase that dates back to 560 B.C.

And we learn with regret that these noble citizen-soldiers are quite content to let the poor Helots, and even the freemen, till the soil and raise the crops, yet regard all workers and craftsmen as an inferior breed. Why? Because all persons who earn wages are socially beneath the defenders of their country.

Spartan money, by the way, was made of iron. It weighed a lot, but was worth very little. And because few people could afford oxcarts in which to carry their wages, no matter how small they might be, foreign traders and merchants, seeking markets in Sparta, were invariably discouraged.

But to offset many of the trials and tribulations of life in ancient Sparta, we note that the females, all good athletes, whose principal task is to aid and comfort their soldier menfolk, enjoy slightly more freedom than the women of neighboring states.

Of course, they are also required to spin, weave, and keep

At left, a vase painting (460-450 B.C.) of Greek women working in an apple orchard; in 1965 (photograph below), women still were doing much of the work in the fields.

house. But they are allowed to own property, which was certainly progressive, compared to other earlier civilizations.

And, to illustrate another phase of the Spartan approach to life, what could compare more favorably with today's do-or-die outlook than the story of a Grecian king who lived near Sparta? Having long been covetous of his neighbors' goods and lands, he wrote a threatening letter to their government.

"Let Sparta and Spartans tread warily," he warned. "Otherwise I shall be compelled to seize their lands, and their goods. And, *if* I do so, all Sparta will be enslaved!"

To which, with characteristic economy, the Spartan authorities replied: "IF. . . ."

THE HOME OF THE ACROPOLIS

Northward from Sparta, our next stop will be the city-state and famed metropolis of Athens. In many respects, Athens was the foremost city-state of ancient Greece, and therefore set the educational and cultural standards followed by the peoples of the many smaller city-states.

Beyond the protective walls, we notice thriving olive groves, rich grain and pasture lands, and a magnificent temple. And, without difficulty, we scale the walls, and the centuries, as before.

For, in the world of make-believe, all things are possible, no matter how impossible they may prove to be in reality.

In the colorful Athenian marketplace, or *agora,* we catch the delicious smell of freshly-baked bread and cakes. Moving slowly through the busy *agora,* we wonder if the handsome slave women who carry their water jars with such an air of queenliness, ever wish they might change places with Helen of Troy. Not too far from where we now stand, all the bankers of Athens are at work in their counting houses.

And, since the *agora* is also a favorite meeting place, no gentleman citizen who is worth his *chiton* (the garment commonly worn next to the skin by both sexes in classical times) would forego a chance to exchange pleasantries with friends and colleagues—and all the local gossip, besides.

The principal article of male covering, we observe, is the *chiton,* or tunic; not unlike a Roman *toga,* in appearance. (But we really must try and remember that we haven't crossed the Mediterranean, yet.)

The ladies of Greece, not to be outdone by their handsome menfolk, also wear long *chitons,* and when outdoors, a flowing mantle, the upper part of which becomes a sort of draped headdress, or hood.

Athenian gentlemen generally go bareheaded, we learn. But both sexes, if they desire, might be seen in public in

An artist's conception of life in the busy and famous agora, the marketplace of ancient Greece.

sandals. And, while the ancient Greeks are averse to lavish personal displays, Athenian ladies wear simple jewelry, when and if they wish.

AT THE SEAT OF DEMOCRACY

Continuing our tour of Athens (which was so named in honor of Pallas Athena, virgin goddess, and guardian of cities), we reach the western approach to Acropolis.

At the foot of this mighty hill, which dominates the city, an open-air meeting of the Citizens' Assembly is already in progress.

One of the council members, responding to questions from interested bystanders, explains that the Acropolis stands about 260 feet high (or approximately one-fifth of the height of New York's Empire State Building, we decide, after hastily dividing 1,250 by 260).

Of course, the latter is only in its middle thirties, whereas the Acropolis, precise age unknown, has existed for over two-and-a-half thousand years, at least.

All citizens, we gather, have an opportunity to hold public office, and all may vote in the Assembly. But not all the peoples of Athens are citizens.

And women, it seems, can neither become citizens, nor, in consequence, are they entitled to vote.

Moreover, this enlightened city boasted a great many slaves. And these, too, were denied the privileges of citizenship.

Even so, ancient Athens is generally regarded as the birthplace of democracy, which, of course, is a Greek word. And our present-day democracies continually strive to improve

From top to bottom: the Greek chiton, a garment worn by both men and women (the styles differed slightly for the sexes) and a typical sandal.

upon their late twentieth-century concept of government by the people, and for the people, a system under which all are granted equal rights.

The system of trail-by-jury also originated in Athens. And jurors functioning as judges, in certain cases, were chosen by drawing lots.

All participants, on oath to their gods Zeus, Poseidon, and Demeter, swore to speak the truth, the whole truth, and nothing but the truth; to listen, with open ears and an open mind, to *both* sides of every question; and to render an honest verdict, when called upon to do so.

Athenian boys attended school from the age of seven to fourteen, and learned to read, write, sing, solve mathematical problems, and play the lyre, a stringed instrument not unlike a small harp.

At first, using a stylus, they wrote on wooden tablets coated with wax. Later, they progressed to papyrus and ink.

They studied and read ancient Greek poetry and literature, much of which was memorized before their teacher, or pedagogue, who recited it to them and to whom, in turn, they repeated it, word for word. Indeed, it is said that a boy's ability to recite *The Iliad* by heart eventually gave him the confidence to speak in public. And, as we already know, the ancient Greeks had quite a way with words—not only in public, but also in private.

They also had a way with competitive sports. And, early in life, Athenian and Spartan youths were trained not only as scholars but as athletes whose watchword must always be: "A sound mind in a sound body." Or, for those of us who prefer the original Latin (adapted from the even-more-original Greek), *"Mens sana in corpore sano."*

The Muse of Music from the Portico of the Muses in the Achilleion Palace on Corfu Island.

The Parthenon on the Acropolis in Athens (below) and a close-up of a frieze on top of the columns (at left).

And, at the temple, when they were received into the brotherhood of Athenian citizens (having reached the age of eighteen), they solemnly vowed:

> "Never will we bring disgrace upon our city by dishonesty or cowardice. In company with comrades or all alone, we will fight for its sacred temples and for its ideals. We will revere and obey the laws of the city. We will always strive to quicken, in others, the sense of duty to the city. In all these ways, we will strive to pass on to our sons a city more glorious and beautiful than that which our fathers entrusted to us."

Having agreed to assume this responsibility, they undertook compulsory military training. And after two years' service, they returned to assume their duties as good Athenians.

THE FIRST OLYMPICS

Religion was a powerful tie that bound the Greeks together. They worshiped many gods and oracles, whom they identified with the forces of nature. These gods and goddesses, according to ancient Greek myths, loved, quarreled, and feasted among themselves, in the manner of their mortal subjects.

Athenian silver coin (tetradrachm, fifth century B.C.) with the head of Athena on one side and an owl behind an olive branch on the other.

Ruins of the temple of the goddess Athena in Delphi.

No Greek citizen ever made an important decision without some sign from an oracle, or priestess, who spoke for the gods.

Each city had its special patron god or goddess, but all the Greeks worshiped at certain famous temples and frequently sought advice, or prophecies about the future, from the same oracles.

One such place was Olympia, which lay under the wooded mount of Cronus where the river Cladeus flows into the Alpheus, in the angle between the two streams. Zeus was supposed to have claimed the sacred grove for himself.

When the days of the stone temple arrived, an older shrine to Zeus, with columns of wood on a foundation of sun-baked bricks laid upon lower courses of stone, was overshadowed by the new great stone temple built in his honor. (The foundations of the first temple are still preserved in Greek soil!)

A colossal image of Zeus, wrought by the skillful hands

of the great sculptor, Phidias, who had worked on it in his workshop for five long years, enhanced the new temple.

The bearded Zeus looked down from a lofty throne. His hair was wreathed in olive branches, and he was richly clad in a flowing robe of gold. In his right hand, he held a Victory; in his left, a mighty sceptre.

On the northern side of the sacred grove, there stood as many as twelve treasure-houses.

That the ancient Greeks should pay homage to a god with a program of competitive sports may come as a surprise to us. The tradition, however, seems to have had deep roots, for *The Iliad* describes the funeral games for Patroclus, the friend whose death sent Achilles back to battle in the Trojan Wars. Hence, they were a feature of Greek life in the ninth century B.C. Scholars don't really know how far back the ancient institution dates; they do know that such a program was always included in these ancients' religious festivals.

Nike, the goddess of victory, driving a quadriga, a chariot drawn by four horses (a fifth -century B.C. painting).

Held every fourth year at the time of the second full moon after midsummer's day, the Olympic Games became famous wherever the Greek tongue was spoken. When the feast-tide came around in each cycle of four years, there thronged to the Olympus—from all quarters of the Greek world—countless athletes and horses to compete in the contest and even more spectators to watch them. The camps on the banks of the Cladeus and the Alpheus were endless and must have been quite a sight to behold at night when fires glowed.

The Olympian festival helped the colonies of the west to keep in touch with the mother country. And, with the advent of the Olympics, a center sprang up where Greeks from all parts could meet and exchange ideas and experiences. Over the years, a feeling of fellowship—even though they were a scattered folk—was nourished by the event. Today, the influence of the Olympics is not confined to such feeling of fellowship among a single people; it brings those of the whole world closer together.

Today, women may also participate (a fact of modern life

Paintings on vases and statues found in Greece show the importance the Olympic Games had in classical times. Above, vase painting of a foot race; on the opposite page, a statue showing a wrestling match in progress and one showing a discus thrower.

which would be the death of the venerable gods—if they hadn't long since given up the ghost). The women of ancient Greece were forbidden to compete at Olympia. They weren't even permitted to watch from afar, much less enter, the gymnasium!

Later, perhaps to even the score, they were allowed to take part in womanly sports known as Heraea. But alas, the Roman tyrants eventually put a stop to their innocent fun and games, and the ladies went back to their household chores.

The first Olympiad is said to have occurred in 776 B.C. with Spartan exercises which tested strength and endurance under the direct supervision of the supreme Greek deity, Zeus (or so the ancients were convinced).

However, the list of contests was soon expanded to include such activities as running, jumping, wrestling, discus- and javelin-throwing. And, in succeeding tournaments, chariot- and horseracing were added.

As we know, monuments were erected in honor of the victors. Epic poems and songs extolled their virtues and

their triumphs. But they received no prizes or monetary rewards; no trophies or medals. The single tribute was a crown of olive leaves, which was placed upon the head of the winner.

Victorious Spartan youths were accorded the honor of fighting side by side with their kings—at the close of the Olympiad, however, for no wars were waged during the games. Indeed, if any Greek city-states were engaged in hostilities at that time, a truce was immediately signed.

AN ARMY OF 100,000—DEFEATED!

By the year 499 B.C., the fast-growing Persian Empire was steadily advancing toward its next objective, Greece. And, during the bloody half-century that ensued, the Persian Wars raged furiously.

Darius the Great had already conquered a number of city-states along the coast of Asia Minor. He now delivered ultimatums to both Athens and Sparta. By way of response, they promptly mobilized for action.

Then, determined to punish these city-states for sending troops against him, Darius ordered them to surrender at once, or face destruction.

Both Athens and Sparta refused. Indeed, the Greek city-states further stiffened their resistance and resolved at all costs to stand firm against their Persian oppressors.

Darius was determined to subdue the Greeks. He gave them the chance to save themselves from *total* destruction by surrendering. Before setting out to conquer Greece, he sent messengers to all Greek cities, demanding that each send him a bit of its earth and water as a token of submission to Persian rule. Many of the Greek city-states were terrified of Darius' mighty armies and navies; and they hastened to send some of their earth and water, as requested. But Athens and Sparta refused. The men of Athens threw the messenger into a well, crying, "There you will find both earth and water for your king! Help yourself!" Sparta, that small city of tough fighters, was no less gentle with Darius' messenger and his threats.

This made Darius so angry that he sent his ships with an army of a hundred thousand men to vanquish Greece. When the Athenians heard that the Persian Army was on its way across the sea, they were greatly alarmed. They sent Pheidippides, their famous Olympic runner, to Sparta with a message asking for help. He ran night and day, hardly stopping to eat or rest. In two days, he reached Sparta. But in spite of this heroism, this almost superhuman effort, on the part of Pheidippides, the rulers of Sparta stated they would have to wait five days until the full moon had passed, when it was their custom to sacrifice to Apollo, before they could help. To break this tradition would be to insult the god.

When Pheidippides returned with the message, the Persians had already landed near Marathon. The Athenians could not wait for the Spartans; they had to meet the powerful enemy by themselves.

While the Greeks were outnumbered almost ten to one, the men of Athens were better equipped for the battle. They wore metal armor and shields; the Persians wore only thin garments of cloth. The Athenians used long spears, while the Persians had only short spears, and bows and arrows. The invaders, for the most part, were slaves who were fighting for a cruel king. The men of Athens, on the other hand, were not only fighting for their very lives, but also for their homes and loved ones. At that very moment, wives, children, and old men were in the temples, or at their home altars, praying for their Athenian fighting men.

Rather than wait for the Persian soldiers to attack, the Athenian general, Miltiades, ordered his men to charge down the plain. The maneuver caught the Persians by surprise, and they did not have time to use their bows and arrows effectively. And the Greek's longer spears served them well in hand-to-hand combat with the Persians. Again and again, the Athenians attacked and broke through the Persian lines. Finally, the remaining Persians fled to their ships and sailed away.

Pheidippides was at Marathon, and again, this famous runner was pressed upon to deliver the news to Athens—twenty-six miles away. That distance, urged by his own joy, was covered without stopping. But he had not yet had the chance to rest from his recent run to Sparta, and he had taken part in the battle itself. As soon as he reached Athens and gasped out the glad tidings, "Victory is ours!" he dropped dead.

Pheidippides, who died in 490 B.C., is honored to this day in Olympic games. There is a special event called the Marathon race; it involves running the exact distance covered by the brave athlete who sacrificed himself for his country.

But a small band of Greek patriots had beaten a great king with a vast army of slaves and hired killers. The Persians were disgraced before the whole world. Darius was now furious, and even more determined that he would yet destroy the Greeks. He swore that he would not rest until Athens was leveled to the ground. With this unshakable purpose in mind, he began the task of gathering together a huge army and navy. No one would stand a chance against Darius this time.

But the angry king died before he could carry out his solemn oath to destroy Greece. His son, Xerxes, succeeded him, and, like his father, he set out to conquer the Greeks. But the people of Greece were equally determined not to be beaten. Knowing that the Persians would sooner or later seek revenge, they had prepared for them.

Accordingly, Athenians, under the leadership of Themistocles, the warrior, feverishly contrived to defend themselves. Throughout the city, there was the din of the pounding of many hammers as more and more ships were built. Themistocles felt the only way to defeat the Persians was with a strong navy. While the fleet of triremes were materializing, most of the other city-states in Greece had formed an alliance. If Persia attacked one of them, all the others would come to the rescue. Sparta, because of its fighting fame, was made leader of the defenders in case the Persians attacked by land; Athens, if the attack was by sea.

Just ten years after Marathon, Persia had formed an army so large that it seemed no nation, or group of nations, could ever stand up to it. This new army was supposed to have had 2,000,000 soldiers! Xerxes decided to cross his huge army into Greece at a place called the Hellspont, a narrow strait that separates Europe from Asia. (On modern maps, this strait is called the Dardanelles.) There was no bridge across this body of water; it was about a mile wide.

Xerxes, however, had his men fasten some of the boats

of his fleet together until they formed a bridge for the army to cross. But hardly had the boats been tied together from shore to shore when a storm destroyed the bridge of ships. Xerxes was so enraged that he ordered the sea to be whipped as if it were one of his slaves. It is hard for us to picture an army of men along the shore of the Dardanelles today, each with a whip or stick, beating the waves with great fury. And Xerxes was naive enough to believe that the Hellespont obeyed him when the water again became calm.

The Persian king rebuilt his bridge of boats, and the army crossed. It took all of seven days and seven nights, two men abreast, before the whole army had reached the other shore. The navy followed closely through the waters as the army moved on land. The Persians destroyed everything in their path. It seemed that nothing could stop such a large body of men. They reached the northern part of Greece.

In order to reach Athens, the masses of Persian soldiers had to go through a pass called Thermopylae that had high mountains on one side and the sea on the other. It was here that the Greeks decided to make their stand before the enemy could reach Athens. Here it might be possible for a few Greeks to fight with some advantage against the formidable enemy.

Leonidas, King of Sparta, decided to lead the fight at Thermopylae himself. His total force was 7000 soldiers. Three hundred of these were Spartans. Since the Olympic games were in progress, the full Spartan Army could not be spared. They would join their king upon completion of the games. Actually, when Xerxes found this ridiculously small

Xerxes and his army crossed the Hellespont on a temporary bridge supported by hundreds of ships. Most likely this was the first pontoon bridge in history.

group of Greeks blocking his way, he benevolently sent word that he would accept their surrender. But Leonides was a Spartan. "Come on and fight," he hurled back at the Persian king and his 2,000,000 soldiers.

Two days later, the Greeks still held the pass. Not one Persian had managed to get through. Instead, the bodies of Persians piled high as they perished at Thermopylae. But a Greek traitor (not a Spartan), fearing for his life, betrayed his comrades, and informed the Persian king of a secret path over the mountains. Soon Leonidas learned that some of the enemy had bypassed Thermopylae and were approaching from the rear. He sent troops to defend the road, but many of these had deserted the battle.

There was still one way of escape for those who wished to leave. Leonidas announced that anyone who wished to save his life could do so. "All those who want to remain with me, step forward," Leonidas said. It was indeed a choice between life or death.

"We have been ordered to hold the pass," the 300 Spartans said in one voice as they stepped forward. And others, too—a total of 1000 men—remained to die with their leader.

After Xerxes and his army marched through the pass of Thermopylae, they went on toward Athens. As they approached, the people of Athens sent messengers to Delphi to ask the oracle what was going to happen. The priestess, interpreting the words of the gods, said that Athens would be destroyed, but the people themselves would be saved by "wooden walls." The Athenians were greatly puzzled by this strange reply. Themistocles, however, immediately knew the answer. "There are the wooden walls of which the oracle speaks," he said, pointing toward the ships of the Athenian Navy which lay in the bay of Salamis.

When the Persians arrived at Athens, they found the city deserted. Themistocles had already sent the women and children to nearby islands, and the Athenian soldiers had taken

Xerxes, from a throne built on the shore, watches his Persian fleet suffer a crushing defeat by the Greeks during the battle in the strait of Salamis.

to their ships. As predicted by the oracle, Xerxes burned down the city.

By this time, the great Persian fleet was getting ready to attack the small Athenian fleet. Xerxes was so sure he would win that he had a throne built on the shore in order to watch the battle. Themistocles, however, had some plans of his own. His ships were in the narrow bay. Actually, Themistocles was now very much in the same situation with his ships as Leonidas had been with his soldiers.

This gave Themistocles an idea. He would play the part of a traitor, like the betrayer at the pass of Thermopylae. He sent a secret message to Xerxes suggesting that he divide his fleet and bottle up the Greek ships in a two-way trap. Xerxes thought this was an excellent idea. It had worked on land, and he concluded that it would be equally effective on the water. One-half of the Persian fleet stayed at one end of the strait; the other half closed off the other end.

Xerxes sat back on his throne to enjoy the destruction of the Greek fleet. Instead, he got the surprise of his life! With the enemy fleet thus divided, the Greeks could fight each half separately. And the strait was so narrow that the large number of Persian ships got in one another's way and bumped their own ships in the scramble to reach Athenian ships. In the confusion of rammed vessels, the masterful strategy of the Greeks brought them victory.

After the humiliating defeat of his navy, Xerxes decided to leave Greece forever. Realizing that the Athenian Navy might break down his bridge of boats across the Hellespont before his army could march across, he and most of his troops hastened toward Asia. The Athenians met what was left of the Persian Army the following year and defeated them thoroughly. The remaining few Persians who were not killed fled from Greece never to return.

A GOLDEN AGE

Under the leadership of Pericles, a great statesman, and patron of the arts, Athens became the focal point of Western civilization. New temples and shrines replaced those destroyed by the Persians. The finest marble was quarried from nearby hills. Sculptors shaped the massive blocks into objects of rare beauty. The hand of man had never before wrought such masterpieces in stone.

Much of their craftsmanship enhanced the Acropolis, in the heart of Athens. And the Parthenon, temple of Athena, with its imposing columns and carved ivory-and-gold statue of the goddess, was a triumph of early Grecian architecture.

The *agora,* the same marketplace we visited before, had indeed become an interesting place. It had been extensively reconstructed, but remained the center of Athenian life. Men still met there daily and talked about all that was going on in their world. It was a small world, but that could not be said of the men who congregated there.

Watched by his weeping friends, Socrates drinks the poison cup of hemlock and dies.

The Greeks were the first people to ask: "What is the world made of? Why is it the way that it is?" Their early philosophers thought the world was made of one basic thing,

Objects once used in daily life in Greek antiquity today are priceless collectors' items and museum pieces.

and they constantly searched for it—even in their conversations. One philosopher, Democritus, actually worked out an atomic theory that is surprisingly like the scientific views of today!

Among those for whom the *agora* was a favorite meeting-place at that time were Socrates and his followers. Socrates, who was dedicated to his mother-city and believed that *good* government depended on the *good* conduct of *good* citizens, felt it his duty to try to help his fellow Athenians become wiser. He haunted the marketplace, always ready to entrap men of all ages into argument. He was a familiar figure in the streets of Athens and could be recognized easily; nature had marked him out among other men by a grotesque satyr-like face.

Socrates' guiding rule of behavior was: "Know thyself." Goodness in man, he taught, is based on wisdom; wickedness, on ignorance. No wise man would deliberately choose what was bad for him in the long run. Unfortunately, through ignorance, most men may choose an evil that *appears* good at the time.

Socrates' influence extended outside the realm of philosophy. He always sought the truth, and was the first man to demonstrate that knowledge can come only from ideas or concepts such as whiteness or hardness. Think how important these attitudes are to men of science, to give only one example of many.

A funny story has been passed down about Socrates. His wife's name was Xanthippe and, evidently, she was as difficult as her name is to pronounce. Socrates often said that, by living with her, he learned to get along with the rest of the world! We seem to owe that ill-tempered lady a great debt.

Life, unfortunately, did not deal with Socrates with the same good ethics as he approached it. When the growing popularity of his ideas got in the way of some important politicians, they banded together to falsely charge him with introducing new gods to the people and corrupting youth. (Many a grudge was owed him by conceited powers whose foggy minds he had exposed to ridicule by means of his interrogation.) Although he brilliantly defended himself in a speech described by his pupil, Plato, in *The Apology* (Socrates left no writings of his own; it was Plato who recorded his teachings), he was judged guilty and sentenced to death.

His last days were spent in a dank prison. He was allowed but one final meeting with his followers, during which they discussed the immortality of the soul. With the setting of the sun, Socrates drank the cup of poison that the jailer brought him and, it is said, died in peace.

So, while the history of Greece was being directed by

Much has changed since the days of ancient Greece, but the way a stray animal is carried back to the flock remains the same. Far left, a relief from 570 B.C.; left, a present-day shepherd.

The Greek waters were always rich in fish, and fishing was as important in ancient times as it is today. Left, modern Greek fishermen casting their nets; above, vase painting of a fisherman from 520 B.C.

Pericles, the interests of the whole world were far more deeply affected by the doings of one eccentric Athenian. Greece can well remember him with pride, for he gave to mankind its most precious possession–fearless freedom of thought.

We can thank him, too, for two other geniuses destined to move the world: Plato, a true "child" of Socrates; and Aristotle, pupil of Plato. The school that Plato founded lasted for nearly 800 years after his death; his twenty-seven dialogues on beauty, good, love, pleasure, immortality – indeed, the whole nature of man – still endure. Aristotle brought to ancient Greece an atmosphere like that of modern science. The father of organized and methodical research, he laid massive foundations for all the world's halls of knowledge.

Pythagoras was another learned Greek. But he lived quite a while before any of the gentlemen mentioned above–and originated a sort of ancient "numbers game" in mathematics which many of us nowadays associate with geometry and stacks of homework.

But, during this fruitful era, there were also individuals who did more than sit and think, or walk and talk; and map out loads of homework for posterity. For instance, there was the great Hippocrates, a physician and healer of the sick.

Universally recognized as the father of medicine, his writings and teachings have inspired countless generations of medical men and women through many centuries. And the Hippocratic Oath is as familiar to modern medical practitioners as it was to doctors who lived and practiced 400 years before the birth of Christ.

Herodotus, the historian, spent much of his life compiling the epic story of the Persian Wars. He also traveled through Asia Minor, and is reputed to have visited Egypt, Babylon, and Mesopotamia—to all of which countries we, too, have journeyed via the magic of our hard-working imaginations.

Nor must we overlook Thucydides, the Athenian soldier-citizen who served as a general in 424 B.C., and compiled an impressive military history of the Peloponnesian War in which he served.

The Greeks were also outstanding poets. At religious festivals, their works were recited or sung by trained choruses. In fact, the word "chorus" is also of Greek derivation. Most of their early dramas and tragedies – especially tragedies – were written in verse.

The actors, accompanied by a chorus of singers, always performed outdoors. And masks were worn to depict such emotions as fear, rage, sorrow, and joy.

These "props," as we would now call them, were fitted with mouthpieces which amplified the voices of the players so that they might be heard by a large audience. Today, reproductions of these ancient Greek masks are sometimes used as decorative motifs in our modern theaters. And let's not forget the masks used at fancy dress balls, or masquerades, or the feasts of All Souls, or Halloween; and at various seasonal pageants such as the Mardi Gras and the Mummers' Parade.

The Golden Age of Greece lasted for less than half a century. Within this span of years, however, the great city-states built up powerful military and naval forces; as well as magnificent shrines, temples, and public buildings in honor of their gods. Yet, they were unsuccessful in uniting all their peoples under one central government. Old jealousies, fears,

Traces of the Golden Age of Greece are still in evidence within the modern city of Athens. The Temple of Nike, shown here, is but one of many beautiful architectural relics on the Acropolis.

and rivalries—legacies of the past—remained. And at last, the smoldering hostility between Athens and Sparta erupted into war.

The war was to endure for almost three decades and result in much death and destruction. The city of Athens was again brought to its knees. Many citizens lost their lives, and the mighty Athenian fleet was reduced to barely a dozen vessels.

But, worst of all, the Spartan conquerors tore down the walls that had long protected the city. The defeat of Pericles, under whose leadership Athens had flourished, was the final indignity.

After the death of Pericles, in 429 B.C., Sparta subjugated other city-states and wrought considerable havoc in Asia Minor before a new oppressor seized control and, as some of our modern strategists might say, cut Sparta down to size.

Athens recovered the independence for which her great soldiers and statesmen had fought and died, and an uneasy peace was restored.

But, as we of this century might also say, things were never quite the same again.

THE CONQUEST OF THE WORLD

In the ancient country of Macedon to the north of Greece, the natives were not only restless, but under their ambitious ruler, King Philip II, they were now ready, willing, and able to make war upon their good neighbors to the south.

By stratagem and trickery, therefore, Philip II won the confidence of Greece, annexed such territories as he and his troops could lay hands on, and imposed the will of Macedon upon all those peaceful city-states which offered resistance.

It was thus relatively easy for his son, Alexander the Great, following in his murdered father's footsteps, to complete the takeover.

A clue to Alexander's greatness is given in this story of him as a boy. One day, he stood watching some of his father's men as they tried to tame a wild horse. Each time the animal was mounted, it roared and kicked so that the rider was soon thrown to the dirt.

"Let me try," Alexander pleaded. His mouth was resolute, and his eyes shone with anticipation.

The king opened his mouth to refuse, but a look at his son's expression stopped him. "Alexander, my son, wants to try. Let him ride the wild horse." The soldiers, holding their breath, stepped aside. Surely, the lad would be killed. But no one questions a king's command.

The young Alexander tames Bucephalus.

You see, Alexander had noticed that the horse seemed to fear its shadow; young colts are often afraid of dark moving objects. So Alexander merely placed the horse so that it would face the sun. The animal's shadow would thus be behind its line of vision. The boy mounted the horse, and calmly rode away.

King Philip was overjoyed to learn how clever his son was. He gave him the horse for his own. In all the years that followed, Bucephalus, as Alexander named the horse, carried him through many battles. When the animal died of old age and weariness, Alexander named a city "Bucephala" in honor of his faithful steed.

A vase painting from the fifth century B.C. shows a soldier giving first aid to a comrade.

All the same, Alexander the Great (whose official title was Alexander III) had considerable respect not only for the bravery of the Greeks, but also for their artistic attainments.

Had he not read of Pheidippides, the heroic Marathon ruler; of Leonidas, who fought at Thermopylae; of Themistocles, the valiant naval commander? Their illustrious deeds were known far and wide—even to their foes in distant lands.

And had not Alexander's father sought to unite Greece? To restore to its former glory, Athens, the historic capital? That, at least, had been the impression Philip II left with his son.

But, as the youthful conqueror pressed forward, it became increasingly obvious that not everyone was in accord with the Alexander plan. Nor had Philip really convinced the Greeks that Macedon held the key to their future. Quite the reverse.

One Demosthenes, indeed, was violently opposed to all such grandiose schemes. And said so—on twelve separate occasions in the presence of a great many witnesses.

But not even the silver-tongued oratory of Demosthenes, the Athenian youth (whose mentors had once despaired of his ever being cured of a speech defect, much less inspiring thousands in the marketplace) could, in the end, prevail against the armed might of Macedon.

Besides, Alexander was not the sort of general who sat brooding in his tent. Having earned his title the hard way, he was determined that no man, or woman, should ever lose sight either of him, or his greatness.

First and foremost a man of action, he was perhaps the do-it-yourself type of military genius who never missed a battle and seldom, if ever, lost one. Yet, as a pupil and champion of Aristotle, he was also an admirer of the traditions and cultural achievements of ancient Greece. These, he avowed, should be carried to the remotest corners of the earth, and by none other than Alexander himself.

Meanwhile, such tiresome city-states as Athens, Sparta, and Thebes must be united under one government or heads would certainly roll—always excepting his own, of course.

We are not surprised, therefore, to find ourselves riding through Greece with Alexander and his war horse, Bucephalus. Naturally, *our* own prancing steed is invisible to the naked eye.

We might also call attention to the fact that crossing the Hellespont into Asia Minor is far less hazardous (for chair-borne campaigners such as we) than it must have been for those who actually made the expedition in the year 334 B.C.

And to say that the conquering hero took everything in his stride is putting it mildly.

Tyre, Gaza, Syria, the Persian Empire, and Egypt fell like leaves before the winds of autumn. In Egypt, furthermore, in honor of himself, this remarkable strategist founded the city of Alexandria, at the mouth of the Nile.

And, on the homeward journey—with stopovers in Syria, Mesopotamia, and Babylon—he left no stone unturned, and many demolished.

The second and third times around, Alexander helped himself to several North Indian provinces, incurred the wrath of many of his followers, and died of a fever at the age of thirty-three.

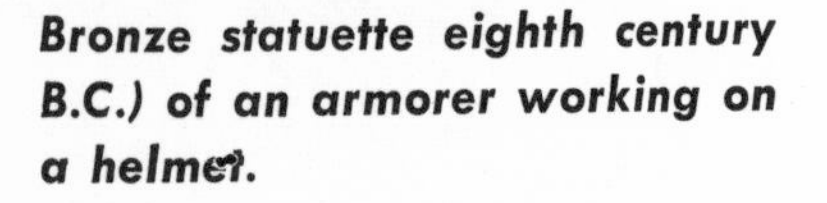

Bronze statuette eighth century B.C.) of an armorer working on a helmet.

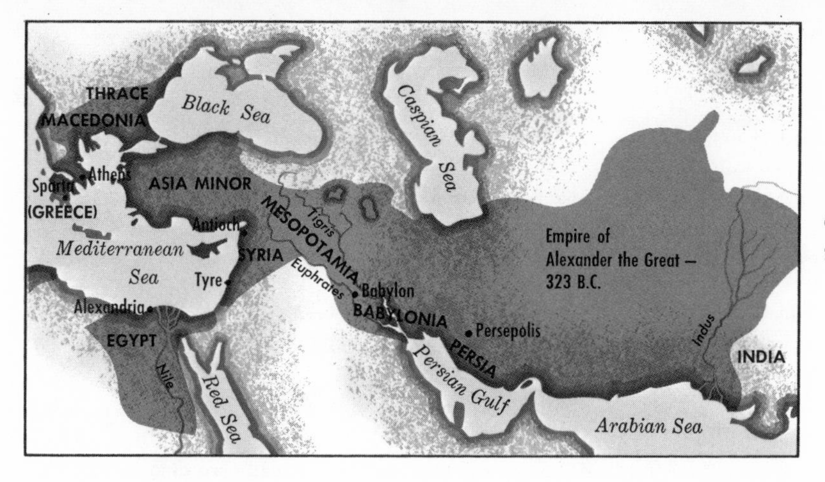

The map shows the empire of Alexander the Great at the peak of his glory.

The two sides of a Greek coin from about 290 B.C. depict the head and seated figure of Alexander the Great.

Meaning no disrespect to the departed leader, we heave a sigh of relief. But only because we weren't exactly counting on even a let's-pretend ocean voyage to Arabia (the next spot on his list), immediately after all that roughshod riding and marching through Asia.

It has been said that, toward the end of his brief but colorful career, Alexander was obessed with delusions of grandeur, and that his disenchanted officers finally repudiated him as a tyrant. And while the subjugated peoples of Greece had long ago resigned themselves to the Alexandrian way of life, they certainly had no intention of accepting this mere mortal (and a Macedonian, to boot) as one of their beloved gods.

They were spared the need for complying with this outrageous request, however, when in 323 B.C., the great man breathed his last.

But, across the Mediterranean, a neighboring republic was very much alive—and in search of new lands to conquer.

So, treasuring our memories of Greece at the height of her splendor, we pack our imaginary suitcases and take wing.

And, even though we had definite mental reservations about joining the late Alexander the Great on the Arabian excursion he was fated never to take, we look forward to our next flight of fancy.

In fact, we can hardly wait to explore the highways and byways of mighty Rome, the Eternal City. . . .

circa 1000 B.C. Terramare peoples settled in Italy; they are probable ancestors of Samnite, Sabin, and Latin tribes.

circa 900 B.C. Etruscans appeared in Italy, possibly coming by sea from Lydia.

circa 753-616 B.C. (Historically unproved). Traditional founding of Rome. Four early kings: Romulus (753-715), Numa Pompilius (715-673), Tullius Hostilius (673-641), Ancus Marcius (641-616).

458 B.C. Cincinnatus made dictator to save Rome from invading Aequi. Returned to farm after military success.

390 B.C. Rome sacked by Gauls. Capital allegedly saved by geese.

367-349 B.C. Four wars fought against Gauls.

264-241 B.C. First Punic War with Carthage (North African city-state). Annihilation of Carthaginian fleet.

235 B.C. Closing of temple of Janus indicating that Rome was at peace with all nations.

218-201 B.C. Second Punic War. Hannibal, Carthaginian general, reached Po Valley through Alpine pass. Quintus Fabius Maximus made dictator to protect Romans against Hannibal.

204 B.C. Roman General, Scipio, defeated Carthage. Recall of Hannibal.

202 B.C. Carthaginian army destroyed by Scipio. Hannibal escaped. Scipio named "Africanus" in honor of victory.

149-146 B.C. Third Punic War. Destruction of Carthage (146).

58-51 B.C. Caesar conquered Gaul.

54 B.C. Invasion of Britain by Caesar, defeating King Cassivellaunus.

48 B.C. Caesar defeated Pompey who fled to Egypt where he died.

45 B.C. Roman calendar reformed according to Egyptian computation of 365½ days per year.

44 B.C. Caesar assassinated. Succeeded by Marcus Antonius (Mark Antony).

31 B.C. Battle of Actium; Octavian defeated Antony.

31 B.C.-A.D. 14 Reign of Octavian (later called Augustus), first Roman Emperor.

29 B.C. Octavian closed the temple of Janus signifying peace throughout the Roman Empire.

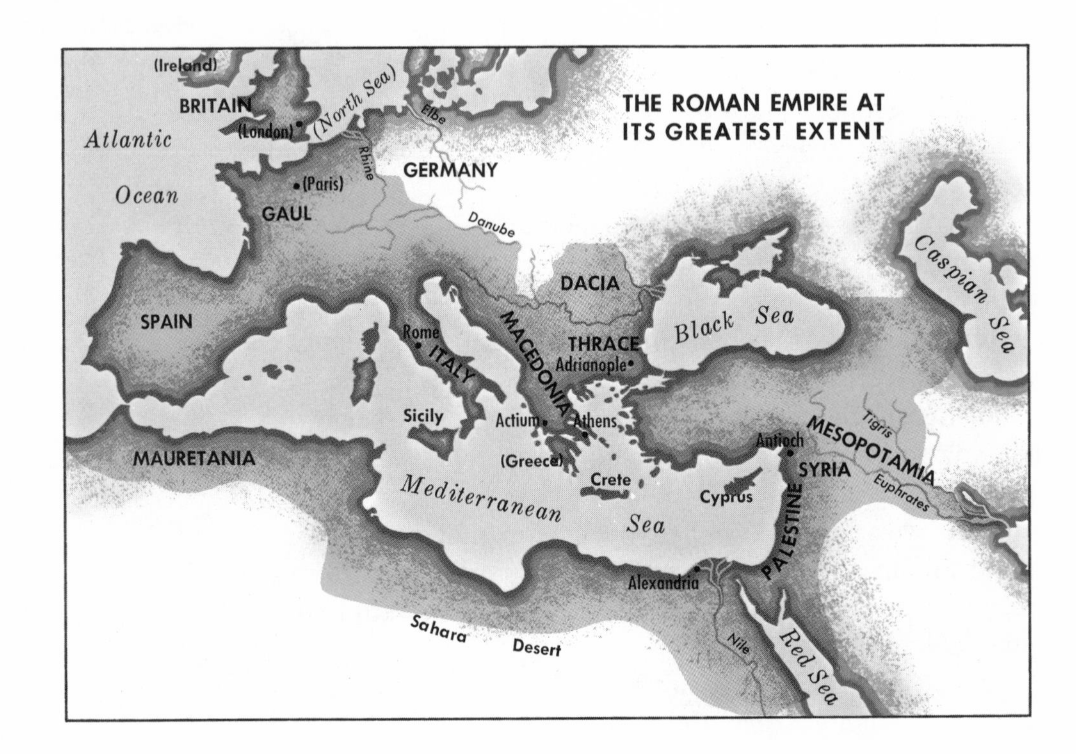

A.D. 1 *(anno Domini:* Year of our Lord), follows 1 B.C. because there is no year 0.

circa A.D. 33 Pontius Pilate allowed Jewish Council to crucify Jesus.

A.D. 54-68 Rule of Nero. Fire destroyed most of Rome (64) as Nero, accompanied by a lyre, sang a poem on the burning of Troy. Nero died in disgrace.

A.D. 79 Mt. Vesuvius erupted and buried Pompeii and Herculaneum.

A.D. 132-135 Jews rebelled in Judea. Revolt was crushed and they were dispersed among other peoples.

A.D. 376 West Goths (Visigoths) crossed Danube and attacked Balkan region.

A.D. 407 Romans left Britain.

A.D. 410 Rome sacked by Alaric, leader of Visigoths.

A.D. 441 In Britain, Saxons gained foothold of mouth of the Thames.

A.D. 419 First barbarian kingdom established in Spain.

A.D. 452-453 Italy invaded by Attila. Rome saved by Pope Leo I. Attila died, and Huns withdrew.

Mistress of the Ancient World

During the very years that the Greeks were at the height of their glory, a little town was growing up on the peninsula which is now Italy. That little town was Rome, which was located on seven hills by the side of the river Tiber. No one knows very much about this early period of Roman history, but a wealth of legend has grown up around those days. One of the stories is about the founding of Rome.

It is said that in early times there were twin princes named Remus and Romulus. Their wicked uncle, Amulius, who wanted to be king of the land, had them put in a basket and set afloat on the Tiber River. He thought that the basket would pass out to sea where the babies would surely perish. But the servant who had been charged to drown the infants left them in the shallow water on the bank thinking it would be deep enough to drown them. But the Tiber had over-

Etruscan figure of a she-wolf (the figures of Romulus and Remus were added later).

flowed its banks. When the river went down, the boys were left on dry ground. There the cries of the hungry children were heard by a she-wolf. This poor beast had just lost her cubs at the hands of a cruel hunter. So, instead of devouring the babies, the she-wolf nursed them as if they were her own. A woodpecker was supposed to have brought the twins fresh berries to eat.

Thus kept alive by the care of a wolf and a bird, Romulus and Remus remained on the edge of the river, until Faustulus, a shepherd of the king, passed that way. He found the children with the wolf. The shepherd, knowing who the boys were, carried them home to his wife, who brought them up with the knowledge and secret assistance of their grandfather, Numitor, the rightful king, who had been dethroned by Amulius.

When the boys had grown up, Remus, Romulus, and their friends set out to find a location for a new city of their own to govern. (They had learned who they were; Amulius had long been slain, and Numitor replaced on the throne.) They chose a spot on the banks of the Tiber, in a place where seven hills rose above the surrounding plain. But, first, the two brothers thought it would be well to give the city a name. Each wanted the honor of naming it, and each wanted to rule over it when it was built. As they were both hot-tempered and obstinate, they soon began to quarrel.

Their companions then suggested that they should stand on separate hills the next day, and let the gods decide the question by sending a sign from the heavens. Remus, watching the sky carefully, suddenly cried that he saw six vultures. A moment later, Romulus exclaimed that he could see twelve. So the right to name the city was awarded to him. He said it should be called Rome.

Romulus chose a hill and started to build a protective wall for the city. Remus laughed at the wall. "It is too low to keep out an enemy," he said, and jumped over it to prove it to his brother.

This so enraged Romulus that he killed him. "So shall it be henceforth with everyone who leaps over my walls," he said. Thus Romulus became sole ruler of Rome.

THE FIRST OF SEVEN KINGS

The city of Rome was at first composed of a series of mud huts, and, as Romulus had been brought up among shepherds, he was quite satisfied with a palace thatched with rushes. As the number of his subjects increased, however, the town grew larger and richer, and, before long, it became a prosperous city, covering two hills instead of one. On the second hill, the Romans built a fortress atop some great rocks, making it a safe place in case of an attack by an enemy.

As all the robbers, murderers, and runaway slaves of the

Etruscan bronze war chariot from the sixth century B.C.

Terra-cotta head of an Etruscan warrior.

kingdoms nearby had come to settle in Rome, there were soon plenty of men there. Only a few of them, however, had wives, so women were very scarce, indeed. The Romans, anxious to secure wives, tried to coax the girls of neighboring states to marry them, but, as they had the reputation of being fierce and lawless, their wooing was all in vain.

Romulus knew that the men would soon leave him if they could not have wives, so he resolved to help them get by deceit what they could not secure by fair means. He sent trumpeters out into all the neighboring towns and villages, to invite the people to come to Rome and see the games with which the Romans were going to honor one of their gods.

As these games were wrestling and boxing matches, horse- and footraces, and many other tests of strength and skill, all the people were anxious to see them. They came to Rome in crowds, in holiday attire and unarmed. Entire families came to see the fun, and, among the spectators were many of the young women whom the Romans wanted for wives.

Romulus waited until the games were well under way. Then, upon a sudden signal from him, all the young Romans caught the girls up in their arms and carried them off despite their cries and struggles. The fathers, brothers, and sweethearts of the captive maidens would have defended them, but they had come to the games unarmed, and could not strike a single blow. When the Romans refused to give up the girls, they rushed home for their weapons. When they came back, the gates of Rome had been closed.

While these men were raging outside the city, the captive maidens had been forced to settle down with their captors, who vowed that no one should rob them of these maidens, and prepared to resist every attempt to do so.

Most of the women came from Sabine villages. It was easy for the Romans to conquer their enemies until they were called upon to fight the Sabines. The war with them lasted a long time; neither side was much stronger than the other.

At last, in the third year, the Sabines attacked Rome with

great fury. First, the Romans, and then, the Sabines were beaten back. Finally, both sides paused to rest.

As battle was renewed, the Sabine women of Rome rushed out of their houses, and flung themselves between the warriors. They appealed to their husbands on one side, and their fathers and brothers on the other, not to fight. Those who had little children held them up between the lines of soldiers; the sight of these innocent babies disarmed both sides.

Instead of fighting any more, the Romans and Sabines agreed to lay down their arms and to become friends. A treaty was made whereby the Sabines were invited to come and live in Rome, and Romulus even agreed to share his throne with the Sabine king, Tatius. Thus the two rival nations became one, and when Tatius was killed by an enemy, the Sabines were quite willing to obey Romulus, who was an excellent king and made many wise and just laws.

As it was too great a task for him to govern the unruly people alone, Romulus soon formed an assembly of the oldest and most respected men, whom he named senators. They were at first the advisers of the king, but, in later times, they made laws for the good of the people and saw that these laws were obeyed.

The younger and more active men were the cavaliers, or knights. These were the men who fought as horsemen in time of war, but, before long, the title was given only to those with a certain amount of wealth. The sons and relatives of the senators and knights, and all the earliest inhabitans of Rome, were known as patricians, or nobles. The people whom they had conquered, or who came to dwell there later, were called plebeians, the ordinary people.

After Romulus' death, an old enemy of Rome, the Etruscans, conquered the Romans. For over a hundred years, Etruscan kings ruled Rome. The last of these kings was Tarquin (not an Etruscan by birth, but he had married into one of the foremost families in Etruria). He was so tyran-

Etruscan mirror from the late fourth century B.C.

nical that the Romans rose against him and drove him from the city. Tarquin, however, persuaded two of the cities of Etruria to become his allies. An interesting story about the battle between Tarquin and the two armies from these cities and the Romans is told.

The invading armies advanced so close to Rome that only a wooden bridge over the Tiber separated it from its goal. The Romans' only hope was to destroy the bridge before the enemy could cross it. Horatius, a brave noble, volunteered to hold off the enemy while the others cut down the bridge behind him. Lartius and Herminius, two other Romans of high birth and renowned courage, offered to help Horatius.

The three brave warriors stopped the invaders momentarily. When the bridge cracked and began to crumble, Horatius told his two companions to run back for their lives. He, however, remained and fought until the bridge fell. Single-handed, he had held back Rome's enemies. But, alas, the bridge crashed into the river, and Horatius found himself in the water. Although he was pulled down by his heavy armor, and although many of the foe's missiles fell over him, he still managed to swim to the Roman shore. Even the enemy cheered him for his bravery when he reached the other side. In gratitude, a statue of him was set up in the Forum, and he was awarded as much land as he "could plough in a day."

There was another Roman hero called Cincinnatus. He had a small farm on the bank of the River Tiber where he often went to rest. Enemies frequently attacked Rome and, during one of the more serious of these attacks, the people asked Cincinnatus to be their leader.

He left his plow, organized an army, and defeated the enemy. Within twenty-four hours, he was back in Rome. The people were indeed grateful, and wanted to make Cincinnatus their king. But he refused, and returned to his fields, preferring its quiet to high honours and wealth. He could have been a king, but he chose, instead, a humble abode in the country.

Remains of the Roman forum with the temple to the god Saturn in the foreground and the Colosseum in the distance.

WHEN ALL ROADS LED TO ROME

After the Romans defeated the Etruscans and other neighboring tribes, they declared that never again should a king rule them. In 509 B.C., about 250 years after its founding, Rome became a republic. A republic is a form of self-government in which citizens, who have the right to vote, control the country.

The Romans elected two consuls to head the government for one year. Each consul had equal power; each could stop the other if they did not agree. The duties of the consuls were somewhat like those of the President of the United States.

The lawmaking body of Rome was the Senate. Its 300 members, chosen by the consuls, held office for life. Because of this, Senators gave all their time to Rome. Gradually, they became the real rulers of Rome and, as they grew in their knowledge of men and government, they became true leaders.

Members of the Senate were chosen from the patrician class. Although the plebeians could not become members of the Senate, they had the right to elect two tribunes. The tribunes could attend Senate meetings at which laws were discussed. When a law was proposed which a tribune felt would hurt the plebeians, he cried "Veto!" This meant "I forbid!" and no law could be put into practice after a tribune had vetoed it. Today, we often hear much about the use of the veto in United Nations' proceedings. This practice comes to us from ancient Rome.

Most of the people were farmers. Cultivating small farms of maybe three or four acres, they took great pride in their crops. They raised grapes, olives, and grain as well as carrots, onions, turnips, cabbage, and beans.

The home of the average plebeian consisted of a single room and an *atrium*. The *atrium* was an open court where the family took their meals, entertained friends, and cooked their food. Sometimes, a householder built other rooms around the sides of the *atrium*. One of these rooms then became a kitchen. In the center of this room, there was a hole in the roof to let the smoke out from the hearth when cooking was being done. This hole also permited rain water to fall in the pool below which served as a water supply for the family.

Inside the house, furniture and possessions were few: a couple of stools, one or two chests for clothes, some cooking pots, and various household jars. Even the homes of wealthy patricians were fairly simple when compared to those of the wealthy Egyptians, Babylonians, and Greeks. But no matter how poor a Roman home was, it always had an altar to the gods.

The father was the head of the family. When a son married, he brought his wife to his father's house and they all lived as one family until the father died. Then the son became the head of the family. The father made all the rules for his household. All money earned by the children was his. He could punish any wrong deed by a member of the family. His commands had to be obeyed. Even so, the

Roman in the days of the Republic was usually a kind parent.

The mother in a Roman family was almost as important as the father. She was in charge of all the work in the house. She nursed and trained the young children. She helped receive guests and sat at table with them. The mother and father talked together about household matters. Roman women did not themselves have the right to vote, but they did openly campaign and influence elections. The Roman women were much more free than were the women of Greece.

It was the duty of the father to make the offerings to the household gods. He had to teach his son about the religion of the family, so that when the son became the head of a household, he, too, could make offerings. The Romans had almost the same beliefs as the Greeks, though they changed the names which the Greeks had given to the gods. They worshipped Jupiter as the king of the gods. Mars was the god of war; Juno, the wife of Jupiter, the protectress of women; Janus, god in charge of welfare of the home; Neptune, the ruler of the waters; Mercury, the messenger of the gods; Saturn, god of agriculture; Venus, the goddess of love and beauty; and Minerva, the goddess of wisdom.

One of the most honored of the goddesses was Vesta, protectress of the hearth; she watched over the household and her symbol was the fire which glowed upon the hearthstone. Temples were built in her honor, and the six maidens who were chosen as her priestesses tended the sacred fires in these temples. These girls had to promise to remain unmarried for the thirty years they dedicated to Vesta. All honor and respect was given to these women, because the safety and prosperity of the city was believed to depend upon the faithfulness with which they performed their duties and kept their vows.

Before every meal, the gods were honored by the father. He threw bits of food on the fire, and sprinkled a little wine

This bronze coin with the head of the god Janus (336-280 B.C.) originally weighed 12 ounces.

on the floor. This was his way of offering his respects to the gods. With this act of devotion, the family sat down to their porridge of pounded grain or to other simple fare.

Romans looked upon worship as a sort of bargain with their gods. They believed that their prayers would be answered if they prayed at the right time, in the right place, and with the proper form. When a man wanted a favor from a god, he promised to make a gift to the god if his prayers were answered. The Romans believed that they would be punished if they failed to make the proper sacrifices. On the other hand, they thought, many favors would come to them if they gave due respect to the gods.

The forum was the very heart of Rome and was far from a dull place. There were many kinds of trade. Farmers, their carts loaded with grapes, grain, or vegetables, haggled over the exchange of their produce for animals or other valuables.

There was no money; barter was the chief method of trading. One person would give vegetables for sandals; another, a certain amount of grain for fish.

However, livestock was often used as a kind of money. In other words, cattle, horses, goats, or other domestic animals were used to buy other things. The ox, for example, was recognized as valuable by everybody, which is one of the essentials of money. A suit of armor was worth about five to fifty oxen, depending on the armor's workmanship. From time to time, other items were thus used for trade. For example, salt, because of its great value, sometimes served as money.

Silver coin from the first century B.C. shows the head of the goddress Juno on one side and her temple in Rome on the other.

Roman men and boys dressed in short tunics, somewhat like those of the Greeks. In cold weather, they often put on one or two extra tunics, and perhaps, a sort of mantle. Over the tunic, a Roman citizen wore a *toga,* a long oval scarf, sometimes ten feet wide. It was folded lengthwise and draped over the left shoulder, under the right, and over the left again. One end hung down in the back; the other was tucked into the fold or loop in front. Both the *toga* and tunic were made of white woolen cloth, but members of the Senate were distinguished by the broad purple stripe down the fronts of their tunics. Slaves wore tunics and sometimes, in cold weather, cloaks; but they were never permitted to wear the *toga,* for that was regarded as the special dress of the Roman citizen. The Roman boy's *toga* was bordered with a broad purple band until he reached seventeen. Then his father and a company of friends led him to the forum to enroll his name as a citizen, and after this, he was permitted to wear the "manly *toga,*" as it was called.

In the house, Roman males wore sandals on their bare feet, but, for the street, they donned shoes and boots somewhat like those we wear today. Hats were worn only for travel and when the sun was uncomfortably hot.

The Roman woman wore a tunic and vest, and, over these, another tunic long enough to touch the floor, the stole, kept in place by a girdle. When the Roman lady went outdoors, she put on a *palla,* a shawl of white wool, draping it in much the same fashion as the men did the *toga.*

Women usually wore sandals both in the house and on the streets.

Roman boys were sent to school, usually in the care of some trusty slave whose duty it was to make them behave. They did little actual studying as we know it except for some reading, writing, and arithmetic, but they were taught

The ruins of the temple to Fortuna, above, and the temple to Vesta, at left, still stand in Rome today.

to ride, swim, and use arms in order that they might be of value in defense of the state. They were most carefully trained to worship the gods, to love their country, obey their seniors, and to always tell the truth—in short, to be fine citizens for the good of the state.

THE MISTRESS OF THE MEDITERRANEAN

While Rome was growing and the Romans were gaining control over all of the Italian Peninsula, the city of Carthage —across the Mediterranean Sea in North Africa—was growing rich through trade. This city-state had been founded by the Phoenicians in the eighth century B.C. As the years went by, Carthage became more and more powerful. Its prosperous trade brought it great wealth. It even controlled parts of the Iberian Peninsula (now Portugal and Spain) and a part of Gaul, the land that became France. The people of this African city boasted that the Mediterranean was a Carthaginian lake and that no one could wash his hands in it without permission from them.

It was difficult for Rome to avoid conflict with arrogant Carthage. With everything going well within Rome, its leaders began to take more interest in Mediterranean trade. Naturally the Romans resented the attempts of Carthage to keep it all for itself. Carthage, on the other hand, feared that Rome might shortly become a real trade rival. The two cities grew more jealous of each other every day—and more hostile toward each other. Each began to rally its forces for battle.

While the Romans had a large army, they had no navy to match the great fleet of Carthage. The Romans had to have ships to combat Carthage, but they knew very little about building them. Then, one day, around 260 B.C., fortune brought a wrecked Carthaginian quinquireme—a five-banked ship—to the Italian shore. The Romans hauled the quinquireme out, studied her, measured her, and so learned how to construct a galley. Crews were taught to row in a framework of benches set up on dry land. The Romans built and launched a fleet in but sixty days after the felling of the first timber.

This first Roman fleet was badly beaten by the more experienced sailors of Carthage off the Italian coast, but the Romans hastened to build a more powerful fleet. In the new fleet, the inventive Romans constructed what was called a *corvus,* a bridge that could be dropped onto an enemy vessel and that would hold its place by a heavy iron hook that fastened into the deck. By means of this bridge, Roman soldiers could board the enemy ship and fight the enemy hand-to-hand, a form of combat in which they had long been successful on shore. The new fleet defeated Cathage at Mylae in 241 B.C. and Carthage was forced to make peace, thus ending the first Punic War.

Roman citizen wearing tunic and toga.

The peace which followed the first war between Carthage and Rome was an armed peace. The first clash proved to be only the beginning. As its own trade increased, Rome continued to resent the arrogance of Carthage. The Carthaginians could not forget the defeat, nor Rome's growing power.

In Carthage, a general named Hamilcar was preparing for another war with Rome. One day, he took his nine-year-old son, Hannibal, to the altar of the gods. "My son," said Hamilcar, "do you wish to go to war with me?"

"Yes," the boy cried eagerly.

'Then lay your hand upon the sacrifice," said Hamilcar, "and swear that you will never be a friend to the Roman people." The child repeated his father's words solemnly. He never forgot his oath.

Hannibal and his father then went to Spain, where Hamilcar trained the men of this land to be soldiers. He taught Hannibal how to fight, how to plan a war, and how to lead an army. When Hamilcar was slain in battle, Hannibal was chosen the leader of the Carthaginian forces in Spain.

Hannibal decided there was only one way to beat the

To shade young Roman women from the sun, slaves followed them holding parasols.

Hannibal crossing the Alps.

Romans: to march through Gaul into Italy and capture the city of Rome itself. This was a difficult thing to do because Italy was a great distance from Spain and the highest mountains in Europe, the Alps, lay between. Thus, in the spring of 218 B.C., Hannibal gathered together thousands of foot soldiers, cavalrymen, and elephants, and set out for Italy. Elephants proved to be very useful in battle, and served much the same purpose as modern tanks. The elephants carried on their backs little wooden forts from which bowmen shot arrows.

HANNIBAL

It was late fall before Hannibal reached the towering Alps that guarded northern Italy. Little wonder his men were discouraged when they saw the steep, dangerous, snow-covered mountains. Day by day, the army crept along a narrow pass. The men were hungry, cold, and weary. Unfriendly natives rolled huge stones down upon them. Snowslides hurled animals and men to their destruction over the dizzy precipices. Roads had to be made in many places so that the elephants could pass. Half of Hannibal's men, and most of his elephants, were lost in crossing the Alps. The surviving half made their way into Italy.

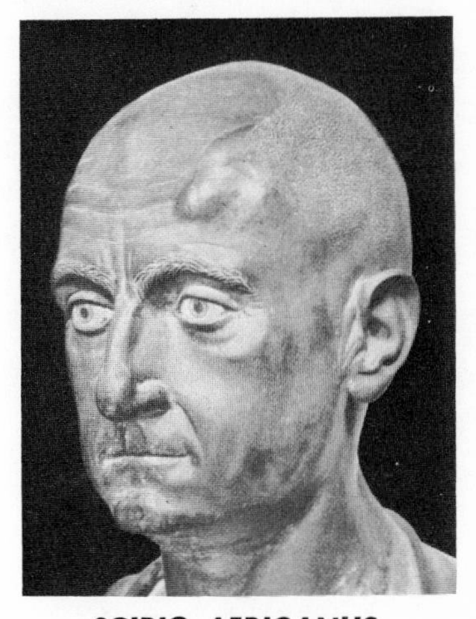

SCIPIO AFRICANUS

The Romans were surprised, and alarmed, to discover Hannibal approaching from the north. The Carthaginians battled their way south, conquering town after town. More than once, Hannibal won major battles with the Romans, but he could not take Rome. He remained in Italy for almost fifteen years!

With Hannibal so close at hand, a Roman consul named Scipio decided to go across the Mediterranean and attack Carthage itself. He assumed that the best way to defend Rome was to march on Carthage, that the best defense was to attack. The Carthaginians found their lives at the mercy of Scipio and his ally, the King of Numidia, while Hannibal and his vast army were far away in Italy. A Carthaginian victory in Rome would have been of little comfort to Hannibal if his own country had been defeated. In panic, the

Carthaginians sent word to Hannibal, and he and his men sailed from Italy back to Carthage.

Outside Carthage, at a place called Zama, Hannibal got ready to fight once more. In the front of his army, he put eighty armored elephants. Behind the elephants, he placed foot soldiers of every rank and regiment. On each side, he put cavalry. The Romans also lined cavalry along each side, and they now had more cavalry than Hannibal. Hannibal opened battle by ordering the elephants to charge. But the Roman trumpeters blew their trumpets all along the line, terrifying the elephants. They turned back on Hannibal's troops and killed many of them even before the battle started! In the battle itself, the Carthaginian Army was badly defeated. The Roman Army then marched to Carthage where the city gave itself up without a fight. Thus the Second Punic War was ended, in 202 B.C.

In the years that followed, Carthage again became a leading trading state. The hatred between Carthage and Rome flamed anew, and, in 149 B.C., a third Punic War started. This war was a short one and the victorious Romans, three years after it began, decided that Carthage must be totally destroyed. The soldiers rampaged through its streets, killing every man, woman, and child. Then they set fire to the city, and, when the fires had burned out, they scattered the bricks and stones. They plowed over the land where the city had been, and sowed it with salt to prevent the soil from ever again producing.

At the time of the Punic Wars, "the world" meant the countries encircling the Mediterranean Sea. Even before Carthage was totally destroyed, the Romans began to send armies into lands along the eastern Mediterranean. Greece, Macedonia, Syria, Asia Minor, Palestine, and Egypt were all conquered by the Romans. By the end of the Punic Wars, the Mediterranean was *Mare Nostrum* ("Our Sea"), the exclusive property of the Romans. Rome became the capital of "the world."

PIETAS, GRAVITAS, AND DIGNITAS: DUTY, PURPOSE, AND WORTH

By now, the Romans had become quite civilized. Having, through all their provinces and settlements in southern Italy, absorbed much of the culture of Greece (as well as much of Greece itself), they were quite pleased with their progress as empire-builders.

At first, they used the Greek alphabet and methods of counting. Finally, however, they evolved a system of their own. And today the Roman alphabet and Roman numerals are familiar to all, though, to be sure, many of us find it easier to write the Arabic "1-2-3," instead of the Roman "I, II, III." For not a few of us are quite bewildered by numerals above 10, try as we will, when in Rome, to do as the Romans do.

Prior to the third century B.C., the written Roman language was largely a crude imitation of Greek.

But, during the Punic Wars, the written histories, poetry, architecture, and cultural attainments of Greece exerted considerable influence upon the Romans. They learned to read Greek poetry and drama, built theaters, and translated Greek words into Latin, their mother tongue.

Ultimately, they developed their own literature, dramatists, historians, and poets.

They also dispatched to Athens a special investigating body to study Greek law and methods of government. This led to the construction of twelve bronze tablets of written law, which were exhibited in the Roman forum for the benefit of citizens, visitors, and scholars.

Roman children were required to memorize and repeat the Twelve Tablets. Indeed, the ancient solons, or lawgivers, formulated an impressive code of Roman laws, many of which are still in use throughout our modern world.

All conquered territories were identified as Roman provinces. And their inhabitants were in duty bound to pay

Roman soldiers in front of an important aqueduct (below) and at right, remains of the Claudian Aqueduct, one of the finest in its time.

taxes to Rome. Moreover, the Senate appointed provincial governors, and stationed detachments of troops in each province to maintain law and order—*Roman* law and order, of course.

They stripped their "provinces" of virtually all their possessions, invariably returning home bearing such spoils of war as vessels of gold and silver; jewels of every description; fine silks; richly carved furniture; and priceless sculpture and paintings.

However, their foreign victories also fostered endless domestic problems in the areas of food, housing, and employment. For wherever Roman legions set foot, they looted, destroyed, and enslaved. Thus, a vast segment of Rome's population consisted of victims of war, pressed into service as slaves and laborers. In fact, there were so many alien slaves that native Roman freemen and farm workers were unable to find employment. And this greatly increased the misery of all concerned.

Moreover, the irreparable loss of Roman youth in endless wars and an oppressive system of internal taxation eventu-

Even today the Via Appia Antica (the ancient Appian Way) carries traffic over its somewhat bumpy course, just as it once carried Roman war chariots and centurions.

ally undermined the strength of the republic. Thus, the ill-gotten gains of the conqueror, in certain respects, proved to be losses.

At this period in their history, Romans might be divided into two classes: the self-indulgent rich, who cared for little but wealth and pleasure; and the poor, who grew more and more resentful of those who exploited them, when all they sought was food, shelter, and a decent way of life—with a minimum of hard labor.

After all, if their self-styled betters could luxuriate on elegant couches all day, and spend their nights carousing, why should the worthy poor be denied the right to "express" themselves?

Stern and forbidding as taskmasters, the Romans had grown callous and cynical. In the field of sports, they were no longer content with chariot races and wrestling matches. They demanded fist fights and blood sacrifices.

At first, they were amused by the spectacle of wild beast pitted against wild beast; of lions, leopards, panthers, and elephants—sometimes scores of them—clawing and mauling each other in the arena. But this form of diversion soon lost its novelty.

It is said that those who ill-treat animals are often brutal humans.

And many Romans had reached the point where they craved the excitement of violence and sudden death. But not their own, you may be sure. A quaint Etruscan custom favored combats among prisoners at the gravesides of fallen warriors. The Romans found this so diverting that it soon degenerated into an orgy of mayhem, wherein trained fighters, or gladiators, and slaves (who also happened to be convicted criminals) were promised their freedom, if they fought for a certain number of years and emerged unscathed.

Training schools for gladiators did a thriving business, and also supplied graduates upon short notice. These men battled furiously, but not always dexterously. And the Romans soon grew tired of their inept and clumsy performances.

Upper-class Romans often abused their slaves, branding them with hot irons, as they did their cattle. Nor did they care unduly if these unfortunates were overworked and underpaid; if indeed they ever received a single *denarius* for their pains. Many of them died miserably in the service of their masters. But traders and merchants could always obtain replacements—as they might barter tin or wheat for silk. And children born of slaves were also the personal property of the master, to dispose of when, as, or if he saw fit.

THE DEATH OF A REPUBLIC

But, even as the Roman republic widened its boundaries and daily grew mightier, unrest stirred. Civil wars, often hinted at, finally erupted. Roman citizen fought against Roman citizen. Brother betrayed brother. General rose up in arms against general. Julius Caesar, conqueror of all Gaul and many Germanic lands, crossed swords with Pompey, deliverer of Syria and Palestine. The great Caesar assumed control of an empire that extended from the North Sea to the Euphrates.

Under his leadership, Rome changed in 49 B.C. from a republic to a dictatorship, with all powers vested in one man for the duration of his lifetime. And all subordinates, such as consuls, senators, and tribunes, were responsible to the head of the state instead of to the people.

A brilliant general and an astute statesman, Caesar served his country wisely and well. During his reign, he improved the living conditions of the impoverished, appointed more senators, and stipulated that commoners, as well as noblemen, be given seats in the Roman Senate.

He limited the amount of property individuals might own, and reformed colonial tax structures, so that unscrupulous governors could no longer appropriate moneys to which they were not entitled.

He specified that the calendar devised by the Egyptians be modified by Roman astronomers and used throughout his dominions. And, with remarkably few changes, we moderns still use the ancient Roman calendar to this day.

From Caesar and the Roman astronomers, we also inherited the months of our year. January is named in honor of the god Janus. February comes from *Februarius,* the feast of purification. March honors Martius or Mars, god of war. April derives from the Latin *aprilis* which means "to open," and perhaps signifies the blossoming of flowers and plants. May is named for Maius Jupiter, the chief Roman god; June comes from Junius. July honors Julius Caesar. August is named for the emperor, Augustus Caesar. And the Latin equivalents of seven, eight, nine, and ten: (*septem, octo, novem, and decem*) provide the names for the remaining months of our year.

As we recall, the months of the Egyptian calendar were all thirty days in length, with five extra days at the end of the year. In rearranging this calendar, Caesar decided to have thirty-one days in every other month. There were, however, only enough days in the year to have five months with thirty-one days. Caesar subtracted a day from February, the last month in the Roman year, leaving it with twenty-nine days.

Later, when Augustus became the Roman emperor, the month of August acquired another day. For, if great Julius Caesar's month of July numbered thirty-one days, almost-as-great Augustus Caesar must be no less honored.

So, eventually, we inherited seven thirty-one-day months, one twenty-eight-day month—except in Leap Year, when there are twenty-nine days—and four thirty-day months.

World conquest was, of course, the ultimate goal of Caesar. He envisioned a splendid empire that would flourish and endure forever.

But, as we have seen, conquerors rise and fall. Vulnerable to forces from without, and to foes from within, empires seem fated to sow the seeds—and reap the harvests—of their own destruction.

And, although many Romans had abiding faith in their ruler, others, seeking to revitalize the republic, feared that

Roman coin* (denarius) *showing citizen voting.

Denarius with the head of Caesar.

Many wars were fought by Rome, many victories won, and after each victory the winner was given a triumphal reception in the capital.

Caesar would ultimately restore the hated monarchy. Thus, they were suspicious of his noble intentions.

Finally, his enemies, led by Brutus and Cassius (all of whom pretended to be Caesar's friends), decided to proceed against him.

In the year 44 B.C., on the fifteenth day of March, the Senate convened.

The conspirators surrounded their leader, under pretext of asking his advice.

At a given signal, they unsheated their swords. Mystified, Caesar drew back a few paces. Then, sighting his old comrade, he gasped: "Et tu, Brute!" Stabbed many times, he then fell to the ground, and died.

Civil war followed the death of Caesar. And three rivals contended for the leadership of the Roman Empire.

THE FIRST EMPEROR

Octavian, a grandnephew, finally succeeded his granduncle, Julius Caesar.

When Octavian assumed control of the government, he

restored to the Senate the powers it had vested in his predecessor. But, to a man, they insisted that he remain their consul, and their "First Citizen."

Octavian also held the posts of tribune, provincial governor, and dictator. Since "dictator" was a term he disliked—nor was he anxious to be called king, a rank despised by the people—Octavian in 27 B.C. became known as *Imperator,* or "head of the empire." And, in time, he was honored with the added titles, Augustus Caesar Octavianus—or Augustus, for short.

During his thirteen years as Emperor, Augustus appointed honest governors to serve the Roman provinces and their peoples.

He instituted a fair system of tax levies, whereby revenues were apportioned to roadbuilding, aqueducts, bridges, and other civic necessities. The aqueducts guaranteed an uninterrupted supply of water for all regions; and contributed to the good health and general well-being of the people.

Nowadays, we merely turn on the faucet, and water flows freely. But as we have learned, in our make-believe travels through many lands and many centuries, water in the early days of civilization came almost entirely from wells and springs, which, in some cases, might be polluted.

The ancient Romans surmounted this difficulty by making pure water readily available to all peoples. First they sought out lakes and other bodies of water; then connected them with enormous conduits, or aqueducts, which are artificial channels for the conveyance of water from one place to another.

The Romans also built underground sewers that would dispose of all waste matter in such a way as to keep their community free from disease. Before they employed the aqueduct system, however, the most unsanitary conditions prevailed.

Nowadays, almost all cities and communities take such

The ruins of the Temple of Hercules in Agrigento, Italy.

"modern" conveniences as aqueducts and sewers for granted.

And most of us have heard of the Appian Way, 350 miles long and built in the fourth century before Christ, and the familiar saying, "All roads lead to Rome." For these splendid highways and winding ribbons of stone (traces of which are still to be found) were known to all merchants, soldiers, charioteers, and travelers, from near and far.

By building splendid palaces and temples, after the style of those in Athens and in other Greek cities, the Emperor Augustus beautified Rome.

Men, he thought, were forgetting their gods, and he wished to inspire them; to restore their faith in the great Roman deities. The Pantheon was, of course, the temple of all gods, and a magnificent structure. There were now several imposing forums in the city, too. And these, as well as the temples, were adorned with statues. There were many attractive parks and public gardens. Along the Campus

Much of what we know of life in a Roman city comes from the city of Pompeii in Italy, which was buried on August 24, in the year 79 A.D., by the ashes of the erupting Mt. Vesuvius, a volcano still active today. Pompeii was dug out of the ashes and partially restored only in this century. Our picture shows an artist's conception of the day the earth started to tremble.

Martius there were porticoes, with roofs upheld by columns. Here, people might walk in the shade. Augustus is said to have often boasted, "I found Rome of brick and will leave it of marble."

WHEN IN ROME....

And now, let us briefly retrace our steps through ancient Rome during the reign of the Emperor Augustus.

In the early days of the Roman Republic, we recall, living conditions, except for the wealthy, were fairly simple. But,

as the national coffers were enriched by taxes from various conquered peoples and provinces, many of the middle-class residences increased in size and splendor. And, of course, all were equipped with baths, of which, we might say, the early Romans were the originators.

And, in the well-regulated Roman household, no *atrium,* or courtyard, was complete without a couch, not especially comfortable by modern standards, but suitable for reclining purposes in case of fatigue.

As to the early Roman diet, their food sounds a bit stark to us. Yet, had we lived then instead of now, we doubtless would have eaten heartily of peas, onions, beans, other vegetables, and a sort of wheaten porridge. Meat was not a staple item, we learn.

But, as time passed, the meals became slightly less monotonous for the privileged. Indeed, they progressed to eggs, fruit, fish, various meats, fowl, and many kinds of wine. Furthermore, if you were in the higher social brackets, you were likely to be entertained by conjurers, who seemed to make dishes vanish into thin air—and by rope-dancers, who made themselves do likewise. You, however, were only expected to make the food vanish. And judging by the busts of certain Roman nobles, they most certainly fulfilled *that* requirement.

And, since fingers were made before knives and forks, your spoon, a slice of bread, and your fist never caused the invisible goddess of etiquette to turn thumbs down on your table manners.

In case we were carried away by all these old Roman customs, and perhaps omitted a few important details about school, we ought to explain that sons of affluent fathers attended private schools, as a rule.

And daughters, rich *or* poor, were taught by their mothers that woman's place was in the home.

Meanwhile, there was always something to be done, even

Remains of the columns of the Temple of Jupiter in Pompeii.

The bedroom of a nobleman's house in Pompeii. The floor is of mosaic tile, the walls are painted, the table is of bronze and marble, and the couch and stool are of carved bone.

in a well-run villa with no servant problem to speak of and plenty of *librae, solidi,* and *demarii*—otherwise pounds, shillings, and pence, or £. s. d., as modern Britons *still* call their money.

And, since every literate Roman citizen was expected to be able to present his own case in court, and perhaps express his views in the assemblies, the boys also studied rhetoric and public speaking, as well as Greek and Latin literature.

Later, they advanced to Roman law and history. Many studied medicine, engineering, or music. And, in rare instances, a few completed their education at the Universities of Alexandria, in Egypt, or Athens, in Greece.

The rich Roman breadwinner, having inherited everything from his ancestors, was a breadwinner-in-name-only. So, after a morning of reading and writing, he snatched a quick goblet of wine, some bread and honey, and greeted visitors in the *atrium*.

Later, he strolled down to the forum, attended to nonexistent business, and strolled back home for a light lunch and maybe an afternoon nap.

Upon arising, he bathed, joined guests, if any, and prepared for the next meal.

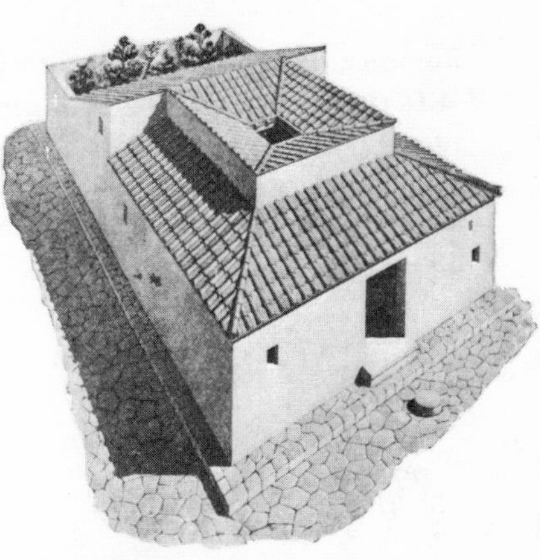

Above, an early Pompeian house (restored) and below, a look into the atrium of a Pompeian house owned by a rich Roman.

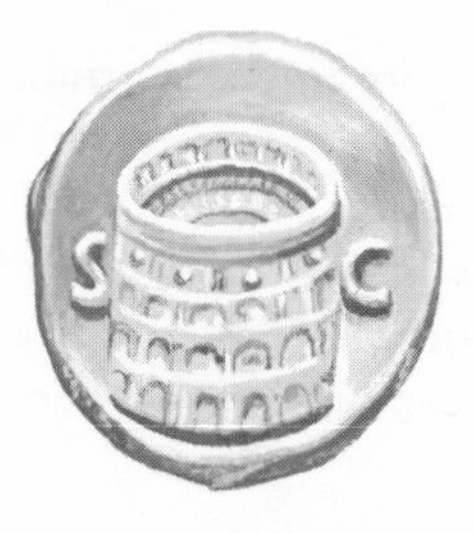

Roman coin from the first century A.D. (bronze Sesterce) with a picture of the Colosseum (above).

Aerial view of the ruins of the Colosseum in Rome (at right).

In sharp contrast, the Roman poor worked like slaves (which, of course, they were) from dawn till midnight; huddled together in wretched tenements. And, lacking the amenities of their masters, they seldom bathed.

During the reign of Augustus, their lot was slightly improved, it seems. But to what extent, and for how long, we have no clear idea.

However, rich or poor, most Romans enjoyed chariot races, and contests between gladiators which took place at the Colosseum. This impressive structure seated thousands of spectators, and was the scene of many thrilling events.

Gladiatorial contests were especially popular, we find. Tense with expectation, the audience sat on the edge of their seats, as swords clashed and shields flashed.

And, in the center of the arena, brave men faced each other, and death, while the crowd, with thumbs up, indicated that *both* lives must be spared because, met in equal combat, two Romans had had the courage to face death unflinchingly.

Gladiators asking the spectators for the verdict (picture at left); thumbs down meant death for the loser. Above, a charioteer about to round the goal during one of the dangerous races.

Relieved that no "thumbs down" signs will mar our imaginary visit to the Colosseum, we shall wend our way toward the Circus Maximus, built during the reign of Tarquin I, and rebuilt by Julius Caesar.

We are just settled down in our seats when a procession of charioteers enters, followed by young men on foot and on horseback, each racing driver wearing his special color: red, white, green, or blue.

The priests, carrying images of the gods, are the last to enter. A great shout of approval is drowned out by thunderous applause. The judge takes his place, the chariots line up, and the races begin. Four horses draw each of the two-wheeled vehicles, which must circle the course seven times.

Round and round they go, with the crowd shouting excitedly.

Neck and neck, the horses run. Will it be victory for the red or the blue? Five times around the track, and the blue regains the lead. The driver of the red gives his horse more rein. Six times around, and the horses are running side by side. We jump to our feet, cheering and clapping our hands, impartial spectators—but may the swiftest win the race! One inch of gain, then two, three, five; and, by a length, the driver in red has won the race!

Our make-believe tour of ancient Rome has almost ended, we remind ourselves.

But, even as we prepare for our next adventure, we learn that in the Palestinian village of Bethlehem (an outpost of the Roman Empire, beyond the Mediterranean), the life of an infant named Jesus, born during the reign of Augustus, is just about to begin. . . .

A CARPENTER'S SON....

The birth of Jesus, son of Mary and Joseph, a Nazarene carpenter, will also mark the beginning of the Christian Era. So, henceforth–instead of "before Christ," or "B.C."– we speak, write, and think in terms of *"anno Domini,"* or "A.D.," meaning "in the year of our Lord."

Many centuries before Jesus was born, as we have already learned, the ancient Hebrews believed in *one* God. And their faith remained unshaken through all the ensuing years.

But countless other peoples of the ancient world, paid homage to *several* gods. The Greeks, for example–and the Minoans who preceded them–had numerous gods. Likewise, the Romans.

However, even as a youth, and later, as a preacher, journeying from village to village, Jesus urged His listeners to accept God as the Father of all. And, as God's children (friend and foe alike), He bade them love one another.

In effect, as His teachings were interpreted, He wished us to "do unto others as we would have them do unto us."

This basic advice in various forms has been adhered to as "The Golden Rule" by peoples of all races, creeds, and color. We, of course, realize that not *all* peoples are (or were) Christians. And that Jesus, born a Jew, was circumcised and confirmed according to Jewish law.

But the frontiers of faith are boundless. And we have also been taught to "live and let live" at peace and in harmony with *all* our brothers and sisters under one God.

Byzantine ivory plaque (tenth century), Christ in Majesty.

And since the Jews (who believed themselves to be the chosen people of God) had long awaited a sign of His love in the guise of one who would deliver them from oppression and bondage, many welcomed Jesus as their leader, or Messiah.

Others failed to comprehend His teachings and feared Him, as all mortals tend to fear that which they cannot understand.

And, throughout the far-flung empire of Augustus, there were many such citizens. But Jesus continued to exemplify brotherly love and the Golden Rule. Preaching and teaching in Galilee, He fulfilled a three-year mission. And, on the eve of the Passover, He entered Jerusalem with His disciples.

He partook of His last meal in their company and then retired to the Garden of Gethsemane. Betrayed by Judas Iscariot, one of His followers, Jesus was seized while at prayer, charged with blasphemy, tried before Pontius Pilate, the Roman governor, and crucified on the hill of Calvary.

The Romans had never denied people the right to worship as they chose—providing that they also worshiped the emperor.

But the Christians refused to follow this rule. And some declined to serve in the Roman Army. Thus, because of their faith in one God only, they endured torture, persecution, and lingering death.

As firm in their Christian belief as the ancient Hebrews had been (and still were) in theirs, they willingly sacrificed their lives, rather than abandon their religion.

And, in the fullness of time, many came to accept the faith of those who had suffered and died for it.

FOUR HUNDRED YEARS OF THE ROMAN EMPIRE

Under Augustus, meanwhile, the nation was united as never before. Industry and commerce prospered, and with it, the Roman Empire.

Tiberius succeeded his stepfather, Augustus, and dispatched General Germanicus Caesar, his top general, to conduct what proved to be a futile campaign in Germany.

Caligula ("Little Boots"), son of the general and also a son of infamy, met death at the hands of an assassin, after a four-year reign of terror.

Claudius I, conqueror of Britain, succeeded him. And considering that he was supposed to be the ancient counterpart of every timid little soul in the world, he seems to have fared moderately well; that is, until one of his wives put him to sleep forever.

After Nero arrived on the scene, public bloodbaths were the order of the day. He murdered his mother, and a wife, among others. And, while he is said to have been partly, if not wholly, responsible for the great Roman fire of A.D. 64, he attributed this disaster to the Christians, and made them pay dearly for their alleged crimes against the state.

Thousands were tortured and put to death. And many believe that Peter and Paul, disciples of Jesus, were among Nero's victims.

His replacement, Trajan, managed to restore some of the empire's tottering prestige, by adding Mesopotamia and Armenia to the eastern boundaries of Rome's imperial outposts.

And Hadrian, a military expert and administrator, reorganized both the army and the Senate. He also concerned himself with the welfare of the poor and supervised the rebuilding of the Pantheon. He was responsible for the construction of Hadrian's Wall (of which there is still *concrete* evidence in Britain) and for several "protective" walls in Germany.

But Rome's twilight hours were fast approaching. And, after a fitful Golden Age, under Marcus Aurelius, who died in A.D. 180, the great Roman Empire passed beyond the point of no return.

To be sure, Septimius Severus campaigned successfully against the Picts, a tribe from North Britain.

Caracalla, his son, granted Roman citizenship to all free men, and also enjoyed the distinction of lending his august name to the famous baths at Caracalla.

Then Decius, arch-foe of all Christians, fought against the Goths and lost everything–including his life. Indeed, these fierce Germanic tribes were soon to give the vanquished Romans a great deal more than they had ever bargained for, even in their prime.

And, in the year of our Lord 313, after an impassioned plea for religious tolerance, Constantine decreed that the persecution of Christians must forthwith cease.

Above, the stone head of Constantine, the emperor who ended the persecution of the Christians; below, the Arch of Constantine.

THE END OF AN EMPIRE

In the 300's A.D., Emperor Constantine moved the capital of the Roman Empire to the ancient city of Byzantium that stood on the Bosporus, the entrance to the Black Sea. He rebuilt and enlarged the city, which became known as Constantinople. (In modern times it has been renamed Instanbul, and it now is the capital of Turkey.)

For a time Constantine's successors ruled the entire em-

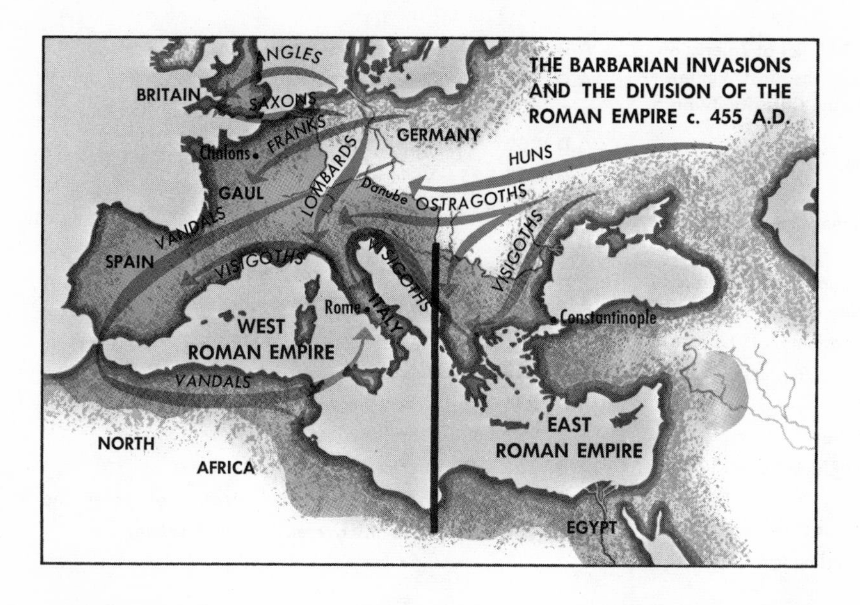

pire from Constantinople. Then in A.D. 395, after the death of the Emperor Theodosius I, his sons Honorius and Arcadius divided the empire into two parts. Honorius ruled the western Roman Empire centered in Italy, while Arcadius ruled the eastern Roman Empire from Constantinople.

Honorius was unable to defend Rome from the attacks of Alaric the Goth, who sacked the city in 410. Other barbarian invaders whittled away province after province from the western Roman Empire until little of it remained except the toe of the boot of Italy.

Eleven weak emperors followed Honorius in rapid succession, some of them holding the title for only a few months. Most of them were figureheads set up by various barbarian chiefs. The last Roman emperor, fourteen-year-old Romulus Augustulus, was overthrown by the barbarian general Odoacer in A.D. 476—marking the official end of the once-proud empire.

A.D. 311-313 Emperor Galerius issued Edict of Toleration, legalizing Christianity as a religion in the East. Emperor Constantine issued Edict of Milan placing Christianity on a par with pagan cults.

A.D. 486 Clovis, King of the Franks, defeated Sygarius, the last Roman governor of Gaul.

A.D. 486-493 Theodoric, King of the Ostrogoths, conquered Italy.

A.D. 529 Western monasticism developed as reaction to harsh society. Founding of Benedictine Order.

A.D. 531-534 Franks overthrew kingdoms of Thuringia and Burgundy.

A.D. 622 Mohammed fled to Medina.

A.D. 670 Arabs began conquest of North Africa.

A.D. 700-730 *Beowulf* composed, oldest English epic poem.

A.D. 732 Charles Martel defeated Arabs at Tours.

A.D. 768-814 Charles the Great (Charlemagne). Frankish Empire.

A.D. 782 Arabs raided Constantinople.

A.D. 788 Charlemagne annexed Bavaria.

A.D. 800 Charlemagne crowned Emperor at Rome.

A.D. 802 Tribal laws codified by Charlesmagne.

A.D. 802-825 Vikings invaded Ireland.

A.D. 835-836 Danes raided England and sacked London.

A.D. 846 Arabs pillaged Rome.

A.D. 847-855 Pope Leo IV fortified Rome.

A.D. 875 Charles II (the Bald) became Emperor.

A.D. 871-899 Alfred the Great, King of England.

A.D. 893-929 Charles III the Simple, King of France.

A.D. 936-973 Otto I the Great, German king.

A.D. 953-955 Germany rebelled against Otto I.

A.D. 962 Otto I crowned Emperor at Rome.

A.D. 982 Eric the Red began colonization of Greenland.

A.D. 1000 America discovered by Leif Ericsson.

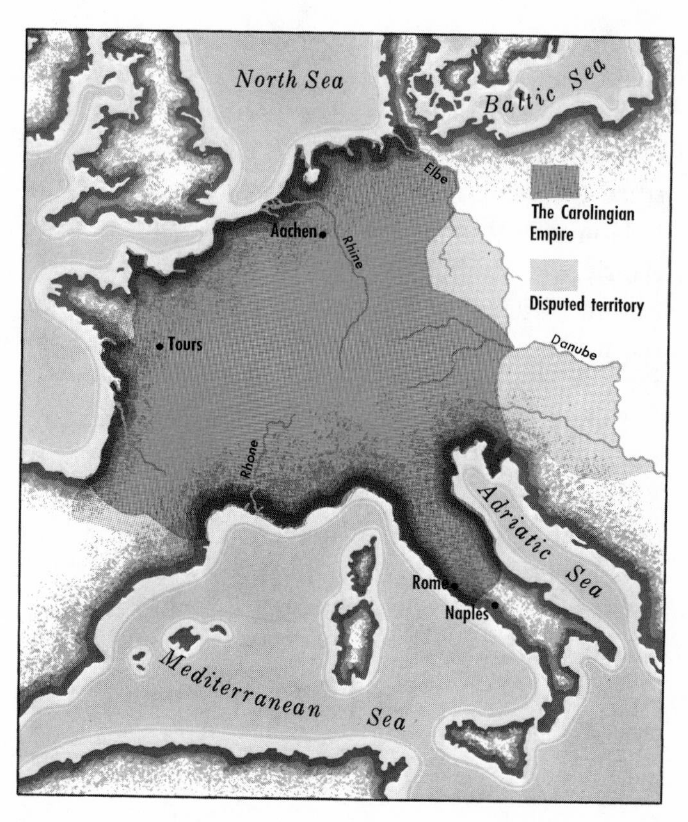

CHAPTER 7

The Middle Ages

AFTER the downfall of the western Roman Empire, the history of the world entered an era of roughly a thousand years that is generally known as the Middle Ages, because it lies between ancient times and modern times.

The eastern Roman Empire, which later became known as the Byzantine Empire, survived throughout most of this period, ruling southeastern Europe and western Asia from the luxurious capital of Constantinople. It stood as a Christian bulwark between Asia and Europe, preserving the culture of ancient Greece and Rome while absorbing some of the oriental customs of Asia. Its artists and craftsmen designed elaborate mosaics and ivory carvings. Its architects built huge domed churches, the most famous of which, Saint Sophia in Istanbul, was constructed during the reign of Emperor Justinian in the 500's A.D. The Eastern Orthodox form of Christianity, which later spread to Russia, developed under the rulers of the Byzantine Empire.

At the opposite end of Asia, a great civilization matured in China. The Chinese protected themselves from barbarian invaders of the north by the Great Wall of China, a tremendous feat of engineering that took hundreds of years to complete. This twenty-five-feet-high and twenty-five-feet-thick Great Wall wended its way more than 1500 miles across the mountains and valleys of China—a distance greater than from New York City to Denver. During the Middle Ages, Chinese emperors of the Han, Sui, T'ang, and Sung dynasties succeeded each other. Chinese inventors discovered printing and gunpowder and Chinese craftsmen made beautiful porcelain vases—all hundreds of years before similar achievements took place in Europe.

And in the Americas, although no one in Europe knew it at the time, the Incan Indians of Peru, the Mayan Indians of Central America, and the Aztec Indians of Mexico all were achieving states of civilization roughly equivalent to those of ancient Egypt and Babylonia.

But civilization in Europe moved somewhat more slowly during the Middle Ages. Most of Europe had been overrun by barbarian tribes who had not yet learned to write or appreciate great works of art.

A LIFE FULL OF DANGER

Clad in animal skins or homespun tunics, the German barbarian tribes, without roots and leaderless as a rule (although individual groups were answerable to one person), lived in small log huts with thatched roofs and roamed the woodlands in quest of food and plunder.

The tribal chief has called the warriors together to vote on an important issue.

A Germanic tribal village.

Often at war among themselves, they constantly seized each other's lands, villages, crops, animals, and weapons. And, when not so occupied, the men hunted wild animals in the forests while, as in Mediterranean lands and remote Middle Eastern regions, the women kept the home fires burning, the animals tended, the children fed and clothed, and their small patches of earth planted. When the year's harvest was insufficient to feed their rapidly growing numbers, the wandering tribes either moved on—or starved.

A freedom-loving people, the ruler, or chief, of a Germanic tribe was chosen by a group of warriors. And, when important decisions had to be made, the warriors assembled and called for votes. If the warriors agreed with the suggestions of their leaders, they struck their weapons against their shields. And, if they did not agree, they probably just struck.

Their women were held in great respect and treated with kindness and courtesy. On the other hand, it was they who rallied their menfolk in battle and taught their sons that bravery and manliness were a young warrior's secret weapons, to be prized above all else.

For a man might steal, murder, or destroy. But, if he were also brave, nothing else mattered.

The Germanic peoples preferred their own pagan gods to those of the Greeks or the Romans. And they revered

Woden, the king of the gods, or Odin, as he was sometimes called.

As their supreme deity, Woden directed the affairs of the world. Valhalla was his home, and all brave warriors who perished in battle joined him at this mythical abode.

Attended by the Valkyries, or handmaidens of Woden, the gallant dead slept peacefully until the end of time. And, speaking of time as measured by our days of the week, Wednesday (once spelled *Wodensday*) is named after Woden. But the first "d"—like the departed warriors—has long been silent.

Woden's eldest son, Thor, was the Teuton god of thunder and lightning. He is said to have wielded a heavy celestial hammer, with which he wrought havoc in the heavens and hell among the clouds. Even so, somebody made him a present of Thursday long, long ago. And, thus far, no one has dared to question his right to it.

Indeed, four out of the seven days in our week were named after pagan gods. Tuesday comes from Tiw. Freya, goddess of love and beauty, gave us Friday. And, to refresh our memories, Sunday honors the sun; Monday, the moon; and Saturday comes from Saturn, the Roman god of seed-sowing.

A monk, in the solitude of his cell, copies a book by hand.

A monument to the spirit of the Middle Ages, the famous Abbey of Mont-Saint-Michel, off the coast of Brittany, was founded in 708.

After their conquest of the western Roman Empire, the barbarians settled in small villages and lived much as they had before. Roads, bridges, and aqueducts were neglected. Theaters, baths, temples, and public buildings crumbled into ruins.

A glimpse into the garden of the medieval monastery of Maulbron in Germany.

KEEPERS OF THE FLAME

As time passed, the Germanic invaders adapted themselves to the Roman way of life and culture. During their mass migration, many had also embraced Christianity. Many more were to follow their lead.

Zealous priests and monks in isolated communities solemnized marriages, baptized, buried the dead, and conducted religious services.

Often, they were the only literate persons in the village and so became teachers, counselors, and wise friends to all. They visited the poor, the rich, and the sick, and spoke of the brotherhood of man and the way of the Cross.

Others thought that they might better serve Christianity by removing themselves from the confusion of the outside world and dedicating their lives to prayer, meditation, teaching, and good works. These retired to a monastery, or abbey.

And, if after a trial period, they proved themselves religious, they were admitted to the monastic community.

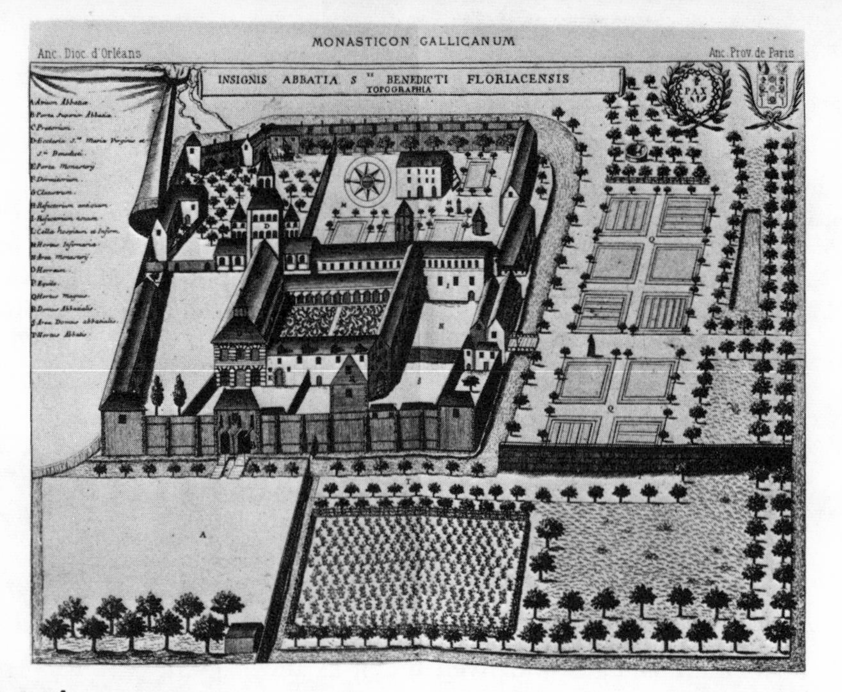

Grouped around an open court—the cloister—were the church, buildings for sleeping, eating, and cooking, and space for workshops, orchards, and gardens, making the medieval monastery a self-sustaining "household."

In those dark days, the monasteries (which were self-sustaining institutions) were a haven of refuge for oppressed travelers. Preyed upon by highwaymen, robbed, beaten mercilessly, and often killed by their assailants, they came to regard these kindly men as their benefactors.

No one was refused, and no one was ever turned away from the gates of a monastery. There were always food, shelter, and a bed for the asking, and without charge, though grateful wayfarers often insisted upon making contributions.

Since they have long been noted for their kindness and hospitality to strangers, let us visit one of the monasteries. We enter through a well-tended garden and see a group of friars on all fours, weeding and pruning. Although they are not members of a closed order sworn to perpetual silence, they do not speak; in fact, they seem quite oblivious of the presence of visitors from the outside world.

Brother Caretaker ushers us past the kitchen gardens, as they used to be called, and into the reception hall. Here, a plump and friendly monk receives us, shows us around the chapel, and smilingly apologizes for the practicing choristers, who, he whispers, have never been in worse voice. "As for the organist. . . ." he adds, and good-humoredly shakes his shaven head. After a brief exchange of courtesies, he asks us to remember the brotherhood in our prayers, and bids us Godspeed.

As we depart, we notice several of the brothers, eyes fixed upon on their prayer books, walking in the gardens, and learn that they are saying their daily "office."

We also notice a cluster of buildings we somehow overlooked, and make so bold as to ask the brother at the gate if we might just look in.

And, almost before we can say we're sorry to have troubled him, we are being shown through a small hospital, an adjoining guest house for visitors such as we, a sizeable workshop, and a school.

Here, boys are taught reading, writing, arithmetic, and Latin, the language of the Church. Nowadays, of course, there are few such monastery schools in existence. And most young male students are educated outside the cloister, unless they are studying for the priesthood, in which case they enter a seminary.

But, in the early days of civilization, everyone, in some

Above, a beautiful Romanesque baptismal vessel from a German abbey, and at left, an old woodcut showing monks singing, an important part of the medieval church service.

degree or other, depended upon the good friars (as they were often called) for virtually all their education. And, in time of need or ill health, the monks willingly provided sustenance and medical care, too.

Also, they were skilled craftsmen in many fields; their handbound, beautifully illustrated (or illuminated) books are now treasured as priceless works of medieval art.

The foremost monk of the time was Gregory I (590-604), also known as Gregory the Great. Gregory, the son of a noble Roman family, had left a high official post to become a monk. Through piety and ability, he rose rapidly in the Church and was soon elected pope.

While in office, Gregory the Great not only built schools and hospitals and helped the poor, but established a strong government in Rome. When a new invasion of German barbarians threatened Rome, he organized defensive forces that successfully held the besieged city against the fierce attacks. He constantly sent out missionaries to convert the Angles and Saxons and other pagan peoples.

He also found some spare moments in which to write hundreds of hymns, sermons, and religious treatises that have remained popular for centuries. The beautiful Gregorian chants not only are sung in churches throughout the Christian world, but can often be heard at concerts and over the radio.

The monk, Benedict, established more than a dozen monasteries. He composed a set of widely-adopted rules that required monks to divide their time between prayer, manual labor, and good work.

Many monks went forth to bring the inspiration of their faith to the heathen barbarians. Although some of these missionaries suffered martyrs' deaths, they won over, in the fourth century A.D., the Visigoths and other Germanic barbarians along the Danube.

In the fifth century, the British monk, St. Patrick, so adored by the Irish and thought of with affection throughout the world, carried Christianity to Ireland.

THE AGE OF FAITH

At first, the Christian religion appealed mainly to the poor, lowly, and oppressed because of the message it brought that the humble are more beloved of God than the rich and powerful, and that all men are equal in His sight.

Gradually, however, the upper classes turned to Christianity, too. They were impressed by the courage of the Christians in withstanding persecution, and their attacks on the evils that beset the world. It has been said that "the blood of the martyrs became the seed of the Church."

Eventually, nearly all the inhabitants of western Europe lived and died within its fold. So completely did it dominate people's lives that the Middle Ages are often called the Age of Faith.

So the Church prevented barbarism from engulfing western Europe—by protecting and serving the people, keeping learning alive, and converting the German tribes to Christianity.

Above all, it kept alive in men's hearts the ideals of peace, justice, and morality in a world of widespread brutality and lawlessness.

Under the leadership of the Church, the peoples of western Europe would slowly begin the long and difficult task of building a greater civilization.

Statue of an Abbot in Benedictine habit, a French sculpture from the second half of the fifteenth century.

THE PROMISE OF THE PAGAN KING

Clovis the First, pagan king of the Franks, who lived in the fifth century A. D. and was the founder of the Frankish (or French) monarchy, now comes to mind as one of history's madmen who, at some turning point in his life, repented of his countless misdeeds, and became a powerful influence for good.

Perhaps, in the course of his travels, he heard the words of one of those dedicated holy men of whom we learned just a short while ago?

At all events, he insisted that his children be reared as Christians. Or, so it has been said. And he vowed that, if he triumphed in battle over the fierce Alamanni tribes, he also would accept Christianity.

After his overwhelming victory, he and many of his soldiers were converted.

Later, he subjugated the Visigoths, and the Burgundians, and eventually found himself in possession of nearly all of Gaul (now France) and a goodly portion of southwest Germany.

So, leaving Clovis I of the Merovingian dynasty, founders of the French state, among the honored Christian dead, we press forward into the sixth century A.D., pay a fleeting visit to the holy city of Mecca in Arabia, where Mohammed, Prophet of Islam, was born; and vividly recall to mind the imaginary journey we didn't quite make with Alexander the Great long years ago.

Above, the mosque of Mohammed Ali, one of the oldest temples in Cairo, was built more than 800 years ago; below, the tower from which the muezzin calls for prayer.

THE PROPHET OF ISLAM

Five times a day, 300,000,000 people turn toward the Holy City of Mecca in Arabia, drop to the earth, and prostrate themselves. As they pray, a voice, loud and clear, singsongs, *"La ilaha illa-illahu Muhammed rasul allahi"* ("There is no God but Allah and Mohammed is His Prophet").

When Mohammed was about forty years old, he fell into a trance while alone at prayer. When he awoke, he related that the Angel Gabriel had come to him and told him that there was but one God and that he, Mohammed, once a lowly camel-driver, had been chosen as His Prophet.

In Mecca, Mohammed's attacks on idol worship—the city's temple was guarded by more than 360 idols—almost cost him his life and he was forced to flee to Medina. Many people there believed in Mohammed. They had heard him preaching in Mecca when they went to worship at the temple. So, in Medina, Mohammed was well received.

A group of Moslems answer the muezzin's call to public prayer before a mosque in Alexandria, Egypt.

The new Prophet determined to build a house of worship for Allah in the city. With their own hands, Mohammed and his followers made walls of earth and stones, put up pillars of palm-tree trunks, and roofed the construction with a thatch of palm branches and leaves. This building was the first *mosque* (the Arab word for "temple").

This took place in A.D. 622, a year called *Hegira* by the Arabs, meaning the "flight." This date is important to Arab people because it marks the starting point of the Moslem calendar. We will recall that it was not unusual for the ancients to count the years from an important event. We have already learned about the first Olympiad of the Greeks, the founding of Rome, the birth of Christ.

Mohammed had a disciple call the people of Medina to worship Allah at his mosque. Five times a day, the man summoned them to prayer: before the sun rose, after midday, before sunset, after sunset, and when it had grown dark. More and more of the men and women of Medina flocked to the mosque to pray. Mohammed taught them to be brothers and sisters to one another; to let their slaves and animals live as freely as themselves; to be honest and brave and humble; to make no sacrifices to idols; to drink no wine or eat rich foods; to believe in nothing but the one true God. If

Above, a portrait of Mohammed, and below, a page from the Koran, the Moslem Holy Book.

الذكر والأنثى إن سعيكم لشتى
فأما من أعطى واتقى وصدق بالحسنى
فسنيسره لليسرى وأما من بخل واستغنى
وكذب بالحسنى فسنيسره للعسرى
وما يغني عنه ماله إذا تردى إن علينا
للهدى وإن لنا للآخرة والأولى فأنذرتكم
نارا تلظى لا يصلاها إلا الأشقى الذي
كذب وتولى وسيجنبها الأتقى
الذي يؤتي ماله يتزكى وما لأحد عنده
من نعمة تجزى إلا ابتغاء وجه ربه الأعلى
ولسوف يرضى

they did these things, Mohammed told the faithful, they would live forever in Allah's Garden of Paradise. Mohammed called his new religion Islam, which means "submission" (to the will of God).

Mohammed's followers asked for a written record of the angel's revelations to Mohammed and the prayers and speeches that Mohammed had made. But Mohammed could neither read nor write. His followers, therefore, wrote the words down as Mohammed spoke them. These sayings were put together into a little book called the Koran. The Koran is the "Bible" of Islam.

Mohammed taught his converts that it was their duty to go out and make other people accept Islam. Any person who died fighting for his faith would go to Paradise, he said. "The sword is the key to heaven," he had announced. For this reason, Moslems were eager to battle for their religion, and in the name of Allah, they set out to conquer Mecca in the year 630. After several battles in the desert, the Meccans agreed to accept Mohammed if the Prophet would make Mecca his holy city so that pilgrims would still come to the city. To this, Mohammed agreed, but first he went to the temple where he and his friends smashed the 360 idols and pronounced the temple the house of Allah. (Only the black stone, believed to have fallen from Heaven, was not destroyed; it was built into the wall of the temple.)

Mohammed had said that Islam would conquer the world. His armies began by conquering Arabia. After Mohammed's death, the wars continued until the Arabs had established a vast empire in Asia and in northern Africa. From Africa, it was easy for the Moslems to cross the narrow Strait of Gibraltar into Spain. There they found a tribe of Visigoths who had been living in the country for nearly 300 years. In 711, the Moslems defeated the Visigoths and established a kingdom which extended north to the Pyrenees Mountains.

For a while, it seemed that the Moslems would overrun all Europe. Then, in the Christian Franks, beyond the Pyrenees, they found a powerful enemy.

The men of Islam in the year 732, exactly one hundred years after the death of Mohammed, rode northward to conquer the Franks. But an able leader by the name of Charles Martel met the invaders at Tours in central France with a strong army of fighting men from all the Frankish lands. Charles struck such blows with his great battle-ax that from then on he was called Charles "the Hammer." The Moslem armies were stopped at last and forced to retreat toward Spain.

As a result, Europe became a Christian continent rather than an Islamic one. But the Moslems had spread their religion far and wide. In a hundred years, through the force of Mohammed's ideas, the Arabs had built an empire as big as that of the Romans. Never before in history had so much of the earth been conquered in so short a time.

After the Arabs became the rulers of the lands they had conquered, they learned many things from the people in those lands. They did not destroy, as the barbarians had done in the Roman Empire. The Arabs even improved some of the ways of life that they found. They had keen minds, and they quickly learned from the people they governed. In Egypt, they absorbed not only all that the Egyptians had learned, but also the books of the Greeks which were stored in the libraries. As they went on to new countries, the Arabs carried their new knowledge with them. They started

A scene from the Battle of Tours, A.D. 732, in which Charles Martel defeated the Moslems.

schools, libraries and universities. They taught science, and showed people an easy system of numbers.

The "Arabic" numerals which you write every day—1, 2, 3, 4, 5, 6, 7, 8, 9—were given to the world by the Arabs after they had adapted them from people who lived in India. To these numerals, the Arabs added zero (0). These are the ten numerals you use. Roman numerals from one to ten previously used in the west, were written like this: I, II, III, IV, V, VI, VII, VIII, IX, and X. The Arabic numerals became popular because they were simpler than those of the Romans. If we try to work an arithmetic problem with Roman numerals, it becomes obvious how much work the Arabs saved us. The Arabs also gave us algebra, the decimal system, and many discoveries in medicine.

And do you know that alcohol, alchemy, algebra, check, magazine, muslin, tariff, traffic, and zero are but a few of the many Arabic words in our language?

So the Moslems, who were so great a threat to Christian Europe for a thousand years, really helped in many ways the growth of Western civilization.

It is said that Charlemagne often entered the classrooms of the school he founded, to see whether the students were making enough progress.

THE FIRST GERMANIC EMPEROR

Charles the Great, or Charlemagne, succeeded his grandfather, Charles Martel, in A.D. 768.

He took Pope Adrian's side in the dispute between the Vatican and the King of the Lombards, and in recognition of his services, was received as a patrician.

He also took charge of the kingdom of Lombardy; later investigated territorial possibilities in Spain; and was repelled by the Moorish settlers whose territorial possibilities, they felt, were none of Charles' business. He contrived, even so, to pick up Pamplona and Barcelona as he passed through the Spanish peninsula.

And then he decided that those ugly Saxons, for their own good, required his immediate protection.

Successively (as well as successfully) thereafter, he tackled the Slavs and the Pomeranians. And was advancing steadily eastward, when Pope Leo III summoned him to Rome.

On Christmas Day, in the year A.D. 800, he was crowned Emperor of the Holy Roman Empire. And, for fourteen years, he served his far-flung dominions with firmness and rectitude until pirates from the northern lands began casting about for fresh fields, free booty, and new treasures to the south.

Toward the end of his reign, Charlemagne was sorely beset by plundering, restless Norsemen.

But, possibly to keep his mind off their calculated treachery, he instituted a number of helpful social reforms among the poor, sought to improve educational conditions for the clergy, and served as official arbiter in certain religious disputes.

A statue of Charlemagne from A.D. 1300 in a niche of the cathedral at Zurich, Switzerland, which Charlemagne founded.

A man of simple tastes, he was not considered extravagant, although it has been suggested that several of his wives were.

Charlemagne proved to be a wise monarch and a capable administrator, avid for knowledge. While himself an uneducated man, he instituted countless social and civic seforms within the empire.

He named Alcuin, the eminent English scholar and ecclesiastical reformer, as head of a newly founded court academy, and himself became one of Alcuin's most zealous students.

He also supervised the establishment of a school for underprivileged children. The offspring of aristocrats were, of course, admitted, too.

But Charlemagne's ninth-century war on poverty was largely waged in behalf of the needy youth and worthy freemen of his own vast dominions.

Yet, in spite of his power and exalted status, he was by no means averse to practical jokes at the expense of pompous colleagues when, in his opinion, they grew too self-important. On one occasion, in fact, he is alleged to have requested a group of nobles—bedizened in gaudy robes and plumed headgear—to accompany him through rain-drenched forests in search of game. It must have been a chastening experience, we imagine.

Denied the right to plead their cause before judge and jury, citizens unfortunate enough to stray from the path of law and order were most harshly dealt with.

Indeed, under the prevailing feudal system of trial-by-ordeal, these hapless offenders were summarily exposed to red-hot branding irons, and other forms of torture, on the assumption that, if innocent, they would emerge unscathed. Whereas, in atonement for their wrongdoing, if guilty, they would expire by painful degrees and under conditions grimly reminiscent of pre-Christian times.

Full of honors and years, for he lived to be three-score-and-twelve, Charlemagne himself died of old age.

He was succeeded by his son Louis I, who is said to have been a staunch patron of arts, extremly pious—and virtually incapable of presiding over a small household, much less a large empire.

However, he did his very best (which, by some, was interpreted as the very worst) for the Holy Roman Empire. And, as a reward for his efforts, he was deposed by his sons, all of whom were firmly convinced that they could do much better.

After a short trial reign, during which their convictions proved quite wrong, Louis I was restored to power.

And, when he died in A. D. 840, a grandson, Louis II, took his place.

Poor Louis II was perhaps the most conspicuous failure of all. And, having made a lamentable mess of his grandsire's Holy Roman Empire, he was finally reduced to parleying with insignificant local dukes and phantom kings.

As a result, Charlemagne's imperial realm at length shared a fate not unlike that of other earlier empires.

THE SEA ROVERS

Rampaging vikings, or Norsemen, from northern lands now known to us as Norway, Sweden, and Denmark, in their determination to entrench themselves as traders, merchants, and seamen at the earliest opportunity, overran the inviting territories of southern Europe, like a plague upon the inhabitants.

Since even the most squeamish landlubber can brave the most turbulent of paper seas without a qualm, we now step confidently aboard one of the viking longships, a sturdy double-ended craft made of solid oak.

The fact that we remain constantly within sight of land is naturally most reassuring. And, of course, thoughts of seasickness never occur to us. Moreover, our guide is a handsome tow-headed giant with a fund of exciting sea stories and an excellent memory for dates and place names.

Of the ship's food, possibly the less said, the better, for it is vaguely reminiscent of old, unhappy far-off things and black soup long ago in ancient Sparta.

However, we're now steering steadily toward the end of the sixth decade of the ninth century A. D. And B. C. suddenly becomes more remote than the farthermost outskirts of Venus, the evening star.

Our course is duly set. Our expert navigator is at the prow. And our next port-of-call will be Iceland.

Resisting the urge to cry, "Ahoy there!"—there's neither a ship nor a soul in sight—we rest briefly upon our invisible oars.

After all, we've spanned many centuries, scanned many lands, and learned a great deal about many different civilizations.

And now, we really must just pause for a minute or two, if only to catch up with our zooming thoughts before some bright ninth-century police constable (who reads the minds of chairbound tourists from the latter half of the twentieth century) gives us a ticket for speeding.

And what more restful place to spend a few reflective moments than upon the hallowed spot where a band of courageous Irish monks first set foot in the year of our Lord 813, only to be driven away, we learn, by bands of pagan intruders who raided their peaceful haven and ruthlessly dispersed its occupants?

Reflecting upon the sad fate of these kindly Irish friars, we are reminded of Eric the Red, a militant anti-Christian explorer who, more than a hundred and fifty years later, would also settle in Iceland; establish a colony in Greenland; proclaim himself king; accept the homage of all his loyal "subjects"; and resist the spread of Christianity with might and main.

But, then, early in the eleventh century, his son, Leif Ericson rediscovered Greenland–and, in the process, is said to have discovered North America, too.

He was among the converts, and helped to spread the gospel of Christianity throughout Greenland–much to the annoyance of his father, who vainly contended against him.

For, homeward bound from Iceland to Greenland, Leif Ericson, had been blown off course by adverse winds and borne northwestward across the Atlantic to the land we now

Above, Eric the Red (seated), self-appointed King of Greenland. At right, the boats of Irish monks who landed in Iceland before the vikings.

call Labrador. He remained there for several months, repaired his vessel, and at length resumed his interrupted voyage.

It was only natural that attempts at colonization should follow this epic journey. And, in the year 1003, a small fleet set sail for North America.

Captained by a Scandinavian merchant and trader, the expedition disembarked, settled somewhere along the eastern shores, and began to farm the land. But Indian tribes assailed them time and time again. And, alas, the *skraelings,* as the Norseman called the American aborigines, greatly outnumbered the fierce viking warriors.

Finally, in 1006, one lone ship returned to Greenland with but a few survivors. The vikings may have paid another visit to the continent of North America. However, since they left few written records, we cannot be sure.

Most Norsemen, it seems, were concerned with raiding and trading to the exclusion of all else. Not only did they raid the villages of the Holy Roman Empire, but they plundered and sacked seaports and remote hamlets along the shores of the Baltic and North seas.

They shamelessly robbed the islands we now refer to as Great Britain and Ireland, and made numerous forays into Mediterranean regions.

So fierce were these Norsemen that many of the priests were said to close their sermons with a prayer: "God, deliver us from the fury of the Northmen."

In celebration of their return home, after successful freebooting expeditions, they spent the long, icy winter nights in feasting.

Enormous tables laden with meats and fish of every description were set before the merrymakers. There were mountains of cheese and bowls heaped high with fruit. There were crusty loaves of sour bread, black bread, brown bread, and bread sweetened with honey.

And this huge meal was invariably washed down with

drinking-horns brimful of mead, a brew containing water, malt, honey, and yeast (a sort of eleventh-century version of our modern ale, perhaps). Then a *skald,* or minstrel, entertained the assembled gathering with songs and recitations.

THE ONLY KING OF ENGLAND CALLED "THE GREAT"

By the late ninth and tenth centuries, the Norsemen had begun to establish overseas colonies. Many vikings (and especially the Danes) we discover, decided that they rather liked the eastern shores of the land now occupied by the fiercely independent Angles and by the Germanic tribes known as Saxons.

In other words, although "there's no place like home" (even to self-seeking land-grabbers) the green hills of far-off England now beckoned to them. But, among these freedom-loving peoples of Britain, content with their neat little principalities, a monarch named Alfred, King of Wessex, had his own plans. And invaders from across the North Sea were by no means included therein.

Posthaste, therefore, Alfred summoned his counselors, raised an army, and went forth to repel the audacious intruders.

Overwhelmed by superior forces and beaten back time and again, the king and his gallant soldiers were at last compelled to seek shelter in the forests, where they remained until winter had passed.

They emerged from hiding in the spring, and drove the Danes northward into the moorlands of Yorkshire.

After many battles and much blood-letting, during which the foe ruthlessly destroyed everything in sight, Alfred and his followers clung firmly to their precious southern stronghold. And, finally, they drove the savage Norsemen into East Anglia. From that time on, Alfred was honored with the title of "the Great."

"Alfred the Great, King of the Angles," reads the inscription above this old steel engraving commemorating the only king the English called "the Great."

One of the truly outstanding men of early Britain, Alfred, a fearless military and social reformer, was also a great scholar and an able warrior and patriot.

Indeed, he instituted a new code of laws, based upon the proper administration of justice for all; and, having acquired a knowledge of Latin, was responsible for the English translations of works by Bede, Gregory the Great, and Saint Augustine.

Unfortunately, his military innovations were interrupted by renewed Danish onslaughts during the decade which preceded his death in A. D. 899.

And, although *modern* Britons (when very young) still tend to associate King Alfred with burned cakes and the wrath of a fiery old harridan, posterity reveres him as a truly noble monarch, ". . . whose name shall live as long as mankind shall respect the past."

A SUCCESSION OF KINGS

His successors, for a while, maintained law and order; and even kept the implacable Danes more or less at bay. Ethelfleda, daughter of Alfred, who reigned for seven years, stoutly resisted their increasingly murderous attacks, and died beloved by her people.

However, when Aethelred (the Unready) came to the throne, he was all that his nickname implied, and more. Thus, by A. D. 991, the Danes had seized the upper hand, and once again, England was at their mercy.

With the help of Edmund Ironside, his son, Aethelred stood firm against the foe. But to no avail, for between 1009 and 1012, the Danes waged incessant war, robbed, pillaged, and, in the end, took possession of London. In 1016, upon the death of his father, Edmund was proclaimed ruler, but within six months, he, too, had departed this life.

Shortly thereafter, Canute—not yet the great Dane he was destined to become—replaced Edmund on the throne. He immediately discarded his wife and son, married Aethelred's

The Battle of Hastings in A.D. 1066, in which the Saxons under King Harold were defeated.

widow, and by 1028, found himself the crowned head of Denmark, Norway, and, of course, England.

In spite of a tendency to dispose hastily of all who impeded his progress (and among other things, he is said to have ordered the seas to abate!), Canute kept the peace in England. He also restored the Church to its exalted status, and formed an amicable relationship with the Holy Roman Empire.

On October 14th, in the year A. D. 1066, William, Duke of Normandy, crossed the Channel and defeated the Saxon King Harold, in a battle near Hastings in Sussex.

Busy repelling and vanquishing the Danes in northern England, poor Harold sped southward upon learning of the unwelcome arrival of William. His armies disbanded and most of his soldiers returned to their farms. Harold, with a small detachment of troops, was hopelessly outnumbered, and all were slain.

The Conqueror, otherwise William I of Normandy, was also known to his family and associates as William the Bastard (which, in truth, he was, having been born out of wedlock).

In spite of this not uncommon handicap, he ruled over England and much of his native France for twenty-one years.

But, in a sense, during the latter part of the Middle Ages, the actual rulers were the feudal landlords, who, in many cases, exploited the workers, or serfs, and cynically used these simple peasants as a means to an end, the end being power and land. And more power, and more land. . . .

A.D. 1066 Battle of Hastings. Norman conquest of England. William of Normandy crowned William I of England (the Conqueror).

A.D. 1091 Norman conquest of Sicily.

A.D. 1096 Pope Urban II proclaimed First Crusade.

A.D. 1099 Crusaders captured Jerusalem. Godfrey of Boullin elected King and Defender of the Holy Sepulchre.

A.D. 1124 Christians captured Tyre.

A.D. 1149 Byzantine Empire attacked by Normans.

A.D. 1160 Normans forced out of North Africa.

A.D. 1167-1168 Oxford University founded.

A.D. 1171-1774 Saladin became ruler of Egypt and conquered Damascus.

A.D. 1176-1209 London Bridge built.

A.D. 1187 Saladin captured Jerusalem.

A.D. 1189-1193 Third Crusade, led by three kings — Richard I of England, Phillip II of France, and Emperor Frederick I (Barbarossa) of Germany.

A.D. 1200 University of Paris founded.

A.D. 1202-1204 Fourth Crusade.

A.D. 1215 King John signed *Magna Carta*.

A.D. 1248-1254 Sixth Crusade.

A.D. 1265 Birth of Dante Alighieri in Florence.

A.D. 1267-1268 Roger Bacon wrote *Opus majus, Opus minor, Opus tertium*.

A.D. 1270 Seventh Crusade.

A.D. 1338 Start of Hundred Years' War—England against France.

A.D. 1346 English victory over French at Crécy.

A.D. 1348-1349 Black Death in England.

A.D. 1348-1358 Giovanni Boccaccio wrote *Decameron*.

A.D. 1358 Revolt of French peasants (the *Jacqueris*).

A.D. 1387-1400 Chaucer wrote *Canterbury Tales*.

The Knights—Crusaders and Craftsmen

UNDER Charlemagne, most of the conquered peoples were allowed to retain their own particular forms of administration, supervised from headquarters, as it were, by a representative of the Holy Roman Empire, and, of course, subject to periodic inspection by members of the central governing body, to which all states were responsible.

The emperor also instituted a system of general assemblies, to which the provincial outposts sent delegates annually.

SEIGNEUR AND SERF

Immediately after the collapse of Charlemagne's formidable empire, however, Western civilization, urgently in need of a sense of purpose and direction, turned to feudalism.

In the early stages of its development, the kings and princes owned and controlled all the lands. And their noblemen, according to rank, received special grants of land.

The peasants merely tilled the soil and produced the crops each year. In return for their labors, they were provided with shelter, food, and, in effect, the assurance that while the lord remained the head man, so to speak, they would never go hungry or homeless.

Naturally, they were expected to do all the work *and* pay annual tribute (or taxes) in the form of market produce directly to the lord. Ready cash was something they were never permitted to see, much less lay hands on.

Thus, from late in the ninth century and thereafter, the

This schematic drawing of a castle shows the location of the main buildings.

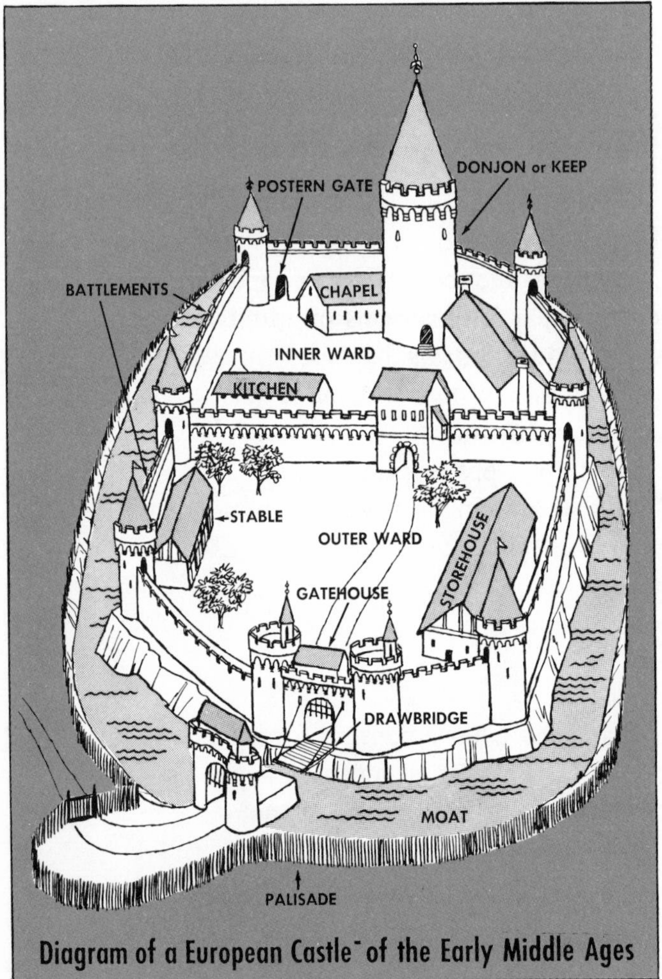

Diagram of a European Castle of the Early Middle Ages

Many old castles, some in ruins, some still habitable, grace the European landscape. Above, the castle of Salzburg, Austria, and below, the castle of Liechtenstein.

early forms of social and economic structure were replaced by the feudal system.

And, toward the end of the tenth century, this type of administration by the lord of the manor was accepted as a matter of course–especially in the Frankish regions, where the higher-ups apparently relished "lording" it over their so-called inferiors.

During this era, the Church was also very influential, within certain limits imposed by the State. For it, too, owned vast tracts of land, having been endowed with monasteries and abbeys by deed of gift from noblemen and other affluent benefactors.

But, inasmuch as *Timeo Danaos et dona ferentes* ("Beware of Greeks bearing gifts") was equally true of all other peoples, the Church, in return for these parcels of real estate, was expected to offer certain "concessions."

Ultimately, the feudal system became as familiar throughout the rest of the European Continent as it already was in the country we now refer to as France.

And, of course, it was William the First (the Conqueror), as we have previously learned, who personally brought his brand of feudalism to England in the year A. D. 1066 when he decided to impose upon his new subjects this

The feudal noble lived in his castle and ruled his subjects, but did not actually own his land. The land (or fief) was given him by a greater lord or the king in return for a promise of military aid, advice, and counsel (often as a judge in the lord's court), and strict loyalty. In the colorful ceremony of investiture, the gift of land was represented by a twig or other symbol of the earth; the noble in turn swore his allegiance to the lord and thus became his "vassal."

unique form of government *by* William, and as it subsequently transpired, *for* William, into the bargain.

And, at precisely this historical juncture, with all powers vested in the monarchy, the feudal system (as others had before it) began *its* slow decline. . . .

Based originally on the idea that the strong should protect the weak, the system of feudalism really began when Emperor Charlemagne divided the conquered lands into countries, and, in return for faithful service in war and in peace, distributed them among the nobles, or vassals. Each vassal enjoyed the use of his particular grant of land during his lifetime. And, upon his death, his eldest son inherited it, with the same obligations and privileges.

This way of life brought a greater measure of economic protection and order to the European people of the Middle Ages. And, although there were no large countries (and the powers of the monarchy were limited), the nobles controlled their own small armies, and supervised the people who occupied and worked their lands.

The warriors, all members of the nobility, were known as knights. Their other recreations included hunting and such sports as tests of strength, skill, and endurance–and kindness toward the weaker sex.

The freemen on a lower rung of the social ladder might farm the land, live on it, or leave it, if they chose to do so. But, at all events, before making a move, they had to pay

their "taxes" to the lord, as every other farmer did, and they must also serve in the armed forces, whenever necessary.

In medieval times the peasants — the serfs — were neither slaves nor freemen. They lived in small cottages on the estate (or manor) and were tied to the soil they worked for their noble master; they could not leave it without his permission. In case of attack, they were given protection behind the castle walls.

But the lowly peasants, unlike the more fortunate freemen, were *forced* to work for their keep. And manual labor was not considered a distinguished service. Also, they automatically became the property of the lord of the manor.

Thus, these humble laborers, or serfs, were semi-slaves, bound to the earth as well as to their seigneur, or lord.

They must farm the seigneur's acres, bake his bread, tend and care for his animals, repair his castle walls, clean and polish his weapons, prepare all his meals, make his clothing, and be constantly at the beck and call of his usually large family.

For such services, they were allowed to raise their own food and livestock. But a portion of all their produce had to be paid to the lord as taxes. The serf was also told when he might marry, leave the land, or aspire to the next rank above him, that of freeman.

He had a few rights, however. He could not be separated from his family and arbitrarily sold. He was allowed a certain amount of time during which he could work for himself, as it were. And he was encouraged to attend church services, to participate in religious festivals, and to join his fellow-serfs in local pleasures.

In a feudal domain, the castle was the center of life and

since we've always been interested in twelfth-century French castles, replete with moats, drawbridges, and towers, let us now pay a visit to one of these Norman strongholds.

THE CASTLE: RESIDENCE AND FORTRESS

A grim-visaged watchman sounds his horn to herald our arrival. This moat, or ditch, surrounding the castle appears to be about thirty feet in width. And, of course, this one is filled with water. The drawbridge is raised. A huge cast-iron door is lowered behind us.

The outer wall of the castle is very thick, possibly twenty feet high, and protected by fortified turrets. Some of these towers jut out conspicuously. And we learn that, from the battlements, arrows can be dispatched and boiling water, tar, or lead showered down upon the unsuspecting foe.

Gunpowder and cannons are not yet in evidence here. Two centuries more will elapse before Europeans make use of those tools of war.

When enemies stormed a castle of this sort, we discover, they pounded battering-rams against its seemingly impregnable walls. And many would-be conquerors resorted to the use of giant slingshots which hurled sharpened stones for great distances and often mortally wounded innocent bystanders.

A giant slingshot is shown in this fifteenth-century engraving.

A battering-ram in action.

Carved on this ivory cover for a mirror from fourteenth-century France you see, on the left, a "noble chess game" in progress, and on the right, a nobleman receiving an honor from his king.

The castle's outer court resembles a sizeable village; it is complete with blacksmith shops, an armory, swordsmiths, saddlers, tailors, carpenters, bootmakers, and other craftsmen. There are also a cookhouse with a large open fireplace, enormous barns, and storage warehouses.

And, of course, stables for the horses and ponies. Cows, pigs, chickens, and other livestock are free to roam about the vast manorial estate.

We now approach another moat, cross a second drawbridge, and enter an inner courtyard.

The main tower here, known as the keep, or donjon, is the home and stronghold of the lord.

The lord and his lady are absent at the moment. But, admitted as well-wishers from afar, we spend ten pleasant minutes or so in quiet contemplation of enormous open fireplaces, exquisite tapestries, and massive (but probably uncomfortable) benches, chairs, couches, stools, and a large private chapel with numerous frescoes and works of art.

In the cavernous dining-hall, the enormous table lives up to the expectations of all who've ever seen, heard, or read of "a groaning board."

And, assuming that the lord and his lady will soon return

to preside over this sumptuous feast, we politely efface ourselves from their donjon, or innermost tower.

We do not inspect the dank prison cells. Nor do we presume to trespass any longer upon the hospitality of our invisible hosts.

After all, even in make-believe land, one must abide by the niceties and courtesies of time and place.

And, besides, speaking of time (which never stands still), we must be on our way.

Before the use of gunpowder, the heavy suit of armor provided good protection against arrows and lances.

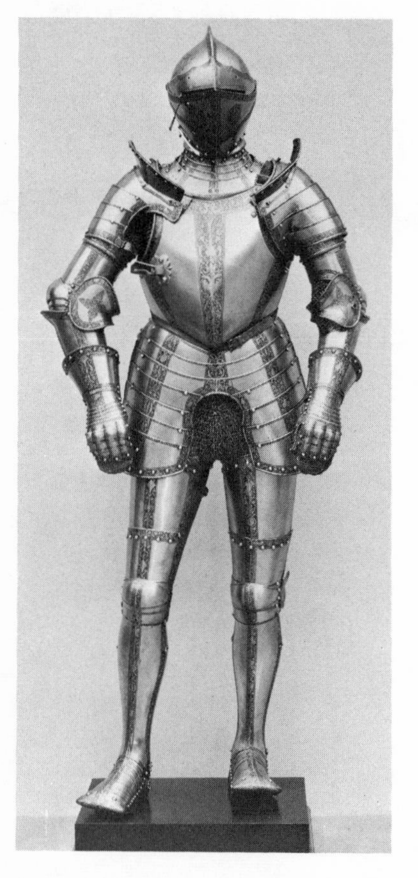

But not before we inquire about the ceremony of knighthood which, upon the return of the lord, will rejoice those spectators now foregathering in the inner courtyard.

Here, we are told, a handsome young man will receive the accolade. That is, in the presence of many lords, ladies, earls, counts, barons (and even squires), he will be dubbed (meaning he will be honored with the title of) a knight.

Clad in white tunic, red robe, shining armor, and a black coat of mail, he will receive this honor at the hands of a noble dignitary. Advancing, the latter will unsheath his sword, administer a tap on the shoulder of the young man, and simultaneously declare him well and truly a knight of the realm, sworn to faithfully serve his liege lord and defend his country.

Nowadays, we are informed, the modern knight is "dubbed" in similar fashion. But *he* may be a middle-aged, even an elderly citizen from *any* walk of life.

And, of course, *his* wife would never let him out of the house in a tunic, robe, and coat of mail, or chain-link armor. He would simply present himself at Buckingham Palace clad in suitable *modern* attire, and the reigning monarch would bestow the honors upon him.

A few years ago, a famous jockey was knighted by the King of England. Rumor has it that he was promptly thrown from his favorite horse, Sir Somebody-or-Other, who just couldn't bear the competition.

In ancient times, incidentally, knights spent most of their

A French ivory plaque from the fourteenth century shows a jousting scene watched by noble spectators.

days in the saddle. Strange as it seems, it didn't matter a dub whether or not they could read or write.

And, from the habit of lifting his visored helmet upon meeting friends, we are surprised to hear, came the gentlemanly custom of doffing the cap, or hat, in the presence of ladies.

But, in the presence of foes, we rather imagine any knight worthy of his armor kept his metal visor firmly closed.

It's possible, furthermore, that the family crest, or coat of arms, originated in medieval times when men were armored.

And, just as the Greeks enjoyed their Olympic games, the Romans, their gladiatorial contests and chariot races, and modern peoples, their great national and international sporting events, so the knights of earlier times were fascinated by jousting contests, combats on horseback in which two participants armed with lances attempted to outmaneuver each other. A skillful lancer was able to unhorse many rival jousters, and often did.

From the sidelines, an audience of lords and ladies cheered on their favorite knights. And to the victor went the privilege of choosing a beautiful lady to reign as queen of the tournament.

And, even as the ancient Greeks (during their Olympic games) called a temporary halt to battles-in-progress, so were tournament enthusiasts allowed to pass without hindrance in medieval Europe.

The horse, as well as the knight, was protected by armor.

Hunting was both a sport and necessity, providing a welcome change in the meat dishes. Woven on this Flemish tapestry from about 1500 is a scene from a typical hunt.

Hawking was a sport favored not only by the knight, but also by his noble lady.

The knights also enjoyed hunting with their hounds or with a falcon, a bird trained for this purpose.

The falcon, secured to the wrist of his master, was hooded. On sight of a possible opponent (perhaps another bird or a small animal), the hood was removed and the falcon swiftly bore down upon its prey.

At harvesttime, we are again reminded, the serfs were obliged to pay the lord with a share of their wheat, oat, vegetable, or fruit crops and with whatever animals they raised, too.

And, as we catch a fleeting glimpse of their miserable one-room huts of stone and brick, these unfortunate peasants have all our sympathy.

Yet, for the most part uncomplaining, the serfs were glad when they could save a little milk, butter, or cheese for their families. On special occasions, they were invited to join in the merrymaking at the castle. And there were times, especially when the lord was in a bountiful mood, when the peasants were allowed extra meat and ale.

THE HOLY WARS

The Church played an important role in the daily lives of most citizens, and many thought a good deal about spiritual influences. Some were inspired to enter monasteries.

Others made pilgrimages to the tombs of those who had loyally served the Church in the past. A few dedicated pilgrims even journeyed to Palestine where Christ had lived and taught.

But, as we may recall, conditions in the Holy Land were no longer serene. Uprisings among adherents to the Islamic, or Moslem, faith were frequent, especially between the Arabs and Turks.

Moreover, the latter seized large tracts of land, hitherto considered Arab territory. And, eventually, fierce Turkish tribes resorted to the wholesale slaughter of all who opposed them, including many of the Christian pilgrims.

Appalled by the wanton destruction, loss of life, and repeated ill-treatment of Christians, Pope Urban II, in an eloquent plea, called upon all to stand firm in their faith—and, should it be the will of God, to die for it.

Among others, Peter the Hermit, a French preacher, led one of the first crusades. Riding donkeys, he and a band of civilian-soldiers of the Cross bravely set out for Palestine. However, many fell by the wayside. Others abandoned their cause or deserted their leaders. Few ever reached their goal.

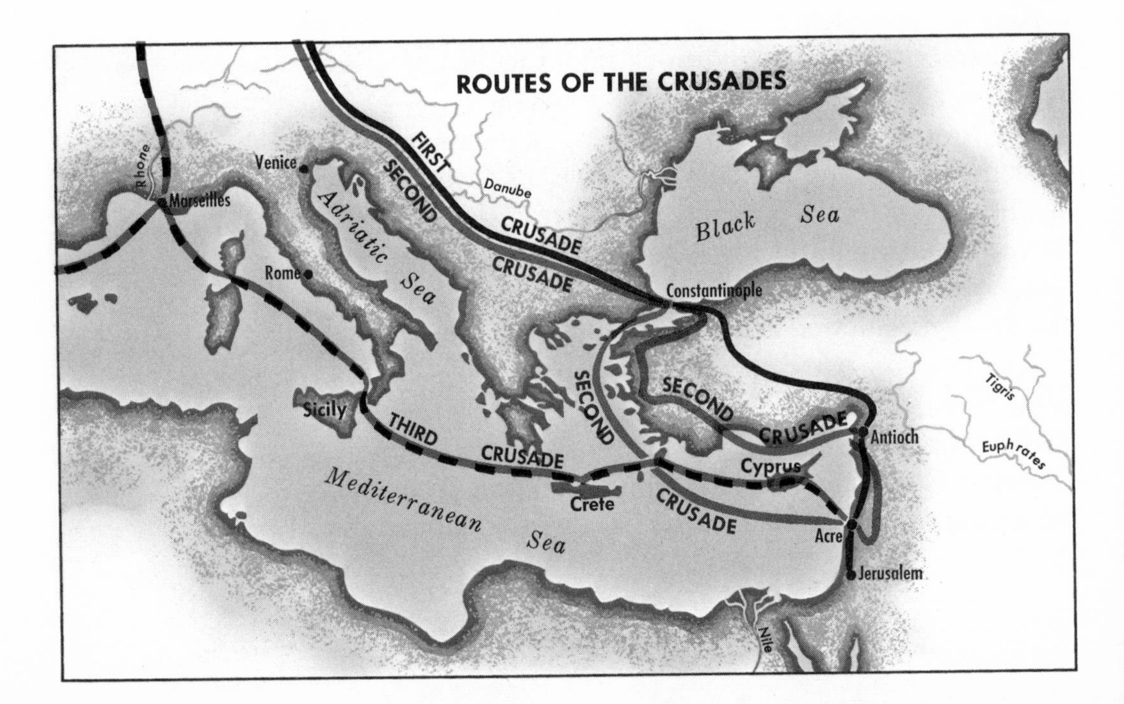

Crusaders on the march: Priests and soldiers lead, women and noncombatants follow.

Most of the crusaders were pious, simple folk. Some, however, were not. Among them were women and children, who gladly accompanied their menfolk, and, if need be, were prepared to give up their lives, too, rather than give up their faith.

But, unfortunately, their food and supplies were totally inadequate. And few of them realized that the homeland of Christ was *so* far from their homes—across high mountains, scorching desert sands, and stormy seas.

Yet, after three years' journeying, incredible hardships, sickness, and death, the five companies of knights making the First Crusade reached Palestine at long last.

Jerusalem surrendered after a bitter struggle. And, for some time, the Holy City was the focal point of Jerusalem's Latin kingdom.

But, a century later, the embittered Moslems reconquered Jerusalem.

THE CHILDREN'S CRUSADE

Perhaps the most tragic misadventure of all came about as a result of the Children's Crusade.

Youthfully confident that they would succeed although their elders had failed, 30,000 children, inspired and led by a twelve-year-old French shepherd boy, set forth from Marseilles early in the thirteenth century.

Imbued with faith, hope, and the will to accomplish their noble mission, the young people were betrayed by unscrupulous merchants and sea captains long before they reached their destination.

Hundreds died of exposure and starvation. Others were kidnapped and sold as slaves.

The pitiful survivors of a German group of 20,000 were later traced to Italy.

Yet, in some respects, the crusades (often described as successful failures) were long to be remembered, for they helped to broaden the horizons of people in many lands, and, in a real sense, furthered the development of Western civilization.

The power of the nobles was greatly diminished because many had joined the crusades and were fated never to return.

Peasant crusaders, who fought side by side with their "betters," gained self-confidence, and thereafter strove to improve their status in every possible way.

Thus, the crusades also contributed to the decline of European feudalism and, ultimately, to the rise of kings.

Never again would brave, but slovenly, knights sally forth from their castles in tarnished coats of mail. Nor would they be seen, either on foot or on horseback, with the medieval counterpart of "five o'clock shadow." After all, if wandering bands of Arabs–in dry lands where water was almost unknown–were able to bathe and shave, surely a gentle, perfect European knight could do no less.

A scene from the Children's Crusade.

For it certainly wasn't enough to bring home such unusual souvenirs as exotic spices, rare fruits, cloves, lemons, dates, endless varieties of perfumes, rugs, linens, and shimmering silks if your Lady Fair (requesting her maidservants to bar the gates) coldly denied you access to the manor because of an unpolished helmet or soiled gauntlets.

IN A FEUDAL VILLAGE

After the crusades, trade between western Europe and Middle Eastern countries increased. And, of course, the Mediterranean lands enjoyed the benefits of a thriving commerce, for they formed the gateway to North Africa and regions beyond.

Villages gradually blossomed into towns. Cities expanded and populations increased.

With open arms, the lords of the manor positively welcomed newcomers to their ancient strongholds, for they were in dire need of skilled craftsmen.

They were also in need of hard cash and fired with a burning desire to retain their sprawling acres, at all costs.

Although the castle still afforded protection, the communities often provided added safety by erecting walls around their towns.

And, as the new townsmen were frequently granted special favors and privileges, they eventually won their freedom from the lords. They formed their own government, elected a mayor, and chose a town council to draw up and enact laws.

Thus, fourteenth-century feudalism showed increasing signs of yielding to the march of progress.

Night watchmen patrolled the highways and byways—carrying their lanterns, announcing the time, assuring the citizens that all was well, and challenging all strangers to advance and state their business.

We notice that the dwellings of the humbler townsfolk are huddled close together. Some are of brick, but most are wooden structures with steep tiled roofs.

But many of the families enjoyed their gardens and ate their meals outdoors in summertime. And, while the young people danced, sang, and played games, their elders sat around talking of the good old days.

We notice that a number of the city streets bear names that identify them with foodstuffs, clothing, trade, and sports. For instance, we pass through Meat Street, Boot Way, and Hatters' Walk in one part of town; Petticoat Lane, Fishmongers' Alley, and Javelin Court in another.

And we notice large, colorful signs directing wayfarers to various taverns and inns. Because many people were unable to read, it wasn't unusual to see these outsized likenesses of jolly friars or plump, pretty damsels inviting passersby to enter and partake of "mine host's" hospitality, as graphically pictured—at a nominal tariff, or charge, of course.

The mortar-and-pestle symbol bespoke an apothecary, or chemist's, in those days. And, somewhere amid the glittering plastic confusion of modern drugstores, they still do.

Red-and-white striped poles called attention to barbers' establishments—red for blood and white for towels. For, as you may know, old-time barbers also practiced medicine and dentistry.

Thus, all medieval haircuts, shaves, toothaches, and headaches were in the hands, so to speak, of your local tonsorial artist.

The marketplace, the church, and the public square are, of course, familiar sights by now. And, since today also happens to be market day, most of the townsfolk are bargaining, as townsfolk will anywhere at any time.

The country folk have already finished their bargaining, for as the old saying goes, "It's the early bird who catches the worm." And country people are apt to rise before even the birds.

Meanwhile, the lord of the manor has just sent a large consignment of unwanted produce to be sold to the highest bidder. And groups of his serfs are lustily hawking their own wares in the side-streets. However, the more sedate citizens remain at their stalls in the market, urging customers to patronize only them and assuring all and sundry that *their* goods are the best and cheapest in the whole world.

Once a year, we learn, a fair is held in the public square.

Many of the old fortifications still stand today in European cities. This is a picture of the "Sun Gate" in the Spanish city of Toledo.

This attracts visitors from near and far—indeed, from lands across the sea.

And knights and their ladies are sometimes seen moving decorously among the crowds, too.

Depending upon the mood of the lord, he either deigns to appear in person or sends his manservants to make purchases for him—and to drive the hardest possible bargain or take the consequences.

During the Middle Ages, money-changers were also a familiar sight, and extremely partial to the fair.

And, since the lord of each manor usually coined his own money, the money-changing business was quite brisk.

Performing monkeys and dancing bears entertained the children and, often, their elders, as well, while minstrels sang and danced and, occasionally, even made people laugh. Gypsies also danced but in rather more frenzied style. And, if some nobleman suddenly found that his pocket had been picked while his broad medieval back was turned, the capering jugglers and acrobats helped to take his mind off his loss—for the time being, at least.

Old customs survive to our day. These are two jumping acrobats on their way to a German city fair.

Majestic old Guild Halls surrounding the market square in Arras, France, give the market day there a look not much different from that of a market day in the Middle Ages.

Many European cities have yearly events commemorating the fairs and customs of the Middle Ages. This is the famous Day of the Palio which brings thousands of visitors yearly to the Italian city of Siena.

Of course, no visit, to a thriving community in medieval Europe would be complete without a brief inspection tour of the famous guild-halls.

Here, the various craftsmen used to ply their trade. And here, too, they held meetings, elected officers, paid membership dues, and perhaps, to some extent, functioned in a manner similar to that of today's craft and labor unions.

There were carpenters', weavers', tanners', gold- and silversmiths' guilds, among others. And only the finest workmanship was acceptable for the artistic standards were very high. Moreover, *non*-members were most unwelcome.

But "the brothers," as they preferred to be called, stood by one another in bad times, as well as in good. And, so long as memberships were fully paid up and the work completely satisfactory in all respects, no one could be dismissed from the brotherhood.

In order to qualify, a young man had to become, successively, an apprentice, a journeyman, and a master craftsman.

Upon completion of the required training, he gained a certain amount of practical experience, worked for a daily wage, and finally, if he chose, was free to set up in business for himself.

We are on the verge of departure when the parish church bell tolls. Suddenly the deserted square is thronged with men carrying pails of water.

One of the nearby dwellings has caught fire, we hear. Fortunately, it will soon be brought under control; its occupants have already been rescued.

The sun is well below the horizon when we are alerted once again. But, on this occasion, the church bell, in less-urgent tones, ". . . tolls the knell of parting day . . ." (as Thomas Gray would write some 400 years later).

It is curfew time, indeed. And firelight and candlelight must soon be extinguished in all the homes and buildings.

Now the church bells are silenced. The market square is hushed and still.

"Ten o'clock!" cries the night watchman, barring the city gates. "Ten o'clock, and all's well!"

In the sabled darkness, his lantern sheds its heartening beams across our path.

Today is almost at an end. In a hundred and twenty minutes, it will be tomorrow.

And medieval Europe, poised upon the threshold of a glorious new dawn, stands ready for the re-awakening.

Both these pictures are old woodcuts from the late Middle Ages. Above, shoes were made and sold on the same premises; below, carpenters like the ones shown here building a house were vital to the medieval community.

Half-timbered medieval houses can still be found in many European cities, making a picturesque and attractive sight. This is a vista of the old part of Nuremberg, Germany.

A.D. 1403 John Huss preached Wycliffism in Bohemia.

A.D. 1415 Henry V of England defeated French at Agincourt. Huss burned as heretic.

A.D. 1419 Rouen surrendered to Henry V.

A.D. 1430 Burgundians captured Joan of Arc.

A.D. 1431 Joan of Arc burned at Rouen.

A.D. 1431-1432 Azores discovered by Portuguese.

A.D. 1431-1433 German peasant rebellion near Worms.

A.D. 1453 Constantinople captured by Ottoman Turks; destruction of Byzantine Empire.

A.D. 1463 Death of François Villon, French poet.

A.D. 1476 William Caxton set up first English printing press.

A.D. 1478-1492 Reign of Lorenzo de Medici (the Magnificent) in Florence.

A.D. 1495-1497 Leonardo da Vinci painted "The Last Supper."

A.D. 1480 Ivan III overthrew Mongol rule and called himself Tsar of Russia.

A.D. 1482 Portuguese colonized Gold Coast of Africa.

A.D. 1503 Leonardo da Vinci's "Mona Lisa."

A.D. 1508-1512 Michelangelo painted ceiling of Sistine Chapel.

A.D. 1517 Martin Luther nailed "95 theses" against church abuses on door of court church at Wittenberg.

A.D. 1520 Luther excommunicated.

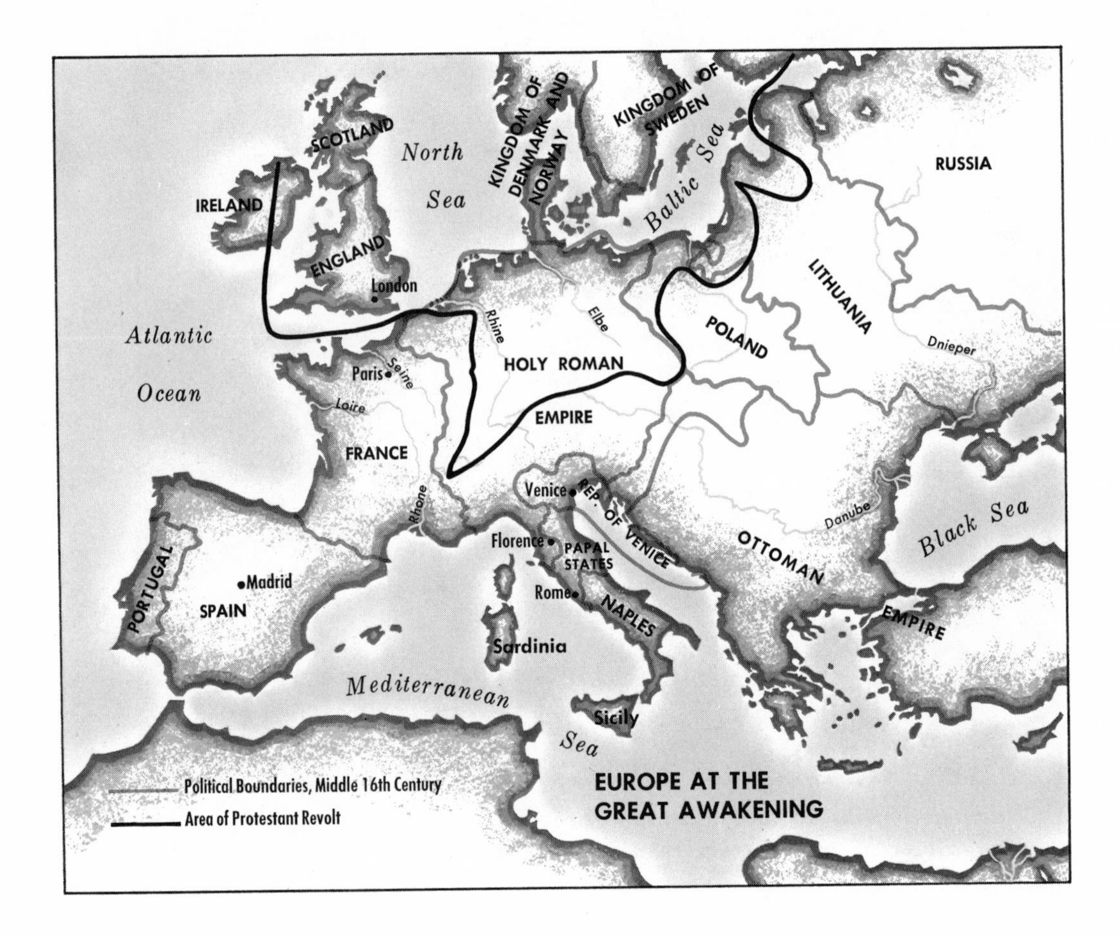

A.D. 1521 Edict of Worms outlawed Luther and his followers.

A.D. 1534 Henry VIII recognized as supreme head of English church. Founding of Jesuit Order by Ignatius Loyola.

A.D. 1534-1541 Painting of "Last Judgment" by Michelangelo in Sistine Chapel.

A.D. 1558 Elizabeth I became Queen of England.

A.D. 1564 Birth of William Shakespeare.

A.D. 1588 Defeat of Spanish Armada in English Channel.

A.D. 1601 Shakespeare's *Hamlet*.

A.D. 1609-1610 Galileo perfected first telescope and discovered four satellites of Jupiter.

The Great Awakening

So many new ideas began to stir the imagination of European man in the years from 1300 to 1600 that this period has been called the Renaissance, a word from the French that means a new birth or revival. This period marked a time of gradual reawakening of interest in architecture, the arts, education, science, invention, and exploration.

During this time the feudal system came to an end; life and society would no longer center around the lords in their castles.

Towns and cities were growing bigger and bigger as more and more people moved into them. Religion still occupied the people's time and thoughts, and churches became too small for their congregations. Many of them, built of wood, were not considered fine enough. It was decided to build larger new ones.

The beautiful Cathedral of Rouen in Normandy, France, towers over the city and can be seen from whatever direction the visitor approaches.

TO REACH HEAVEN

At the end of the Middle Ages, architects introduced a new method of building cathedrals, or churches. Nobles, merchants, craftsmen–even boys and girls–helped in the actual work or gave money for the great projects. Prior to this time, the construction of a church had always followed the basic ideas of the Greeks and the Romans. They had erected blocks of stones upright, and then placed other blocks across the top to form a roof. This meant that thick walls had to be constructed to support the massive stone roof; windows were few and small to avoid weakening the walls. Consequently, the interiors were very dark.

But, the new style, the Gothic, permitted the building of

Above, one of the many priceless art treasures from the famous Cathedral of Cologne, the south portal of which is shown below.

structures that were lofty, light, and graceful, yet just as durable. The architects had discovered how to make thick walls unnecessary. Thus it was possible to build tall cathedrals with many large windows.

When the Germanic tribe called the Goths were fighting Rome, everything these savages did seemed uncouth to the cultured Romans. The word "Gothic" was actually used by the Romans to mean "ridiculous" or "crazy." When Gothic churches were mentioned, Italians shook their heads.

"That building will be shaky," one would predict as he'd watch the strange structure going up.

"It will topple over," another might volunteer.

"That's a crazy way to build a church."

Still another would put in: "It is a Gothic way of doing things."

He meant, of course, that it was a ridiculous way to erect a building. While a few churches designed this way were rickety and did collapse, the vast majority stood for centuries. Many Gothic cathedrals built in the Middle Ages still stand today, and will doubtless last for centuries to come.

The insides of the finest churches were more richly decorated and more beautifully furnished than any buildings in the world had ever been before. The ceilings were often painted in glowing blazes of color by the master-painters of the time. Glassworkers carefully selected hundreds of bits of vividly colored glass, and arranged them in intricate patterns to give the cathedrals their famous stained-glass windows. The polished, or tiled, floors reflected all these marvels.

Magnificent church furniture was designed by craftsmen who painstakingly contrived the most delicate woodcarving on pulpits and altars. Sculptors carved reliefs and statues from the same stone as the cathedral, and thus the sculpture was in harmony with the architecture. Others wrought handsome bronze or iron grillwork on the cathedral's gates. Still others embroidered tapestries for the walls. Diligent men produced artistic manuscripts of religious books for display on cathedral altars.

THREE TITANS

The spirit of ancient Greece and Rome seemed to return, as other beautiful buildings sprung up. Sculptors molded statues as beautiful as any that had been made by the great Phidias of Greece. It was as if the people had suddenly rediscovered beauty.

Michelangelo, an artist of the Renaissance, was more than a talented painter. He was also architect, sculptor, and poet. It is hard to imagine a person being great in all these arts; to master any single one generally takes a lifetime. Michelangelo was equally at home in each.

He would spend years on a single painting or a statue. When he started to work, time stood still. Only his work existed for him, and no one could distract him from the task at hand. But when he finished, people came from far and wide to marvel at the exquisite beauty that he always created.

From the twelfth century, bronze head, a church treasure from the Cathedral of Aachen.

This is the winged altar, late Gothic and dated about 1520, of the Church of Maria Gail in Austria's southern province of Carinthia.

The pope asked Michelangelo to paint the ceiling of his chapel. "No," Michelangelo said. "I am a sculptor, not a painter." But the pope persisted; he would permit no one else to paint his own private chapel. Michelangelo finally

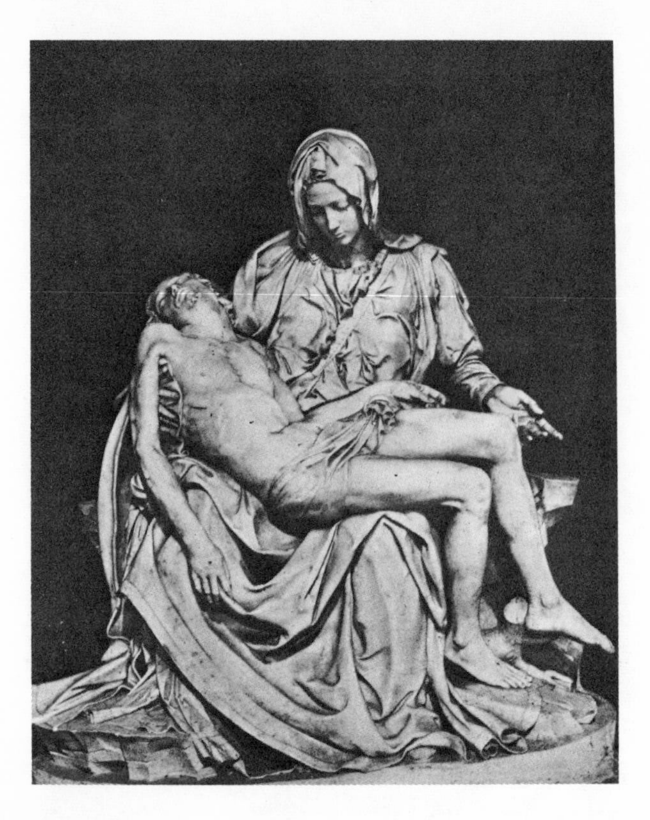

Michelangelo's Pietà, the famous sculpture which stands in St. Peter's Cathedral in Rome, attracted millions of viewers when it was shown at the Vatican Pavilion during the 1964/65 N.Y. World's Fair.

agreed; he set to work as if this were really the most important task of his whole life.

Michelangelo lived in that chapel, the Sistine Chapel, for four years. He hardly left it during those years. He lived, ate, and slept with his work. He built a platform close to the ceiling, and, for days and nights, he would lie there gazing upward without once raising so much as a finger. At times, he read poetry and meditated. He touched his brushes only when he felt the urge to do so. No one could come in, not even the pope. Michelangelo did not want to be disturbed.

The pope could contain his curiosity no longer; he *had* to see what was going on. Would Michelangelo never finish? When would he cease being alone, never wanting to speak to anyone? So, one day, the pope did enter the chapel. A mistake. Just then, Michelangelo "accidentally" dropped one of his hammers. It barely missed the pope's head. Michelangelo said not a word, merely looked back at the ceiling.

Of course, the pope was angry. But he never again interrupted the artist.

Finally, the task was done. Now the pope could look without risking his head. And thereafter, people came from all parts of the world, and gasped at beauty so rare that it might have come from a being greater than human. To view this sweeping painting in all its grandeur, it is necessary to assume the same position that Michelangelo took when working on the project. Some people view the ceiling through mirrors.

The pope called upon him again, to complete the decoration of the Church of St. Peter's in Rome, and to design its massive dome. He did this when he was over seventy years of age.

Michelangelo died in his ninetieth year; his name will never be forgotten.

Meanwhile, another Italian artist of the Renaissance,

The Cathedral of Florence, with its beautiful dome designed by Bramante and its famous bell tower designed by the Florentine architect and painter Giotto.

Raphael, was painting many pictures of the child Jesus and his mother, Mary. He painted so many of them, in fact, that he became known as "the Madonna painter." (The word *madonna* is an Italian one meaning "my lady." When it is spelled with a capital "M," it indicates the mother of Jesus.) Raphael executed "The Sistine Madonna," "The Madonna of the Chair," "The Madonna of the Goldfinch," and "The Madonna and Child Enthroned." His work is characterized by gentleness, sweetness, and grace.

The artist Leonardo da Vinci was considered by many as the greatest man of the age. He painted pictures as great as those of the greatest artists. His two most famous pictures are "The Last Supper" (of Jesus Christ and the disciples) and "Mona Lisa," the portrait of a mysterious lady of Naples.

Leonardo was always working out a hundred and one problems of a hundred and one things. He was an engineer, and many of his engineering plans were carried out in Italy. He studied and wrote about astronomy, anatomy, geometry, and mathematics. He worked out rough sketches of flying machines, steam engines, and many other things which did not become practical inventions until hundreds of years later.

Self-portrait by Leonardo da Vinci.

He had a passion for knowledge, and often would go away alone for days, thinking, reading, and writing. He was a happy man who went to all the gay parties and took the lead in the charades, which were so popular at the time. He was a sportsman, too; and a trick rider upon the horse. He played all the musical instruments beautifully. It seemed he could do almost anything better than anyone else.

Leonardo, Michelangelo, and Raphael were helped by the rich Medici family of Florence, the foremost patrons of culture in all history.

The fame and interest created by the works of Michelangelo, Raphael, and Leonardo da Vinci soon spread over

This is one of Raphael's religious masterpieces, painted for an altar of the Convent of St. Anthony of Padua.

Europe and inspired other artists. In Spain, the name of El Greco became well-known in the field of art, while in northern Europe—in Flanders, Holland, and Germany—the greatest names were the Van Eyck brothers, Albrecht Dürer, and Hans Holbein.

"MY MIND IS MY KINGDOM"

With the development of cities, people began to take a new interest in education. The churches and cathedrals opened schools for boys. The methods of teaching and the subjects covered were the same as those of the monastery school that we visited earlier in our trip through history.

Merchants and craftsmen, however, found that they could carry on their business better if they had someone working for them who could read, write, and keep accounts. They started schools to teach boys reading, writing, and arithmetic. These were the first schools opened to the "public."

This engraving from about 1400 shows a teacher leading fellow scholars in discussion at the University of Paris.

In the larger cities, universities that offered men advanced courses of study were opened. The early university, however, had no beautiful buildings, no lecture halls, no expensive equipment, no football stadiums. It has been said often that universities in early times grew rather than were established. Any learned man who believed that he had something to say about a favorite subject could settle himself near some school and give lectures to as many as cared to listen to him. He held these lectures in a home, a rented room, a barn, or in a field. Other learned men followed him and lectured on other subjects. In short, at first anybody could lecture and anybody could listen; the speaker who brought together the greatest number of students received the most money in fees. The master's only income was derived from the fees collected from his students. After a while, men had to secure a license to teach, and permanent buildings or sites were made available for the lectures.

As time went on, some cities, in order to attract teachers and students, would give them special privileges such as freedom from taxes and exemption from the laws of the city. Thus these students and teachers had their own laws, their own courts, and their own jails. To further set themselves apart from the rest of the city, as well as unite

Lectures and classes at medieval universities were often held outdoors in the shade of a tree.

themselves, they usually spoke the same language, generally Latin.

Naturally, they tried to lodge in the same part of the city, and sometimes they even built lodgings for themselves. At five or six o'clock in the morning, the students would throng to the bitter cold lecture hall, and sit down on the straw or hay with which the floor was strewn. A knowledge of Latin was always vital. Students did not investigate or experiment, but instead had to memorize the works of ancient authorities. Theological students memorized passages from the Bible; medical students, the works of Hippocrates and Galen. They all studied Aristotle. Pupils had to take notes feverishly, for there were few textbooks. They took these notes on waxed tablets.

Some of them then hurried home to go over their notes; others would meet in a meadow playground for wrestling, ball-playing, running, jumping, or swimming. Sometimes those of different nationalities carried on a rough-and-tumble warfare with one another. Sometimes they fought with the townsfolks. The town could do little to control them; and if they chose, teachers and pupils could simply put on their hats, take up their books, and go elsewhere, leaving the merchants of the town to mourn over the loss of several thousand customers.

In time, certain universities became more definitely established and noted for work in special fields. For example, the University of Paris specialized in theology, the study of religious beliefs; Italy's University of Salerno, in medicine; northern Italy's University of Bologna, in law; and England's Oxford University, in philosophy.

Students often wandered from one university to another. As learning was related closely to religion, and the great majority of students expected to become priests or monks, the people thought it their duty to give students food, shelter, and clothing on the way. The medieval student wore a hooded robe similar to those worn by students graduating from our colleges today. Sometimes he would allow the hood to hang down his back so he could carry in it a loaf of bread or other food given him by some kind-hearted person.

The university of the late Middle Ages represented a distinct step forward in educational progress. Great thinkers came from these institutions, and thus, knowledge was spread throughout the whole of Europe. However, education was still for the few, rather than the masses. Women and girls were not among the few.

THE WRITTEN WORD. . . .

Two inventions during the great awakening helped to educate the people. Through the centuries, people had been making books of one kind or another. The Egyptians had made theirs of scrolls of papyrus; the people of Mesopotamia had books of clay tablets; during the Middle Ages, scribes wrote them out by hand on parchment. But, during all those centuries, men were able to produce but one copy of the book at a time. This meant that there were just a few books in existence, and that they were very expensive.

During the Renaissance, both the discovery of a method of making paper and the invention of a printing press meant that books could be made quickly and cheaply.

The knowledge of papermaking had been introduced into Europe by the Arabs centuries before. They had learned the process from the Chinese, who probably had made use of paper even before the first century A. D. Paper made in the Chinese manner came into common use in Europe about 1300, a hundred and fifty years before the printing press appeared. Paper was, of course, a great deal cheaper than the parchment used by the monks.

In the early days of printing, letters and pictures for the whole page were carved on one block of wood.

In the 1100's, it was no longer necessary to copy books by hand, thanks to another Chinese invention that the Arabs brought to Europe. In this contrivance, the letters and pictures for the whole page were carved on one block of wood. After the wooden blocks were covered with ink, a sheet of paper was pressed against the carved words and pictures to make printed pages. Some people still use this kind of block printing to make greeting cards, but it takes a long time to carve out the words.

About the year 1440, Johannes Gutenberg, of Germany, had an idea. Rather than carve the letters of a page all on one block of wood, why not cut each letter of the alphabet separately? He reasoned that he could arrange the letters in words and sentences just as he pleased. He could also use the same letters over and over again in various combinations to form new words. This would, of course, save considerable time and expense in the printing of books.

Quickly, Gutenberg went to work. He sawed boards into small pieces and carved a letter on each piece. In time, he had a pile of all the different letters of the alphabet. He placed these letters side by side to form words. Then, he put the words in a frame. But, when he tried printing with his new letters, he discovered that some kind of even pressure was needed to make a clear impression.

Gutenberg said, "People use a press to squeeze the juice from grapes. They also squeeze the water from cheese with a press. Why not use a press to get a clearer impression of each page of type?" He placed the frame of type in a simple press and inked the faces of the letters. He laid a piece of paper over the type. He then turned the screw until the paper was pressed tightly against the type. Then, he laid this printed sheet aside to dry. He could make as many copies as he desired before he went on to another page. When all the pages of the book were printed and bound together, he would have a cheaper book than could be made by block printing.

Gutenberg's work was not yet finished. The wood letters were too soft and did not last long enough. He solved this problem by using letters cast of metal that could be used over and over again. Gutenberg, after spending several

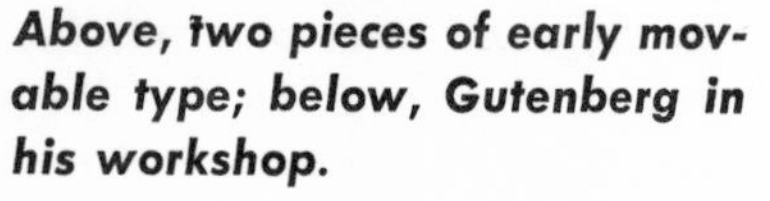

Above, two pieces of early movable type; below, Gutenberg in his workshop.

years on his experiments, finally realized his dream, when in 1456, he printed the Bible.

No one can estimate the full importance of printing to civilization. Many historians go so far as to say that printing was the world's greatest invention. But, certainly in a world without telegraph, telephone, television, and radio, paper and the printing press were the greatest of blessings.

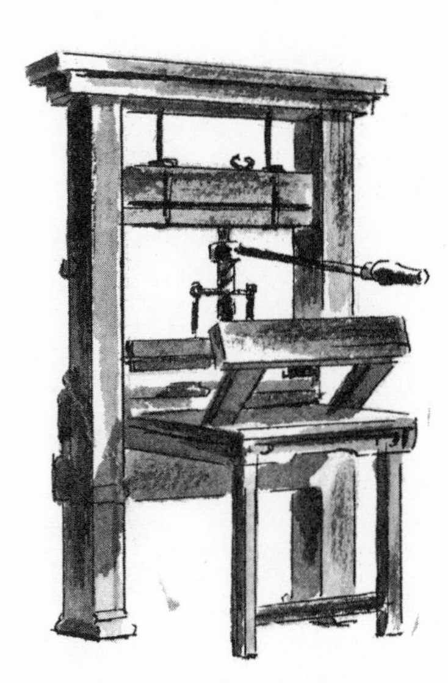

A model of an early printing press.

.... AND THE SPOKEN WORD

Gutenberg's idea spread rapidly throughout Europe. As more books were printed, more persons learned to read. But most of these books were in either classic Greek or Latin, the international language of churchmen, lawyers, diplomats, writers, and students. Most Europeans, however, had never mastered the Latin of Caesar, Cicero, and Horace. Lacking education, they spoke only an unrefined form of the language. Many barbarians pouring into the Roman Empire spoke only their own rough languages.

In time, the people of each geographical area began to speak its own language, based on either the unrefined form of Latin or the language of the barbarians. New words, phrases, and grammar developed. In Italy, the speech of the barbarians almost completely vanished for the Latin of the Romans. Gradually, this became the Italian language. In Spain, the language of the West Goths combined with Latin to form the beginnings of the Spanish language. Many Spanish words, also, were taken from the Arabs, or Moors, whose culture influenced the whole of Spain. In France, the speech of the Franks mingled with Latin to make the French language. These three languages—Italian, Spanish, and French—have a Latin, or Roman, base. That is why we often call them the Romance languages.

The languages spoken in northern Europe beyond the boundaries of the old Roman Empire were not influenced so much by the Latin. Known as the Germanic languages, they include the languages spoken by the different tribes of Northmen (Danish, Norwegian, and Swedish) as well as by the peoples who lived in, or near, the region now called Germany (German, Dutch, and Flemish). The Angles and Saxons also belonged to the Germanic language group because they took that language with them when they migrated to Britain.

The language which grew up in England, however, was a mixture of several. The Northmen who settled in Normandy had learned the French language. This was the language which William the Conqueror and his nobles spoke. After they had conquered the Anglo-Saxons and ruled them, both languages mingled together and each took words from the other. It was this mixture of languages that made our own English language. That is why we have so many words from both the Romance and the Germanic languages.

Some of our words came from one language; some, from the other. The word "commence" comes from the Norman French, but we get "begin" from the Anglo-Saxon; "woman" is from the Anglo-Saxon; "female," from the French. However, we must remember that Anglo-Saxon was the language of the laborer and the conquered. The word "pig," for example, is Anglo-Saxon, while the word "pork" comes from the French. This seemed to indicate that pig became pork when it reached the Norman dinner table. In other words, the Anglo-Saxon took care of the pig in the field; the Norman ate it when it had been prepared for the table. There are many other pairs of words that mean the same thing, except that one was the conquered Anglo-Saxon's and the other was the Norman's. "Sheep," for example, is Anglo-Saxon, while "mutton," which is French, refers to the meat of sheep ready for cooking.

One of the smallest Bibles in the world, printed in 1901 in Scotland; it contains 876 illustrated pages and is perfectly readable with a magnifying glass.

With the development of languages, the common people could express in literature their hopes and fears. Learning, once a monopoly of the few (aristocrats and churchmen), was slowly beginning to filter into the lives of the many. By means of Gutenberg-type printing presses, books began

King James I of England receives the first copy of the "authorized" translation of the Bible.

to be printed in the languages spoken and written by the people of several countries. In England, books were printed in English. In other parts of Europe, books were printed in Spanish, German, Danish, and so on.

During the Renaissance, the minds of men came alive with many new ideas. Dante, who lived in the city of Florence, Italy, was such a man. He wrote in the language spoken by the people of his city. People in Florence read his *Divine Comedy* eagerly because its poems gave voice to the Tuscan language of thirteenth-century Italy.

Some eighty years after Dante, Chaucer's *Canterbury Tales* introduced his countrymen to the vernacular, or native, tongue of fourteenth-century England.

Toward the end of the Renaissance, the scholars translated the Bible into English. They did such a fine job that this Bible became a model for English writers. Since this translation was done by the order of James I, it is called the King James Version. Even today, it remains an example of unexcelled scholarship.

THE RISE OF NATIONS

In ancient times, some men were ready to sacrifice their lives to defend their city-states, such as Athens; or their empires, such as the Roman. In the Middle Ages, some men were ready to do likewise for empires, such as Charlemagne's; or for the feudal states of their lords.

By the end of the Renaissance, a new kind of state was winning the allegiance of many Europeans. A powerful king would unite many feudal states into a national state, or politically independent nation. Confusing rivalries, alliances, plots, assassinations, and wars usually accompanied such unification. Instead of looking like a patchwork quilt of thousands of little feudal states, the Renaissance map of Europe began to look more as it looks today. Among the national states whose boundaries have not changed much since 1600 are England, France, and Spain. On the other hand, Italy and Germany remained divided into small states until the 1800's.

In some countries, however, conditions were opposed to this centralizing tendency, and in these, the Modern Age was reached without national governments having been founded. Yet, even among those peoples where national governments did not appear, some progress was made toward unity through the formation of national languages and literatures, and the development of common feelings and aspirations.

The rise of national kingdoms and the decline of feudalism substituted strong centralized governments in place of the feeble, irregular, and conflicting rule of the feudal nobles or of other local authorities. The monarchy provided more uniform laws for a larger number of people.

QUESTIONS . . . .

There were many kingdoms in western Europe with different rulers. But, during the Middle Ages, all the people of Christian countries were followers of one Church, the Roman Catholic Church. But, as we have already seen, the Renaissance was a time of challenge. Thus, in these transitional days, some people began to question certain teachings and practices of the Church leaders.

Some thought that many Church leaders were more interested in riches than in helping the people.

Some said that the Church leaders had too much power over government.

Still others thought that the Bible should be written in the language of the people, instead of in Latin and in Greek, so that the people could read it for themselves.

A few disagreed with the laws and rules of the Church.

. . . . AND ANSWERS

One man who tried to bring about changes within the Roman Catholic Church was Martin Luther, a monk and a university professor in Germany, who preached vigorously against certain practices of the Church. Luther's ideas spread in many parts of Europe, and finally, he and his followers formed a new religious group, later called the Lutheran Church.

Luther defending his doctrines before the Council (or Diet) of Worms.

After Luther's break from the Roman Catholic Church, other religious leaders followed his example. One of these men was John Calvin. He and his followers established the Reformed Church. A follower of Calvin, John Knox, later started the Presbyterian Church. All of these new churches were called Protestant because they protested against some of the teachings and ways of the Roman Catholic Church.

This time of change in the Christian Church is called the Reformation, from the Latin for "changing to a new way, or a new form."

During the Middle Ages, science had been largely an array of odd-shaped bottles, peculiar mixtures, and–black magic! The men of black magic were called alchemists. They tried to pry into the secrets of nature, and made weird claims. They worked in secret laboratories cluttered with bottles, bellows, and furnaces. They ground powders of all colors and burned a variety of substances. While there are records of some useful discoveries by the alchemists, they mostly pretended to know a great deal more than they actually did and frightened people by threatening to use their magic against them.

It was, of course, easy to frighten people of the time because superstition was so prevalent. Many things were thought to be unlucky. Friday, for instance, was looked upon as an unlucky day, and thirteen as an unlucky number. People wore charms and lucky pieces to keep harm away. Supernatural beings, such as ghosts, goblins, gnomes, and fairies, were thought to roam the earth. Fortunetellers who claimed to have the power to reveal the future abounded. The "science" of the Middle Ages is often described as "the Black Art."

But, with the spirit of the Renaissance at work, men became more ready to shed their superstitions and to seek the actual facts. One of the forerunners of modern science was Roger Bacon, an English monk who lived during the thirteenth century. Though he believed in some of the superstitions and magic of medieval science, Bacon was impatient with the stupidity and ignorance of many of his fellow-scientists. He believed that scientific facts could only be reached by making experiments. In this belief, he showed a truly modern attitude. He also wrote one of the world's first encyclopedias in an effort to gather together knowledge about all things.

Friar Bacon studied in the University of Paris and taught at Oxford University in England. He not only read what early teachers and scientists had written, but he worked out some of their experiments in his own laboratory. He often told his students, "If men would learn to experiment and observe, they could invent all kinds of useful things. The time will come when ships will go without rowers, and with only one man to guide them. Likewise, carriages may be constructed which can move without animals and that men will travel with the swiftness of an arrow without animal and without sails. Machines may be made in which a man may sit in the middle turning some device by which artificial wings are made to strike the air in the manner of a flying bird." In these descriptions, it is easy to recognize the steamship, the locomotive, and the airplane of our present-day world.

Men thought Roger Bacon was a wizard and that evil spirits made him talk the way he did. Curious neighbors sometimes peeped at him in his laboratory and ran in terror, declaring that they had seen the devil spouting fire. The good friar is known to have invented a type of steam engine; very likely it was this, with its fire and steam, which the people thought was the devil or it might have been gun powder, for he was the first European to publish a formula for this important substance. He was even put in prison for a period of time because of teaching and because he was supposedly in league with "the Evil One," as the devil was called in those days. Today, we know that his ideas were far ahead of those of most people of his time.

The two exceptions to this would be Copernicus and

An early lens grinder at his workbench.

Galileo first demonstrated his telescope in Venice.

Galileo. Copernicus, a Polish priest, became very interested in the study of astronomy. Night after night, he watched the heavenly bodies from the tower of the cathedral in his town. Most people of his time believed as the ancient Greek, Ptolemy, did: that the sun, moon, and stars moved around the earth. After observing the stars for years, Copernicus decided this was not true. Instead, it seemed to him that the sun only appears to revolve around the earth. In reality, the earth is moving about the sun. He declared, further, that the earth on which we live is one of several heavenly bodies called planets, and all these planets revolve around the sun.

Because Copernicus knew this discovery would shock most people of his day, he kept the manuscript that told about his theory hidden for thirty-six years. Finally, in 1543, he allowed the book to be published. By the time a copy reached him, Copernicus was very ill. He died a few hours later, having no way of knowing that in years to come, he would be considered "the father of modern astronomy."

In Italy, Galileo, a young university teacher, was refuting another Greek theory. Aristotle had stated that the heavier the weight of a body, the faster it must fall. According to the story, Galileo took two iron balls, of different sizes and weights, to the top of Pisa's Leaning Tower. He dropped them at exactly the same instant. A few seconds later, a number of professors and scientists, who were watching the experiment, cried out in astonishment, "The two balls landed at the same moment!"

Again and again, Galileo tried the experiment to make sure that the results were not accident. But, each time the balls were dropped, they hit the ground at the same time. Galileo proved by experiment that Aristotle was incorrect.

Galileo experimented further with freely falling bodies and bodies rolling down an inclined plane. He proved that not only do all bodies fall faster in each succeeding interval of time, but that this increase in velocity is uniform.

In the course of his teaching, Galileo read Copernicus' book. The theory of the earth moving around the sun interested him. But it was not until after Galileo built a telescope, that he began to check Copernicus' theory. Galileo did not invent the telescope, but he made many great improvements in it. With the improved telescope, he was able to discover several important things about the moon and other heavenly bodies. At last, after many years of observing and studying, Galileo decided that Copernicus was correct in thinking that the earth and other planets moved around the sun, just as the smaller stars moved around the planets.

The news of Galileo's findings spread far and wide. People crowded into his small laboratory to look at the stars

It is very likely that the discovery of gunpowder happened accidentally in China, since the Chinese had developed fireworks displays long before the birth of Christ.

through his wonderful instrument. They endowed it with some magic power. Many learned men of the time refused to look through the telescope. They did not want to change their ideas about the stars, would not accept the theories that Galileo was trying to prove. In fact, the leaders of the Church held a trial of Galileo, forced him to say he did not believe the earth revolved around the sun, and then imprisoned him in his home so that even if he changed his mind again he couldn't tell anyone. But, all through the ages, scientists had met with opposition. Even today, there are people who refuse to look at something carefully because they are not open-minded.

Bacon, Copernicus, and Galileo made other men think. They led other men to use "the scientific method"—to experiment, to observe, to record what happened, and to do the experiment several times again. This method of solving problems has brought about most of modern man's inventions and discoveries.

One of these inventions was gunpowder. Gunpowder is a mixture of chemicals which burns so quickly that it explodes with great force. No one really knows who first made up this mixture. We do know that it originated somewhere in the Far East, most likely in China. The Chinese had been fond of fireworks and had developed them long before the birth of Christ. It is entirely possible that gunpowder was discovered accidentally by some Chinese trying to create a new exciting display of such fireworks. In the thirteenth century Friar Roger Bacon had published a formula for a chemical mixture like gunpowder, and some years later the fourteenth-century German monk, Berthold Schwartz, is said to have mixed a batch of the explosive preparation that blew himself and most of his monastery into fragments. Later a German monk discovered how to use the gunpowder to throw an iron ball from a cannon. Soon, Europeans were making cannons for use in war.

It has been often said that the invention of gunpowder

and the means of firing it gave the final death blow to feudalism. Because gunpowder could destroy strong castle walls, no longer could the lords depend on them to keep out their enemies. The soldier on foot became more powerful than the armored knight. Though the introduction of gunpowder into Europe was the beginning of the terrible tools of modern warfare, at least it hastened the breakdown of the feudal system.

By the early 1300's, elaborate timepieces—far removed from the Greek and Roman sundials and hour-glasses—were popular in Europe. Then, about 1360, Henri de Vick of Württemberg, Germany, invented a clock driven by machinery, the first mechanical clock. The later use of springs made possible smaller and smaller clocks until, by 1600, men were carrying pocketwatches.

The Renaissance was also a time of trade, and the invention of the compass made new routes possible. Before the compass, European sailors had to guide their ships by landmarks, sun, and stars. Men had known for a long time that a piece of iron could be so treated that it would point north and south if it could swing freely. Roger Bacon had told his students about this. He had mounted a steel needle on a pivot and showed that it would point northward. This was the forerunner of the mariner's compass. It could tell the captain, when out of sight of land, which way to head his ship. It could direct the caravan on the desert, or the traveler in the deep woods, to a desired destination.

As the Western World progressed, merchants became more eager than ever to trade with the Far East. Rich luxuries occasionally came from India and China—spices, perfume, silk, wood, exotic foods—but it was a long, slow journey. In our next view of history, we will meet the men who made important voyages of discovery and exploration.

Old engraving of a watchmaker's workshop.

India

circa 3000 B.C. Indus Valley civilization.

2000-1200 B.C. Aryan invasions.

circa 800-550 B.C. Aryan expansion; development of caste system.

circa 600-300 B.C. *Upanishads* (confidential writings) foundation of modern Hindu philosophy.

circa 274-236 B.C. Empire of Asoka included almost all of India.

circa A.D. 320 Gupta Empire united northern India.

circa A.D. 470 Gupta Empire broken up by White Huns.

A.D. 606-647 Harsha, conqueror and ruler of Northern India.

A.D. 1175 Muhammed of Ghur started invasion of India.

A.D. 1206 Sultanate established at Delhi by Kutb-ud-din Aibak.

A.D. 1526-1857 Mogul (Moslem) Empire founded by Babar.

A.D. 1632 Portuguese expelled from Bengal.

A.D. 1632-1653 Building of Taj Mahal.

A.D. 1668 French established trading station in India.

A.D. 1690 English start factory at Calcutta.

A.D. 1744 Robert Clive arrives in Madras.

A.D. 1756 "Black Hole" of Calcutta.

A.D. 1757 East India Company began domination of India. Clive defeated French at Battle of Plassey.

A.D. 1784 East India Company placed under government control.

A.D. 1843 Slavery abolished in India.

A.D. 1857-1858 Sepoy Rebellion.

A.D. 1886 Formation of Indian National Party.

A.D. 1920-1927 Mahatma Gandhi undisputed leader of Congress party.

A.D. 1947 India and Pakistan became sovereign nations.

A.D. 1948 Gandhi assassinated; succeeded by Jawaharlal Nehru.

A.D. 1949 Indian Constitution adopted.

A.D. 1961 Portuguese colony of Goa occupied by India.

China

221-207 B.C. Ch'in Dynasty. Standardization of measures, weights, law. Erection of Great Wall.

202 B.C.-A.D. 9 Western Han dynasty.

A.D. 25-220 Eastern Han dynasty.

A.D. 318 Division of China into Northern and Southern realms.

A.D. 1523 Europeans expelled from China.

A.D. 1644 Ching (Manchu) dynasty gained power (lasted till 1911.

A.D. 1685 Ports of China opened to foreign trade.

A.D. 1839-1842 Opium War of England with China.

A.D. 1860 Vladivostok built by Russians on Chinese territory.

A.D. 1894-1895 China defeated in Sino-Japanese War.

A.D. 1900-1901 Boxer rebellion. China defeated by International army. Open Door Policy.

A.D. 1911 The Republic of China. First republic in Asia.

A.D. 1920-1926 Civil War in China; emergence of leadership of Chiang-K'ai-shek.

A.D. 1931-1932 Japanese occupied Manchuria; beginning of war with Japan.

A.D. 1949 People's Republic of China. Communist government.

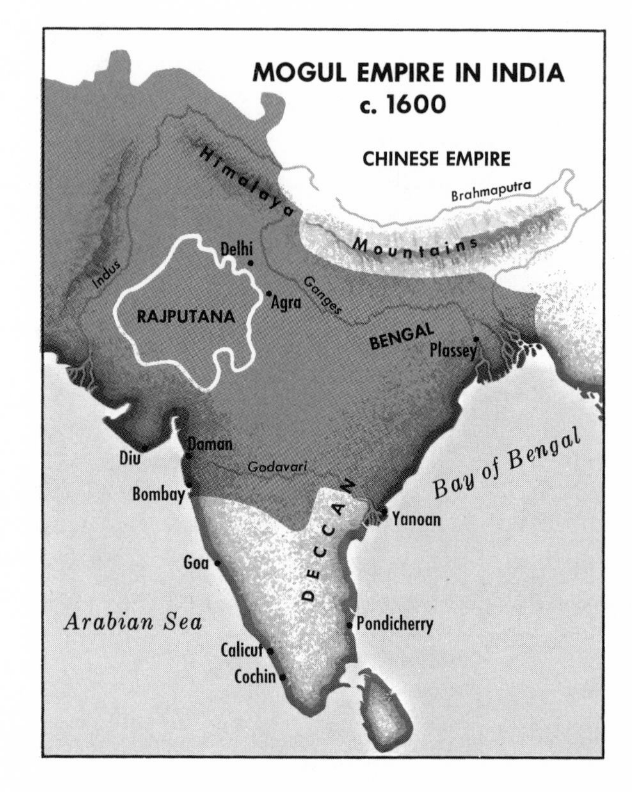

A.D. 589 Reunification of Empire by Ch'en dynasty.

A.D. 618-907 T'Aug dynasty; period of great artistic development.

A.D. 990 Yantu (Pekin) became capital of Northern China.

A.D. 1211-1215 China invaded by Jenghiz (Genghis) Khan.

A.D. 1260 Mongol Yüan dynasty founded in China by Kublai Khan.

A.D. 1271-1295 Marco Polo traveled through Asia to China.

A.D. 1275-1292 Period of Marco Polo's service to Kublai Khan.

A.D. 1279-1368 Mongol Yüan dynasty ruled China.

A.D. 1368-1644 Ming dynasty.

A.D. 1421 Pekin became capital of China.

A.D. 1516 Beginning of expanded trade between Portugal and China.

Europe Looks to the Lands of Tigers and Dragons

DURING the Middle Ages, the peoples of Europe knew little about far-off Asian lands. For, to most Europeans of the medieval period, the world probably seemed even smaller than it had to the ancient Greeks and Romans.

The only lands of which they had any first-hand knowledge were, of course, Europe, northern Africa, and small areas of Asia Minor.

But, during the crusades, they began to hear fabulous tales of remote Eastern countries full of rare treasures, exotic fruits and flowers, priceless jewels, elephants, dragons, tigers, lions—and perhaps even *people* (not quite so civilized, naturally, as most Europeans then believed themselves to be, but people, nonetheless).

Curiosity and a profound interest in world affairs were,

as we have observed, notable characteristics of the Renaissance movement. And hadn't the merchant princes, traders, sailors, and pioneers and missionaries of that era considered it their bounden duty to journey far afield, probing the secrets of mountain wildernesses, discovering new territories, amassing fortunes, furthering the cause of Christianity by enlightening the unenlightened?

Yet, when these voyagers arrived in foreign lands, they invariably found civilizations more firmly established than their own, and considerably more progressive in many respects.

THE LAND BEYOND THE INDUS

In the course of our travels, we've already rested our make-believe caravans at the edge of Middle Eastern deserts, on the banks of the Nile, in the fertile valleys of Mesopotamia, and along the highways and byways of fallen empires.

Now, traveling due eastward, we come upon India: a prosperous land of "modern" cities, an ancient civilization, well-built houses, spacious avenues, and "modern" rural communities.

Ancient civilizations developed in the Indus River Valley of what is now Pakistan about 4,700 years ago. But the peo-

Native boat on the Ganges, India's holy river.

Indians were among the first to spin and weave cotton, and whether in the primitive fashion shown at left, or at a modern factory (below), cotton spinning and weaving is an important industry in India today.

ple of India were enslaved by migrating Aryan tribes from Russia and Turkestan, who originally invaded their country some 1,500 years before the birth of Christ.

The Indian people lived in city-states, governed by princes, or *rajahs,* and *maharajas,* in much the same fashion as the peoples of ancient Greece.

Their religion was called Hinduism and the people who believed in it became known as Hindus. Their chief god was Brahma, creator of the universe. But they also worshiped a number of lesser gods. And their high priests, through whom Brahma was said to have spoken, recorded his utterances in the *Vedas,* or sacred books.

Hinduism passed through many phases and many centuries of development. And countless priests, *rajahs,* and *maharajas* have come and gone since the conquering Aryans swaggered across the Himalayas and staked their claim to this vast and colorful land.

But the strange India "caste" system has endured for thousands of years. And, although to some extent it has been modified and adapted to the demands of contemporary society, the high-caste Brahman in a sense still lords it over his lesser countryman, the "untouchable," who, in the words of a once-popular ballad, has long been scorned as "less than the dust, beneath my chariot wheel."

This exclusive circle of higher-caste Brahmans was composed of priests, rulers, and warriors; merchants, farmers, and craftsmen; menials and slaves. Priests, rulers, and warriors ranked first; merchants, farmers, and craftsmen, second; menials and slaves, or "untouchables," last.

And, if anyone dared to violate the rules of the caste system, he forthwith became what was known as an outcaste.

Moreover, if he had the misfortune to be born an underling or a slave, he remained an untouchable for the rest of his days.

And, while it seems improbable that a high-caste Brahman would ever arbitrarily choose to descend to the level of his inferiors, he couldn't do so—even if he literally begged to be demeaned and pushed around, as they were.

For, in the India of ancient days, if you started life at the top, you stayed there till the crack of doom. After all, you could go no higher. And what more could a first-class Brahman ask?

This being so, no matter how tempted you might be to step out of your class, you could never foregather with inferiors for cozy family outings on the banks of the Ganges or the Indus rivers, picnics under the banyan trees, or occasional *durbars* (receptions) at Delhi.

However, all citizens had one thing in common: They believed in the transmigration of souls; that is, the passing of the soul at death into another body.

For instance, it was taken for granted that the soul of the departed left the body after death, rested for a while on the moon, and then returned to earth to take up residence in the body of another human or even in the body of a lesser animal such as a pig, a dog, or perhaps a reptile, depending upon one's conduct when alive.

Because Hindus believe all animals have souls, they treat all animals with respect. But they particularly treat the cow as a sacred animal. A cow can do no wrong in India and no Hindu may harm a cow.

The staple diet consisted largely of rice, which grew in

abundance. And tea, of couse, became the national brew of India for it also grows in abundance.

Loin cloths were the principal article of male attire below the waist. Heads were encased in turbans.

Women wore loose, flowing robes, or *saris*. And, indeed, today's Indian women, in many cases, still do.

The head man, or chief of each village descended from a long line of head men, or chiefs, and was responsible for maintaining the peace. He was also responsible for protecting and defending his community, in times of unrest. Incidentally, this honor was passed down from father to son through many generations.

THE FOUR NOBLE TRUTHS

And, since no journey to faraway places is ever complete without at least one tale of an incident that "actually happened" (according to local legend, that is), we now sit back and listen to the story of a certain *rajah's* son: a timid youth who hated to see anyone or anything hurt, ill-treated, or in pain.

Strangely enough, although he was a quiet, retiring sort of lad, he is said to have played a fast game of *spellicans,* a form of Indian hopscotch and, when a small boy, to have greatly enjoyed this rowdy exercise.

Since he was the son of a *rajah,* he was expected to be a leader of men. And of warriors. But he disliked cruelty, fighting, and killing.

And, when he walked in the streets of the town, he would often be moved to tears at the sight of poor people trudging from place to place because they were homeless or men and women too old to even move about, homeless, too, and in want.

In great distress, the *rajah's* son went to the priests and implored them to tell him why cruelty and pain were always visited upon the defenseless, the sick, and the aged.

The priests told him about the sun god, the fire god, the god of the air, and the gods of the storm; about Brahma, the supreme god, who watched over all—even the sick, the poor, the aged, and those of lower caste, the untouchables.

But, somehow, their answers failed to satisfy the young man.

He admired the priests, however. But he saw that they, too, despised the untouchables and did little to help them. He also saw that illness and old age came to good men and bad men alike; to princes, as well as to slaves. And, the more he thought about it all, the more perplexed and troubled he grew.

Carving from the famous Elephant Caves near Bombay, showing the three chief deities of Hinduism: Brahma, the creator; Vishnu, the preserver; and Siva, the destroyer.

Now, there were in India at that time a number of mendicants (people who beg for food and shelter) who wandered about the land. They read palms, carried messages from place to place, and foretold the future in the stars. Some of them were miserable men who deliberately mutilated themselves with sharp knives and stones, and deprived themselves of food so that they were emaciated and always hungry. The prince had often invited these homeless wanderers into the palace grounds for he was eager to hear their stories.

Siva, the destroyer, is shown here standing on a dwarf, the symbol of ignorance in Hinduism. Siva is also the king of dancers.

Hindu Temple in Madras, India, is famous for its thousands of carved figures on both the outside and the inside walls (above left).

This representation of Buddha as a teacher, symbolized by the manner of sitting and the position of the hands, was created during the Gupta period of Indian history (above).

Then, one day, five centuries before the birth of Christ, the prince, whose name was Gautama, decided to forsake his gorgeous palace and all his wealth and power to become a poor wanderer.

If he remained at home, he knew he would succeed to the kingdom, or *raj,* when his father died. And then he would be compelled to lead soldiers into battle, and do many other things of which he disapproved.

So, he boldly told his father that he would renounce his kingdom to become a wanderer. This angered his parent, who caused guards to be posted outside the gates of the palace.

Even so, Gautama finally escaped. Pausing only long enough to cut off his flowing hair and beard, he exchanged his fine princely garments for the tattered coverings of a beggar whom he encountered on the road. At length, he found shelter in a cave.

Here lived a number of hermits, one in each cave, who had, they said, retired from the wicked world. They, too, had run away from their homes, wives, and families. Now, they sat under the trees discussing the sadness and mystery

These are not beasts of burden, resting before being yoked to the cart, but holy cows, animals still considered sacred and worshiped as such in India today.

Ruins of an ancient temple in India.

of life, and hoping and praying that they might escape the unhappiness of this world by falling asleep.

The runaway prince listened to their strange, yet fascinating, stories. But, somehow, he felt troubled and sad.

Seeking to gain deeper knowledge by abstaining from food and doing penance, the young prince decided to fast for several days. His problems still remained unsolved. Indeed, his misery became more acute than ever.

Weak from hunger, the poor young man finally collapsed. When he recovered his composure, he excused himself and told his hermit friends that he now proposed to eat his fill. For, obviously, he pointed out, fasting and self-denial were of no consequence. The hermits upbraided him. They called him a coward, and worse.

More distressed than he had yet felt, the prince sat down beneath the nearest banyan tree, and had a quiet chat with himself. "I shall never again," said he, "listen to what any man tells me. I shall think my own thoughts and reflect upon the age-old riddle of the universe. Nor shall I leave this spot until I learn how man should live."

That very night, he received an answer to all the questions that had puzzled him. He hastened to share his joy with the

Scenes from a dance depicting Thaibi, legendary Indian lovers. The Indian dancers have set movements of hands and body for "the expression of the soul."

wanderers. For many days, they mocked and disbelieved him, but at long last, they came to share his joy and to agree that he, the prince, had at last found the four noble truths for which they had sought in vain. They called him Gautama Buddha. (The title "Buddha" means "enlightened.")

After the prince had departed this life forever, his followers honored him as a god and Buddhism became an organized religion with sacred cities and sacred rivers, monasteries and temples, an order of saints and priests, and many idols.

And with many worshipers, too. Not the least of them was the *rajah,* Asoka, a mighty warrior and upholder of peace and the brotherhood of man. When Asoka became a Buddhist, he decreed that this faith be practiced throughout the state.

He treated slaves kindly, was charitable toward the underprivileged, built hospitals for the poor and suffering, and schools for the education of all. He abolished unjust rules and laws, and pardoned many who had been wrongly imprisoned.

Asoka bade his people to honor their parents, to be

governed by charitable impulses toward them and all their fellow men, and to forego the cruel slaughter of animals. Buddhist missionaries were dispatched to neighboring states and other countries.

THE PEOPLE OF THE MIDDLE COUNTRY

To the north of India lies China, the vast land to which the people of the Middle Ages gave the romantic name, Cathay. Cradle of an ancient civilization, the peoples of this gigantic land gradually evolved their own pattern of life.

Many historians believe that China had its origin on the northern plains, in the region of its two great rivers, the Yangtze and the Hwang Ho, or Yellow, River. Here, the farmers tended their crops in much the same manner as the early Mesopotamians.

Rice was raised along the Yangtze; millet (a form of cereal) was the main crop of the fields along the Hwang Ho. The Hwang Ho, however, often flooded the land and wrought destruction.

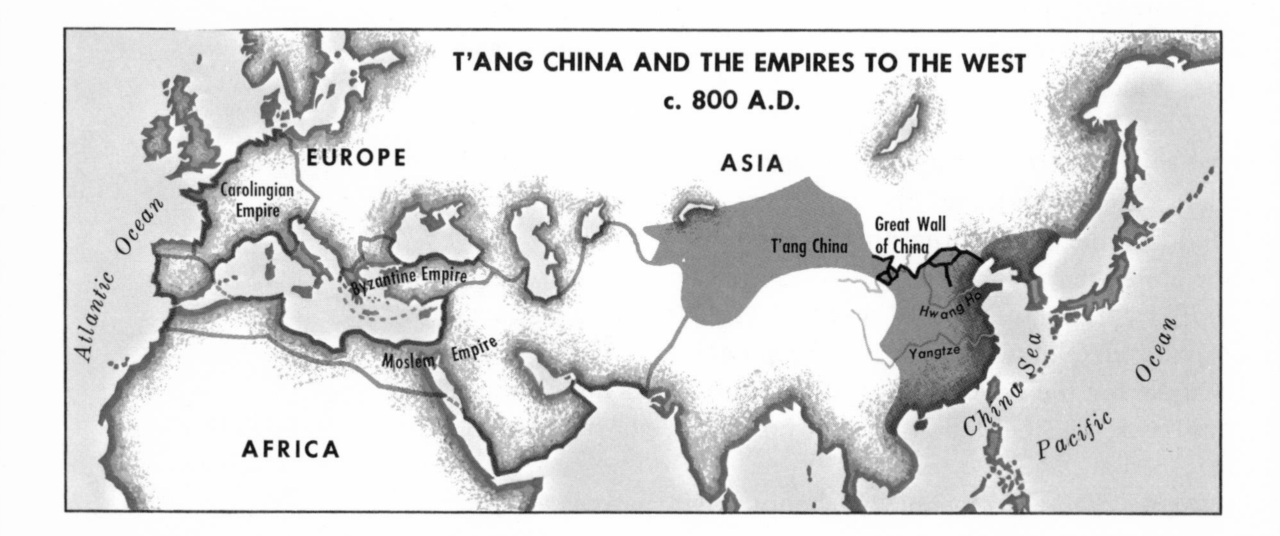

To prevent the annual loss of crops and homes, the Chinese built dikes, but the rampaging river often broke through these man-made barriers.

Unlike the Nile, which enriched and nourished the Egyptian valleys, the Yellow River carried off much of the fertile soil.

Indeed, it frequently carried off everything in sight, including the farms—and, sometimes, even the unfortunate farmers.

The laborers and working people lived in crude, hut-like houses of bamboo or brick with grass roofs. Their clothing was usually made of coarse homespun material. From the earliest times, they domesticated only dogs, oxen, and pigs. Roast pig, incidentally, became in time a choice Chinese dish—and all because one of these unlucky creatures (burned to a crisp through no fault of its own) smelled better in death than it had ever smelled in life. Little did it realize that millions of its descendants were destined to end up in pork butchers' shops from Alaska to Zanzibar, with frilly pants around their nether extremities and apples under their snouts.

As for the Chinese alphabet, or lack of one as we know it, symbols represented the various letters. And since there were innumerable dialects—from Mandarin in the north to Cantonese in the south—we presume that even the native Chinese looked upon their mother tongue as a sort of huge jigsaw puzzle.

Through dozens of centuries, however, they have somehow managed to communicate with each other—and even with the rest of the world.

Most of the early Chinese books were written on long scrolls and rolled up when not in use in a manner not unlike that of the ancient Egyptians.

Religion played a vital role in the history and development of China. The ancient Chinese were convinced that spirits accompanied them at all times; that they peopled the earth, the trees, the rivers, the mountains, and the sky.

Some were good spirits; others were anything but.

The guiding spirit, or supreme lord, was Shang Ti. And, on open-air altars throughout the country, sacrifices of grain, sheep, and oxen were offered regularly. Since ancient China was an agricultural and farming nation, much of the ritual and ceremony concerned the growth and harvesting of crops. And, of course, they constantly besought the spirits of sun, rain, soil, and grain to look with favor upon their lands.

Ancestor worship also formed an integral part of their ritual. They asked their departed kin to protect their families, send them abundant crops, and protect their farms against flood as well as drought. They invoked the ancestral blessing on all important undertakings. And many an affluent family built a temple to the memory of their illustrious forebears; the less fortunate paid their respects before simple, homemade shrines.

Nor were their great men overlooked. However, they preferred men of peace to famous warriors. For instance, there was Fu Hsi, inventor of musical instruments and a Chinese

Not much has changed in hundreds of years in the way of transplanting the rice in early June in the paddy fields.

At left, a Chinese scribe with the paraphernalia of his trade, brushes and ink, in the streets of a Chinese city, and below, a sample of Chinese writing.

聖主迴鑾肅百靈紫雲團蓋翼蒼精屬
劍車復星辰麗先 駕祈常日月明十里春
風傳警蹕萬方和氣協韶韺白頭欣覲朝元
盛願續思文頌太平

system of arithmetic; Shen Nung introduced medicine into China; Huang Ti developed the first Chinese calendar. The unforgettable Yu taught them how to keep the rampaging Yellow River in its place.

"THE FIVE CLASSICS"

Confucius, of course, held a special place in the hearts and memories of his compatriots. Educated by his widowed mother, and trained in the highest ideals of his native land, he learned to respect and honor China's historic figures of the past. And he determined to contribute to a glorious future, for both his country and his fellow man.

He established a school wherein young men might learn to be good citizens, as well as good scholars, administrators, and diplomats.

And, although Confucius was a man of the fifth century B.C., we can readily understand why so much of his teaching and so many of his words of wisdom have endured. For he held that sound, responsible government could forestall wars, hunger, and petilence. And he remained convinced that emperors of the distant past had invariably set a good

The camel is a piece of Chinese tomb pottery from the T'ang dynasty of about 618-907 A.D. The Chinese bronze vessel dates back to the Shang dynasty. The horse, put into the tomb of a nobleman to represent his favorite, is a typical example of the delicate workmanship in ancient Chinese pottery. The ferocious-looking figure embroidered on the satin cloth was the symbol of rank of a military official of the Ch'ing dynasty.

example for their people to follow. "What you do not like done to yourself," he exhorted, "do not unto others."

In other words, his was the oriental version of the Golden Rule, several hundred years before Jesus pronounced it.

Later, Confucius became chief adviser to the city-state of Lu. He was quite happy, and made so many rules of conduct that everyone must have been kept very busy doing as they would be done by and leading blameless lives.

No talking at meals was allowed. And ladies must not walk on the same side of the street as gentlemen. As was often the case in those early days, ladies were not often seen (in public), and they were almost never heard. This was especially noticeable in Far Eastern lands.

Poetry, music, and archery were popular. And good manners, Confucius insisted, rather than good tailoring, made the man or woman.

But, as we have also learned during the course of our travels, there is a time and a place for everything. And, as might be foreseen, even the great Confucius proved expendable when the reigning monarch tired of all the rules and regulations.

Possibly, the ruler was jealous and felt himself over-

shadowed by a wise man and intellectual giant. But, at all events, the philosopher suddenly found himself out of a job and much reduced in circumstances.

Yet, the classical Chinese writings, *The Five Classics,* edited and collected by Confucius, have survived for more than two thousand years as the Confucian Bible.

Succeeding generations of scholars, educators, and philosophers were to contribute enormously, too, to the culture, knowledge, and wisdom of the Chinese people.

INVADERS FROM THE NORTH

But neither the prayers of their honorable ancestors, all the wisdom of the ancients, nor the bravery of their warriors could withstand the might of the Mongolian leader, Genghis Khan, and his barbarian hordes.

Indeed, not even the Great Wall of China was safe against their battering-ram.

Nor could the deadly arrows of flame, or Chinese rockets, stay the inexorable descent of these conquerors from northwestern lands.

But, having slaked his thirst for glory and satisfied his

Bronze statue of Amithayus, the bestower of long life, from the eighteenth century.

Many sections of the Great Wall of China still stand.

hunger for power, Genghis Khan, ruler of an empire that extended from the China Seas to the Persian Gulf, died on active duty.

And Kublai Khan, a grandson, while by no means one of the meek, nevertheless inherited much of the Chinese earth.

To his credit, however, he governed the conquered peoples with a reasonable measure of justice; encouraged foreign trade; was an able administrator; and converted the city of Peiping (then known as Cambuluc) into a splendid capital.

Here, in the year 1266, two adventurous Venetians, the brothers Nicolò and Maffeo Polo, were presented to Kublai Khan.

An admirer of enterprise, the ruler handed them a golden tablet, or amulet, to ensure their safe journey home.

Eleven years later, they returned to China, bringing young Marco Polo, son of Nicolò, who, for three years, controlled the destiny of the city of Yangchow; traveled through Asia and India; and, decades later was to recount his amazing adventures while serving as a prisoner of war in his homeland.

BY CARAVAN ACROSS ASIA

In the service of Kublai Khan, Marco Polo traveled extensively throughout China. He visited the remote mountains of Tibet, explored the China seacoast, and even journeyed as far as Burma in Southeast Asia.

He heard of the wondrous isles of Nippon, or Japan, land of fragrant lotus blossoms and ornate shrines. He heard strange music, played upon stringed instruments, studied the Chinese method of astronomical observation, and at close range, saw the first rockets' "red glare." He watched the flat-bottomed, square-prowed sailing boats, or junks, in the harbors. And, to his amazement, he discovered that the Chinese used paper currency, reproduced by a curious machine which today we describe as a printing press.

He noticed their unusual water-clocks, or *clepsydra.* (We, too, came upon these ancient timepieces in the course of our wanderings.) He saw – but did not recognize as coal – a lump of shiny black stone that burned with a dull red glow.

And he carefully observed a fountain of oil that also burned with a steady flame. In southern Mongolia, he found "serpents" thirty feet long, "with jaws wide enough to swallow a man." Perhaps they were ancestors of the reptiles

Portrait of Kublai Khan.

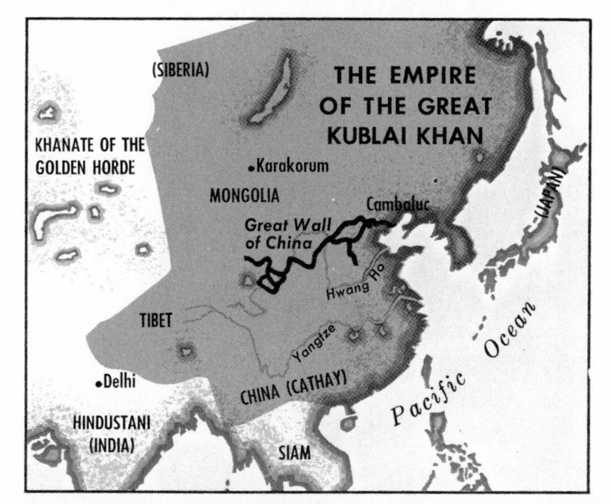

The map shows the extent of the Empire of Kublai Khan and the location of the Great Wall.

Portrait of Marco Polo, above, and a Mongolian house on wheels, an ancestor of our modern trailer, as it was described by the Polos after their return.

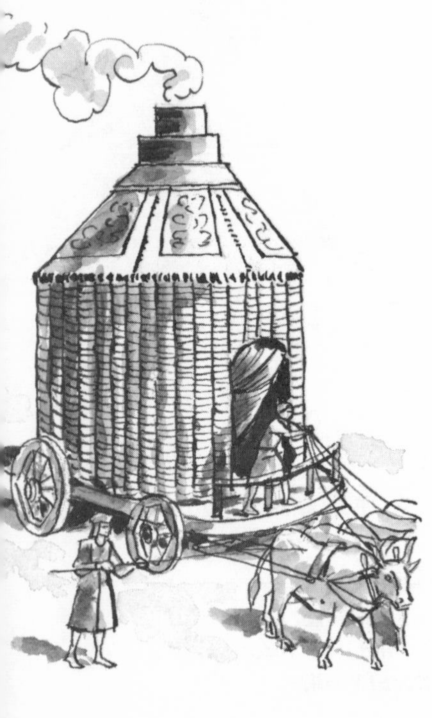

we call crocodiles and do our best to avoid, although the men-eaters seem to confine their unpleasant eating habits to far-off alien seas.

Marco Polo was the first westerner to furnish a graphic description of the Tartars, a nomadic Moslem tribe who wandered through Europe and Asia and ultimately wielded considerable power in Siberia, the Ukraine, and Russia. Their modern descendants now live in the mountainous Ural district of western Russia and around the middle and lower Volga regions.

The Polo family became rich and influential during their long stay in China. But they also grew very homesick for Venice and finally took leave of Kublai Khan, their host and benefactor, who showered them with parting gifts.

On the journey homeward, the Polos traveled by sea, taking a Chinese junk down the coast and around the Malay Peninsula to India.

His mind full of the wonders he had seen and the many voyages he had completed, the seventeen-year-old youth returned to Venice a man, forty-one years old.

Speaking their mother tongue with much difficulty, unkempt, and perceptibly older, the Polos ultimately reached their native land. But, alas, not a soul remembered them. Even their relatives seemed not to know them.

Certainly, they were not the elegant Venetian citizens who had set sail for the Orient so long ago, but they were still members of the esteemed Polo family. Yet, the more they sought to explain this, the more the townsfolk laughed at them.

At length, the Polos held a sumptuous banquet. After the feast, Marco showed them all the costly gems and precious jewels they had brought home from the Orient: Rubies, sapphires, diamonds, emeralds, and pearls cascaded from the seams of their threadbare garments.

Surely these priceless treasures of Cathay bore out the truth of their story, and confirmed their identity?

THE ROAD TO INDIA

Fascinated by the story of Marco Polo, kings, lords, and traders began to dream of traveling afar, and perhaps acquiring rare and costly treasures and amassing huge fortunes.

To journey overland was to invite disaster, however, for the highways and byways spawned robbers and criminals. And kings and nobles were no safer on the road than were humble serfs and laborers.

"But what of the vast, uncharted seas?" Prince Henry, the youngest son of King John I of Portugal, asked himself one morning as he emerged from his bath.

As a very young man, the prince had yearned to eventually travel far afield – even to the Indies. Of course, he had campaigned against the Moors in North Africa. And had he not also helped capture the seaport, Ceuta, gateway to Gibralter, thereby adding to his country's imperial domains?

The fires of adventure burned fiercely within the prince's bosom. He longed to sail the seven seas in search of new lands. But fate conspired against the poor fellow. Save for occasional forays, the navigator remained a stay-at-home explorer until summoned to his first, and final, adventure.

Yet, because of his administrative and organizing ability, Portugal would ultimately acquire a large colonial empire and wield great influence overseas.

Among other things, Prince Henry believed that Africa was a separate continent. Thus, if a ship could only negotiate the southernmost tip, it could sail all the way to India.

Prince Henry also founded one of the most unique training schools of his time, at Sagres: a college for seamen, shipbuilders, and navigators.

There, the finest Portuguese sailors were trained by the prince himself.

He supervised the exploration of Africa's west coast, and

Prince Henry of Portugal is known to us today as Henry the Navigator for the part he played in developing modern navigation.

built up a flourishing trade along the Gold and Ivory coasts of the Dark Continent.

Moreover, he was responsible for the production of a highly maneuverable, square-rigged sailboat, or caravel.

And so, equipped with sturdy vessels, improved scientific instruments, and skillful navigators, Prince Henry's mariners patrolled the seas with renewed zest.

In the year 1432, the Azores (which had already appeared on a map in 1351) were rediscovered. Those inveterate seamen and globetrotters, whom we have met before, the Phoenicians, first discovered these islands in the seventh century B.C.

But the seas were often turbulent, the cross-currents treacherous. And, time and time again, the caravels returned to port because their crews were apprehensive, fearful, and unwilling to complete the voyage.

Year after year, Prince Henry patiently sent his captains forth with orders to continue as far south as they dared. Thus, in the course of time, the strange unknown coasts of the continent of Africa became as familiar to Prince Henry's gallant explorers as his oft-repeated command, "Sail southward!"

Elated by their modest success, the Portuguese Court came to believe that India now lay within their grasp. Prince Henry's sailors would soon bring tidings of a great new discovery!

After the prince's death in 1460, they nobly carried on his work. And, in the year 1488, after an unsuccessful effort on the outward voyage, Bartholomeu Dias (or Diaz), the Portuguese navigator, homeward-bound and driven off course by fog and gale-force winds, accidentally rounded what we know as the Cape of Good Hope, and thereby opened the sea lanes to India, without realizing that he was the first sailor to accomplish this feat.

To this historic landmark on the southernmost tip of South Africa, Dias, because of his recent experience, gave the name, the Cape of Storms.

And, upon his return to Portugal, he went immediately to the king, proudly reported the good news and explained that he had made so bold as to name this elusive point of land Cape of Storms.

As kings will, the monarch hemmed and hawed. "Surely," said he at last, "you can do better than that, my dear Dias?"

But, before the nonplussed Bartholomeu could think of a suitable reply, the king proclaimed it the Cape of Good Hope.

And so it has remained ever since.

A decade later, Vasco da Gama, under orders from Manuel I, set sail for India.

He rounded the Cape of Good Hope (as Dias had in 1488), sailed up the east coast, and crossed the Indian Ocean to Calicut.

Now, all that remained were other lands, other seas: to discover, to chart, to explore—and to conquer. The world seemed to be growing larger.

A.D. 1487 Diaz sailed around Cape of Good Hope.

A.D. 1492 Columbus reached San Salvador.

A.D. 1493 Pope Alexander VI granted New World to Spain and Portugal.

A.D. 1494 Treaty of Tordesillas formalized agreement in Spain and Portugal for division of the New World.

A.D. 1496 Henry VII approved Cabot's voyage to New World.

A.D. 1497 Vasco da Gama sailed past Cape of Good Hope.

A.D. 1498 Calicut in India visited by Vasco da Gama. Columbus discovered Trinidad and mainland of South America. Cabot reached Labrador and the east coast of North America.

A.D. 1499 Alonso Hojeda and Amerigo Vespucci discovered Venezuela and Guiana.

A.D. 1500 Cabral discovered Brazil, and claimed it for Portugal.

A.D. 1501-1504 Four expeditions made to New World by Anglo-Portuguese Syndicate.

A.D. 1506 Death of Columbus.

A.D. 1507 New World named "America" after Amerigo Vespucci.

A.D. 1513 Balboa reached Pacific after crossing Isthmus of Panama. Florida discovered by Ponce de Léon.

A.D. 1518-1521 Spanish conquest of Mexico (led by Cortez).

A.D. 1519-1522 Magellan's ships completed trip around the world after his death on Philippine Islands.

A.D. 1521 Portuguese reached Molucca Islands.

A.D. 1529 Spanish-Portuguese frontiers in Pacific defined by Treaty of Saragossa.

A.D. 1534-1536 Cartier landed at Labrador, and also discovered the St. Lawrence River.

A.D. 1541 Cartier's third voyage to Canada.

A.D. 1543 Fourth Cartier voyage to Canada.

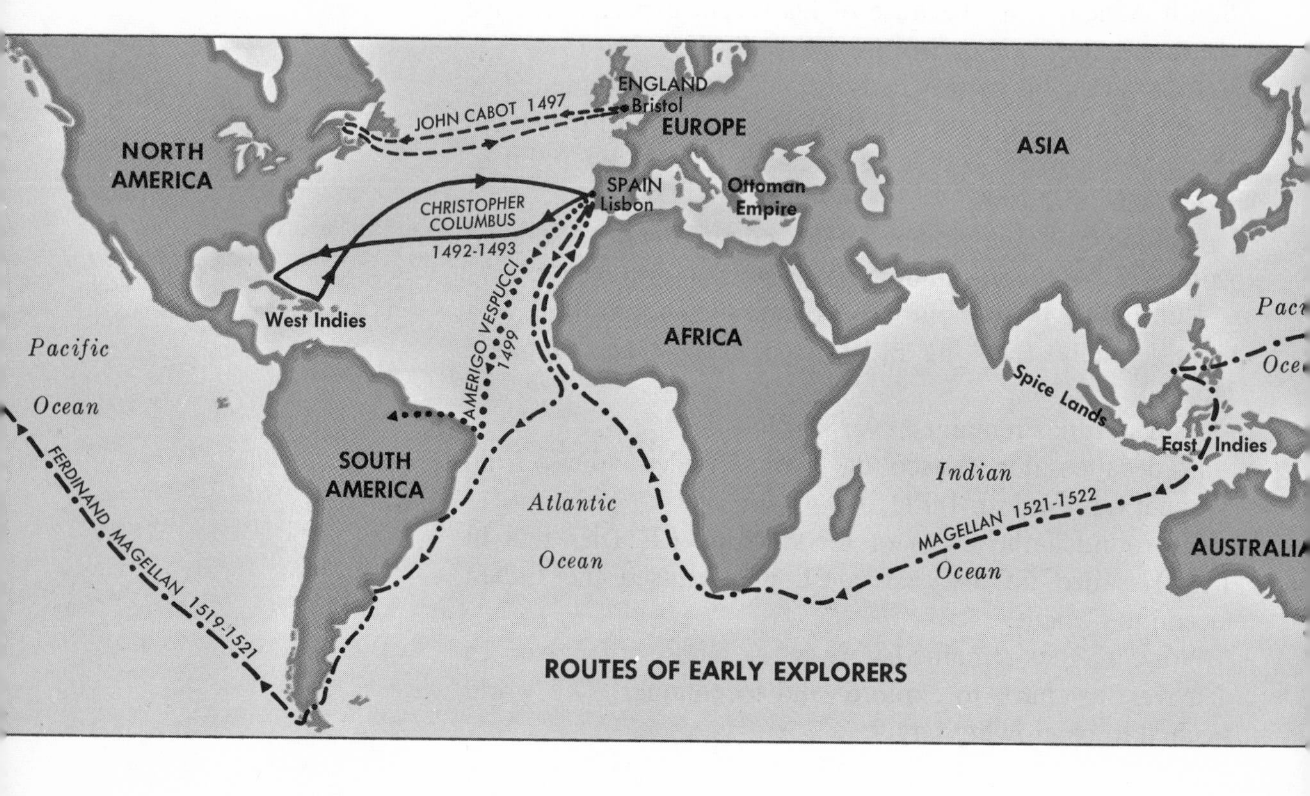

ROUTES OF EARLY EXPLORERS

The Discovery of a "New World"

PORTUGAL was not the only European power with dreams of grand empires beyond the seas. The sailors of other nations had also foreseen the possibility of reaching India, China, and the East Indies by merely sailing westward across the Atlantic Ocean.

They did not know that the two mighty continents of North and South America—of which they were totally unaware—presented a formidable obstacle to the fulfillment of such an ambitious undertaking.

THE ADMIRAL OF THE OCEAN SEA

In the eyes of an Italian mariner named Christopher Columbus, who had long held the opinion (unpopular in many circles) that the earth, of a certainty, was not flat, the time for proving the truth of his belief was at hand.

Nor was Columbus the only individual who made this assertion.

To be sure, a number of scholars, churchmen, and even average citizens, rejected this point of view as preposterous. "Out of the question!" they were prone to thunder even before the question was asked.

But Columbus, a patient man, stood by his convictions and bided his time. His life as sailor, soldier, and wanderer had been filled with adventure. He had studied astronomy, mapmaking, and navigation.

Furthermore, he had once followed the course of the vikings to the north of Iceland. And now he was determined to reach China and India by sailing westward across the Atlantic.

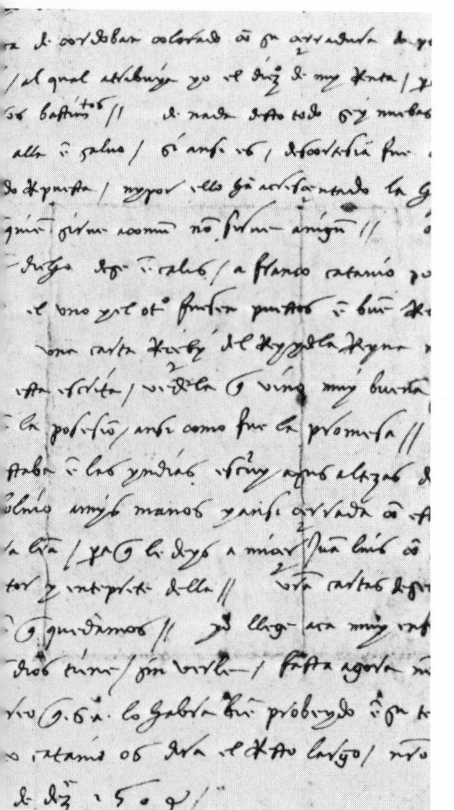

Facsimile of a letter written by Columbus, from a museum display in Genoa, Italy.

After King John II of Portugal declined to finance an expedition in 1484, Columbus journeyed to Spain, where he hoped to enlist the approval and financial aid of Queen Isabella. But again, his plan was viewed with royal disfavor, mingled with suspicion. Besides, the Spanish troops were fighting the Moors, so no money could be spared for uncertain expeditions to far-off places.

Undaunted, Columbus dispatched his brother Bartholomew to England and France to seek the patronage of their reigning monarchs — but to no avail. And now, alas, it seemed as though his great mission was destined to remain but a visionary sailor's dream.

In January, 1492, the Spanish troops conquered the last Moorish stronghold in Spain. Meanwhile, Columbus' friends and well-wishers at the Court of Isabella had finally prevailed upon the Queen to reverse her earlier decision, and now more money was available.

After further deliberation, the Queen decided to sponsor the expedition, with her personal fortune, if need be; and Columbus was recalled to the Spanish Court.

On August 3, 1492, Columbus departed from Palos, Spain, with three small vessels: his own, the *Santa María;*

Columbus' home in Genoa can be seen at the right.

Statue of Columbus at Santa Margarita on the Italian Riviera — one of the many erected in his honor throughout the world.

the *Niña,* whose captain was Vicente Pinzon; and the *Pinta,* under Martin Pinzon.

More than eighty sailors were aboard the three frail craft that left port that morning in August. The little fleet stopped in the Canary Islands for more than two weeks to load food and water aboard. Then they sailed out into the unknown, leaving the last sight of familiar land on September 9.

During the second week of October, mutiny threatened. The masters of the *Niña* and the *Pinta* repeatedly urged the admiral to turn back. Supplies were running low, they explained. The adverse winds had carried them far off course; the crews were restive. Everyone was desperately homesick. (Many were desperately *sea*sick.) Soon, they believed, all would die of starvation. Columbus refused to order the vessels to turn about. He had spent his whole life preparing for this voyage. He aimed to complete it.

However, should land not be sighted by the evening of October 12th, he promised, under duress, the fleet would set course for Spain. The ships continued their voyage west.

At ten o'clock on October 11th, Columbus saw a light far ahead. And, at two o'clock the next morning, the *Pinta's* lookout man sighted land on the horizon.

At dawn on October 12th, 1492, the little fleet cast anchor. And Columbus himself was the first to step ashore and into the New World (unaware that Leif Ericson had preceded him, much farther north, almost 500 years earlier).

To the island upon which he first set foot, Columbus

gave the name "San Salvador." But today we know it as Watlings Island, in the Bahamas.

The great explorer claimed it in behalf of Spain, and thanked the "Indians" for their kind hospitality. He went on his way, convinced that he had at last discovered the East Indies and thus fulfilled the hopes of a lifetime and the expectations of the Queen of Spain. It was many years later, after Columbus had died, that men learned the islands he had discovered were *not* the East Indies.

He and his fleet explored harbors at Cuba (which Columbus believed to be part of China) and the island of Hispaniola, or Little Spain, which now comprises the Republic of Haiti and the Dominican Republic.

The *Santa María* went aground off present-day Haiti, but friendly Indians helped save the supplies from the wrecked vessel. There Columbus supervised the construction of a fort, to which he assigned forty-four men and the name, *La Navidad*. Then Columbus sailed for Spain aboard the *Niña* on January 16, 1493, taking with him some of the friendly Indians as proof of his discovery.

Columbus reached Spain on March 15, 1493. And no conquering hero was ever more cordially welcomed than Cristóbal Colón, (the name he took after he settled in Spain.) The Spaniards called their new hero "the Admiral of the Ocean Sea" and "Viceroy of the Indies."

King Ferdinand and Queen Isabella received him at their Court and showered him with honors and privileges.

A year later, Columbus set forth on his second voyage to the New World. His vessels carried soldiers, settlers, priests, and supplies, in addition to the tools, cattle, and equipment with which he proposed to establish a second colony. But

The only navigational instruments Columbus had on his first voyage were a compass, a quadrant, dividers, and an hour-glass.

On August 3, 1492, Columbus left Palos in his flagship, the Santa María (forground), followed by the Niña and the Pinta.

when he reached *La Navidad,* he discovered that the first settlement and its forty-four inhabitants had completely disappeared. At first, the islanders had treated their seafaring guests with courtesy and respect; it never crossed their innocent minds that today's guests might well prove to be tomorrow's conquerors. However, Columbus' men began to mistreat the Indians, who, in turn, killed them all.

Saddened, but nonetheless determined to try again, Columbus and his helpers established another settlement not far from *La Navidad.*

During his exploratory cruises in the Caribbean where he felt convinced that someday he would come upon India or China – and possibly even both – Columbus left his youngest brother, Diego, in charge of the new colony. And he returned to Spain in 1496.

He made a third voyage in 1498 in which he landed on the South American continent in Venezuela. But unfortunately, public sentiment turned against him because of his failure to discover India, as he long ago had promised. The settlers on Hispaniola denounced him, arrested him, and sent him and his two brothers home to Spain in chains and in disgrace.

An old woodcut showing Columbus talking to his crew aboard the Santa María.

But the Queen released them and sent Columbus on a fourth voyage in 1502.

The fourth voyage ended in disaster when Columbus' ship was wrecked on the island of Jamaica. He spent a year among the Indians, making them believe he was a god who could blot out the sun, because he could predict an eclipse. Finally rescued, he returned to Spain empty-handed in 1504.

But neither failure nor disgrace could dim the glory of his accomplishments. After his death in 1506, many sincerely mourned the loss of a truly great man, and one of the most illustrious master mariners of all time.

At the height of his glory, Columbus had been respected and honored by throngs of admirers, who sometimes walked miles in order to catch a fleeting glimpse, or shake the hand, of Christopher Columbus.

Once, at a ceremonial dinner given especially for Columbus, a certain curious Spaniard had protested that he was tired of hearing the admiral praised so highly for something that anyone else could have easily done.

"Why," said the Spaniard, "even if the admiral had *not* discovered the Indies, are there not other men in Spain who might have done so?"

By way of reply, the guest of honor asked, using an egg to illustrate his point, "Can any of you stand this egg on end?" Several guests tried to do so, but failed, whereupon the admiral struck the egg smartly so that it broke, set it down on its broken part, and smiled benignly. "Any of you can do it now," he said. "And any of you can find the Indies for I have shown you the way."

Thereafter, all the crowned heads of Europe, and many who enjoyed no such distinction, yearned increasingly to "stand the egg on end."

FOR GOLD AND GLORY

After Columbus showed the way across the Atlantic, many other explorers and adventurers sailed westward — some for gold and some for glory.

John Cabot and Christopher Columbus had much in common. Even their surnames began with "C." They were both Italians and seafaring men, and due to faulty sense of direction, were firmly convinced that, by steering a westerly course, they would ultimately glimpse the fabled shores of mystic Cathay (the same place we now call China), the perfumed isles of India, and the deep, uncharted China seas, so loved by their countryman, Marco Polo.

For, as we know, Columbus, who had discovered America on October 12, 1492, went to his grave believing the New World to be the gateway to the Orient.

Cabot, who, twice—in 1497 and 1498—beheld the northern isles of Nova Scotia, off the fogbound coasts of Canada, is said to have harbored a similar delusion until his dying day.

Amerigo Vespucci, another Italian sailing for Spain, explored the mouth of the Amazon and the coast of South America in 1497.

It was a German map-maker who applied Vespucci's first name, Amerigo, to the two continents of the New World — neither of which he had actually discovered.

Vasco Nuñez de Balboa, a dashing Spanish conquistador, who in 1510 made good his escape from the clutches of certain Old World parties to whom he owed vast sums of

Giovanni Caboto (John Cabot), a Genoese-born tradesman, enlisting the support of English merchants for his voyage. He reached Cape Breton Island, off Nova Scotia, in 1497.

money, discovered the great "South Sea," or Pacific Ocean, in 1513.

His old Spanish creditors never did catch up with him, but his New World captors charged him with high treason and poor Balboa lost his head in 1519.

Meanwhile, across the seas – granting more or less that east was east and west was west – certain experts still wondered (with their departed comrades, Cabot and Columbus) if, by any chance, the twain would (or could) ever meet.

Ferdinand Magellan, shortly after Balboa's untimely death, made a gallant, but futile, attempt to prove, or disprove, this fanciful theory.

He crossed the Atlantic Ocean in September, 1519; sailed southward along the coast of South America; and early in 1520, explored the Rio de la Plata.

Amerigo Vespucci led several expeditions to South America. The New World was named America in his honor.

In October of the same year, he passed through the Straits of Magellan off the southern tip of South America. A month later, he entered the Pacific. It was Magellan who named it 'the Pacific," which means "calm"; after all the storms he and his men had endured, it seemed so quiet.

Since Magellan and his men had been sailing in a northwesterly direction for many weeks, their food and supplies had dwindled to the vanishing point. All hands suffered from hunger and thirst.

They came in sight of the Marianas on March 6, 1521, obtained food and water, then continued sailing westward. But, on April 17th, during a battle between his men and the natives, Magellan met his death in the Philippine Islands.

Dispirited and leaderless, the two vessels and their crews eventually reached the Spice Islands of the East Indies.

Here they crammed the holds with much-needed supplies.

Unfortunately, only the *Victoria* under the command of Sebastian del Cano finished the long trip home via the Indian Ocean, and around the Cape of Good Hope. On September 8, 1522, the first vessel ever to sail around the world finally put into port.

Of a total complement of 265, only eighteen men had survived the terrible ordeal.

And, alas, the brave Magellan was not of this number.

BEFORE THE COMING OF THE WHITE MAN

There is some evidence of Stone Age men living in America as far back as 20,000 years ago. It is generally thought that these first inhabitants of America reached the Western Hemisphere by way of the Bering Sea after mass migrations from northeast Asia.

Considerably in advance of the arrival of Columbus, it seems, vast tracts of land to the north of Mexico were populated by more than a million Indians.

Indeed, long before the first white settlers departed from the Old Country, the New World's natives were cultivating patches of corn, beans, and squash; hunting; fishing. Subsisting on a diet supplemented by fruit and raw berries, they wielded their crude stone-and-bone weapons against the forces of nature—and against each other, when necessary.

Unaware that they would someday rivet the attention of prospecting strangers from afar, the Indians blithely trod the

Balboa was the first European to see the Pacific Ocean.

Magellan was killed by natives on April 27, 1521, on Mactan Island in the Philippines.

well-worn paths and practiced the rituals of their ancient forebears.

They remained untouched by outside influences until zealous merchants and traders, seeking to explore and to exploit, began their forays into the North American wilderness.

The earlier waves of immigrants to the New World included the Eskimos, or "eaters of raw meat," whose modern descendants reside in the arctic and sub-arctic regions of the North American continent.

A sturdy, self-reliant breed, of a decidedly Mongoloid cast

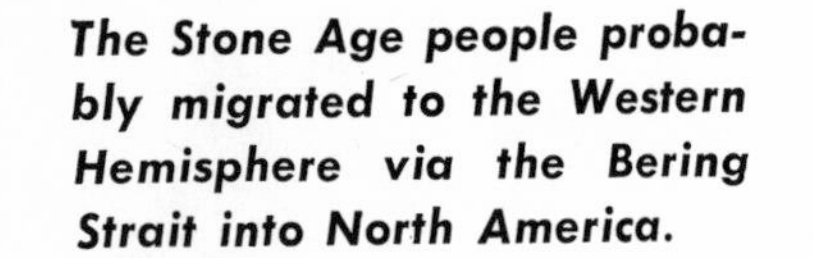

The Stone Age people probably migrated to the Western Hemisphere via the Bering Strait into North America.

of countenance, they retained their common language, which comprised numerous dialects.

We learn, incidentally, that many Eskimo "newcomers" settled in Greenland during the thirteenth century. And we shall soon inspect, from the ground up, their winter homes made of snow and ice, the *igloos*.

Eskimo woman with child.

Other Indian tribes made their way across the northern continent–to the seaboards; into the open plains, the grasslands, and the foothills of the Rockies–hunting bison and trapping bear as they continued south- and westward.

At length some reached the boundaries of North America and gradually progressed from the Yucatan Peninsula into Central and South America.

THE MAYAN EMPIRE

One of the earliest, and most notable, of these Indian cultures was that of the Mayas. But, even with the evidence unearthed by archaeologists and anthropologists, our knowledge of them is still relatively obscure.

At different periods throughout the centuries – both before and after the birth of Christ – impressive ruins gave rise to the belief that the Mayas, an enlightened, agricultural people, had passed through several phases of civilization between 1,000 B.C. and the Spanish conquest in the sixteenth century.

They not only built durable roads and aqueducts, but diligently applied themselves to the study of the natural sciences, astronomy, and mathematics; in all phases of these, they were extremely knowledgeable.

Their handicrafts and pottery were of the finest quality and workmanship. And because wilderness peoples must always be prepared to defend themselves – not only against the treacherous forces that surround them, but also against the calculated treachery of their own kith and kin – they were skillful marksmen and hunters, adept with bow and arrow, dagger, blowgun, knife, and spear.

Sculptured stone slab on the wall of the Palace House in Palenque, Mexico.

The ingenious Mayas also devised a calendar even more accurate than that of the early Egyptians. They formulated a unique method of hieroglyphic, or picture, writing. They were rapidly approaching their most fruitful era when everything suddenly came to a full stop.

No one knows precisely when the civilization of the Mayas actually ceased to be. But, within the span of a few centuries, an entire country, to all intents and purposes, vanished from the face of the earth.

Only a heap of picturesque ruins bore witness to a previous existence as a mighty empire.

In the north, the Yucatan Peninsula, the Toltec Indians lived much like the Mayas. Archaeological discoveries and accounts written by Christianized Mayas after the arrival of the Spaniards suggest that they were related.

THE AZTEC WARRIORS

Another great Indian civilization in Mexico, that of the fierce Aztec warriors, appeared near the end of the thirteenth century, and reached its height about the same time Spanish conquerors arrived in the New World. Originally a backward and savage nomadic people from the north, they settled in the vicinity of present-day Mexico City. Through

Ruins of Mayan temples and temple pyramids in Chichén Itzá in the Yucatan Peninsula of Mexico.

Above, the Great Pyramid of the Sun, a monument of Aztec civilization, over 650 feet across the base and over 120 feet high; Below, an Aztec calender stone.

wars and alliances, they built up a mighty and splendid empire.

The Aztecs, however, were not mere conquerors. They were quick to pick up writing, mathematics, arts, and crafts from other Indian neighbors (who probably learned them from the Mayas). They educated their young, established courts of law, built good highways, created a money system, and encouraged trade.

The Aztecs were ruthless in war. They enslaved the people they conquered. Their priests slaughtered thousands of captive men, women, and children as sacrifices to their blood-thirsty gods. The Aztecs were dreaded by their Indian neighbors. Their empire, made up of conquered people, was held together by fear.

THE KINGDOM OF THE INCAS

Far to the south, there grew up the richest Indian civilization, that of the Incas. The Incan people lived on the west coast of South America in the places we now call Peru, Chile, Bolivia, and Ecuador. To the west, the Pacific rolled and roared; to the east rose the snow-topped Andes, the second highest mountain range in the world. The Incan kingdom contained more people than that present-day giant

among countries, Canada. Their monarch, the Inca, was believed by his people to be a descendant of the sun god.

Like the Romans, the Incas were very good at roadmaking. Their greatest road stretched from one end of their kingdom to the other. It was 3,000 miles long—the distance from Washington, D. C., to San Francisco, California. This road went over the high passes of the Andes, along deep dark mountain gorges, across dizzy canyons. The bridges that crossed the canyons were woven of tough vines and branches.

The Incan roads were nothing like our paved highways; they were, of course, built without the help of machines. The workmen had no trucks to haul stone and gravel. They didn't even have carts; the Indians of America had never learned to use the wheel. They lacked explosives, such as dynamite, to blast away the great rocks that stood in the way. Yet, the workmen managed to cut away the sides of towering cliffs to make roadways. They paved parts of the roads with huge blocks of flat stone. To do this, they first had to cut stones, then shape them, and shove them into place.

The road was always crowded. And what would the traffic look like? Well, it would be mainly llamas; the only beasts of burden in that part of the world, they were the Incas' sole means of transportation. We would meet many

One-piece Incan feather helmet and mantle from Chancay, Peru (at top), and a sample of Incan pottery (above).

The colorful people of modern Peru are to a great extent decendants of the ancient Incas.

Above, the ruins of Machu Picchu, the sacred city of the Incas, and below, the ruins of an ancient Incan palace near Cuzco — both in Peru.

people on foot—soldiers, farmers with their produce (again, strings of llamas), merchants, messengers, high officials—perhaps, sometimes, the Inca himself.

The Inca was probably the most absolute ruler in history. The family of the Inca, the priests, and the high officials were the only freemen. The lives of the people were thought out and ordered by others. Everything went by rule and law. They even had to marry at a certain age. They were assigned to such work as was needed—be it trade or art, field labor, building, mining, quarrying, stone-cutting, street-sweeping. The few at the top lived in splendor at the expense of the many under them. This, of course, was the way of most civilizations; but in no civilization had it been so absolute as under the Inca. The Incas' civilization had other unusual features. The people built the world's most impressive temples and palaces. These structures were made of huge blocks of stone of all shapes. Many of these blocks were as high as twelve or eighteen feet and as broad as six or eight feet. The great chunks of stone were all cut differently and put together like the pieces of a jig-saw puzzle. No mortar was needed; the pieces fitted into each other so neatly that, to this day, diggers can't slip a penknife between them.

The designs drawn on "modern" Pueblo Indian pottery in New Mexico all have traditional meaning.

Just how these stone blocks were cut remains a mystery to modern man; the people had no metal tools. How they were lifted up and sĕt in place to erect the temples and palaces is beyond imagination.

The Temple of the Sun in the city of Cuzco was the tomb of the Incas. The walls, both inside and outside, were covered with plates of burnished gold. Inside the temple was a great sun of pure gold studded with precious jewels. Opposite was a massive moon of polished silver. Scattered on the walls were stars of gold and silver and rainbows of jewels.

Beneath the sun were ranged the mummies of the dead Incas, resplendent in mantles of tapestry and feathers, and golden crowns and masks sprinkled with yet more jewels. Under the silver moon were mummies of the dead queens and princesses, gold and silver images of gods flanking them.

Basket-making is, and has always been, a special skill of the Hopi Indian women.

THE INDIANS THE SETTLERS MET

Among the forests, fields, lakes, and streams of North America, other Indian civilizations were developing differently.

The Eskimos coped with the bitter blizzards of the Far North. The simple igloo is still one of the most efficient dwellings in the world although it is now used only for temporary shelter while hunting or fishing; and Eskimo clothing has been copied for winter dress by modern man. They trained Huskies to pull their loaded sleds, traveled the waters in *kayaks,* and used oil lamps for light and warmth in the long winters.

In the northwest regions of what is now the United States, the newcomers built a way of life around fishing and hunting. They built swift canoes, and used harpoons with great skill. These are the people of the totem poles.

Along the far west coast and down the slopes of the Sierra

Ceremonial Indian dancers of the Taos Indian Pueblo in New Mexico waiting to begin one of their ritual dances.

Nevada Mountains, other Indians were seed-gatherers. Nuts, berries, fruits and edible roots provided their livelihood.

The southwestern part of the United States was the scene of more permanent Indian homes. The Navajos and the Pueblos built dwellings of mud and clay. They created fine pottery, wove baskets, worked metal, and developed a plentiful system of agriculture.

The Great Plains were populated by wandering tribes of hunters who used their spears and bows with great skill. Everything they owned was movable; they followed the migrations of the deer and the buffalo to get enough food.

Because the eastern region of America was heavily forested, the tribes that settled there became fine woodsmen. They learned to track animals silently along shadowy trails and to fish the swift streams. Their agriculture was highly developed. They grew tobacco and corn, and they preserved meats.

Their society was an organized one. Tribes often belonged to a large confederation, whose laws of conduct were strict. These were the Indians the early European settlers first met.

THE SPANISH CONQUERORS

The Spaniards were the first Europeans to learn of the rich Aztec and Incan civilizations, and soon after Columbus' voyages, began to back the treasure hunts of wild-eyed adventurers. The most successful of the fortune-hunters was Hernando Cortez.

There were several interesting reasons for his remarkable feat: The Spaniard's armaments, especially the cannons and horses, terrorized the Indians. Another circumstance that favored the invaders was the assistance of various rebel tribes who had long sought a way to throw off the cruel yoke of the Aztecs. Moreover, many Aztecs believed that the Spanish conquistador, red-bearded and powerfully built—was the fulfillment of an ancient prophesy that Quetzalcoatl, the white god of the Aztecs, would someday come from across the seas.

The Aztec king, Montezuma, received General Cortez with honor. Montezuma was a splendid figure, robed in garments made of fine cotton and the brilliant plumage of tropical birds, all a-glitter with precious gems. His palace was immense and richly decorated; Cortez found it superior to any of the palaces he had visited in Europe.

Meanwhile, some Aztecs had attacked a small force of Spaniards who had been left behind on the coast. When the head of one of these Spaniards was delivered to the capital city, the Aztecs could no longer believe the Spaniard was a god. Cortez was in danger. He seized Montezuma and put him in chains. The fighting that broke out ended once reinforcements arrived from Spain. The Spaniards vanquished the Aztecs in a fierce battle that lasted for a whole week. Montezuma was killed; the city, captured. The Aztecs of Mexico became a lost civilization.

The enslavement of the Incas by the Spaniard, Francisco

Pizzaro, a member of the Balboa expedition, followed in about a decade. Pizarro was welcomed warmly by the Inca, but the treacherous Spaniard murdered the great ruler. The Spaniards displayed the same savagery the barbarians had shown when they thundered down upon the western Roman Empire. Thousands of Incas were killed by the soldiers of Spain; the proud Indians did not make good slaves. And, of course, the wondrous treasures of the Incan civilization were seized by the invaders and shipped back to Spain.

The Spaniards could hardly believe their eyes when they looked upon the gold, silver, and gems in the temples and palaces of the Incas. When they came upon the Temple of the Sun at Cuzco, they tore down the golden sun, the silver moon, the jewelled rainbows, and the gold and silver stars; stripped the mummified Incas and their queens of the fortunes in gems in which they were so brilliantly clothed; ripped off and carried away the plates of burnished gold from the walls. They rampaged through the domains of the Incas in their search for plunder. When they found the gold and silver mines in the mountains from which the Incas obtained their precious metals, they fought among themselves for rights to these rich sources of wealth. Pizzaro is estimated to have taken $100 million worth of gold and jewels from the Incan Empire!

Other Spanish adventurers went deep into the heart of America. Hernando De Soto crossed the great Mississippi River in 1540, and in the same year, Francisco Coronado led an expedition through the American Southwest and up into central Kansas.

These daring men helped strengthen the Spanish claim to the Americas. And Spain became immensely wealthy as gold and other precious resources of the New World were loaded into Spanish galleons and sent to the royal court. Spain had no need to search farther. This was not Asia, but it was just as good.

THE RACE FOR EMPIRE

In 1494, the rights to all of the non-Christian world had been awarded to Spain and Portugal by Pope Alexander VI in an effort to keep the two empire-building countries at peace with each other. He simply drew an arbitrary line across a world map from north to south just east of North America. Portugal was to own all the lands east of the line; Spain, all lands to the west.

But there were other nations that objected to such a division. England, as we have seen, demanded America on the basis of Cabot's discovery in 1497; and France, whose fishermen had for years sailed westward to the shallow banks off Newfoundland for codfish, laid equal claim to American shores.

For years, the French had not openly disputed with Spain; the ships of that nation kept to the south in their search for gold, while those of France sailed northern waters. Verrazano, an Italian sea captain sailing under the flag of France, navigated the coast of North America from Carolina to Nova Scotia in 1542. About ten years before, Jacques Cartier had sailed up the St. Lawrence River as far as Montreal. Other French ships followed, and though Spain grumbled loud threats to those invading Spanish "territories," for a while nothing was done because Spain was occupied with the south and its gold mines.

But then, England awoke to the fact that Spain's greed must be curbed; some of the good things that were being found in America ought to come to her. The King of England quarrelled with the pope in Rome, denying his right to thus give away the New World. King Henry VIII and his daughter, the famous Queen Elizabeth, began to send their ships and fighting-men into the very regions that Spain had held so long, the waters around the West Indies and South America.

Captain William Hawkins, his son, Captain John Hawkins, and Sir Francis Drake were the most celebrated of these early English sea captains who bravely challenged the might of Spain. They worried the Spaniards constantly. They stormed their forts, captured their ships, and seized their stores of goods and merchandise; and by their daring and their audacity, so enraged the Spaniards that, for over a hundred years, the Spanish Main was the scene of many bloody battles and harsh retaliations.

Captain John Hawkins kept his men together by these few words: "Serve God daily; love one another; preserve your victuals; beware of fire; and keep good company." And Sir Francis Drake, who was the first Englishman to sail the Pacific Ocean, and who, in 1578, made a famous voyage around the world, was so feared by the Spaniards, that they called him "the English dragon."

The warring countries attempted settlements on the North American continent. In 1562 and 1564, two Frenchmen, Ribault and de Laudonniere, settled colonies in Florida, only to be killed by the Spaniards in dispute over occupation of that land. In 1565, the Spaniards founded St. Augustine. In 1570, they tried to make a settlement on the Potomac River, but did not succeed. The Spaniards did penetrate into the country as far north as central New York, but all their colonies north of Florida were failures. Sir Walter Raleigh, who gave Europe tobacco, founded the first English settlement in North America in 1587, but it did not prosper.

So, all through the sixteenth century, from 1500 to 1600, Spain, England, and France fought bitterly for almost a hundred years to possess the Americas. The competition was no more than a gold-hunt; few lasting settlements were made, except in Mexico and the West Indies. Europeans would have to be made to understand that the true riches of the New World were in its splendid climate and fertile soil, and that those who made homes within its borders would be the real victors.

A.D. 1530 Portugal established colonies in Brazil.

A.D. 1562 Slave trade between Africa and America begun by John Hawkins.

A.D. 1565 Huguenot colony in Florida destroyed by Spaniards.

A.D. 1568 English defeated by Spaniards off Mexican coast.

A.D. 1572 Spanish harbor in New World attacked by Francis Drake.

A.D. 1577 General patent of colonization granted to Sir Humphrey Gilbert.

A.D. 1579 Drake claimed New Albion (California) for England.

A.D. 1583 English colony founded by Gilbert in Newfoundland.

A.D. 1584 Raleigh discovered and claimed Virginia for England.

A.D. 1585 Virginia colonized by Raleigh. Colony failed.

A.D. 1587 Virginia colonized a second time; colony failed four years later.

A.D. 1603-1604 Expedition to Canada by Champlain.

A.D. 1604 Settlement in Acadia (Nova Scotia) established by the French.

A.D. 1606 London and Plymouth Companies granted charters to establish colonies in New World.

A.D. 1607 Jamestown founded.

A.D. 1608 Quebec founded by Champlain.

A.D. 1610-1611 Exploration of Hudson's Bay by Henry Hudson.

A.D. 1612 Settlers from Virginia colonized Bermudas.

A.D. 1614 Colony established at mouth of Hudson by New Netherlands Company.

A.D. 1619 First representative assembly in America convened at Jamestown, Virginia.

A.D. 1619 Negro slaves brought to Virginia from Africa.

A.D. 1620 Pilgrims departed from Plymouth in Mayflower. New Plymouth founded.

A.D. 1624 Virginia became a crown colony.

A.D. 1626 New Amsterdam (New York) founded by Dutch.

A.D. 1627 Nova Scotia occupied by the English.

A.D. 1629 English settlements in Massachusetts.

A.D. 1634 George Calvert (later Lord Baltimore) founded Maryland; encouraged settlement by Roman Catholics.

A.D. 1636 Settlements by English in Rhode Island and Connecticut.

A.D. 1638 Delaware (New Sweden) settled by Swedes.

A.D. 1646 Bahamas occupied by the English.

A.D. 1667 New Amsterdam surrendered to the English and its name was changed to New York.

A.D. 1669 Constitution for Carolina drawn up by John Locke.

A.D. 1670 Hudson's Bay founded.

A.D. 1675-1676 Indian War with New Englanders.

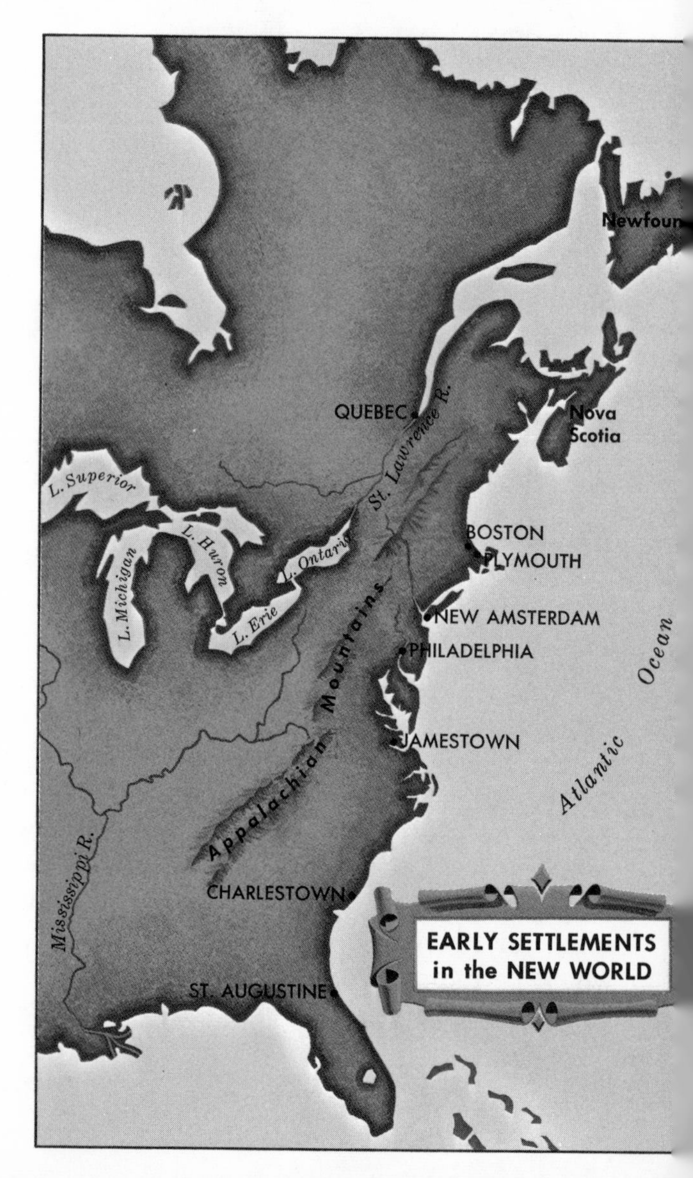

A.D. **1680-1682** French colonies extended from Quebec to the mouth of the Mississippi.

A.D. **1706** Colonists repelled by Spaniards and French at Charleston, South Carolina.

A.D. **1710** Port Royal seized by English.

A.D. **1713** Peace of Utrecht in which English were ceded Hudson's Bay, Newfoundland, and Acadia (Nova Scotia).

A.D. **1755-1763** Anglo-French War in New World (the French and Indian War).

A.D. **1759** Battle of Quebec won by English. Generals Wolfe (English) and Montcalm (French) killed.

CHAPTER 12

Colonial Life in North America

WE have all seen people who would rush ahead of their companions to the best strawberry patch, the thickest blackberry bush, or the best place to watch some passing parade, and then exclaim, "It's mine! I got here first!" Such apparent selfishness is certain to anger their friends, especially if they refuse to share their find.

So each nation, as it took hold in the New World, cried out to the rest of Europe, "It's mine! I got here first!"

For 150 years, from 1600 to 1763, the European settlers in North America spent most of their time trying to push one another off the spots of earth on which they stood, shoving and elbowing each other and growling back and forth: "Get off! This is my ground!" . . . "Get off, yourself; I have as much right here as you!"

The Spaniards shoved away the French; the English elbowed off the Dutch; the Dutch crowded out the Swedes. Then, with one grand sweep, the English pushed off Spaniards, Dutch, French, and all to occupy the whole eastern portion of North America (except for Florida) from the St. Lawrence River to the Gulf of Mexico!

The early settlers still hunted gold. They came for purposes of trade, or because they hoped to make an easier living in the New World. Outlandish stories were told of the riches in America. "Gold," it was reported, "is more plentiful there than copper. The pots and pans of the folks there are pure gold, and, as for rubies and diamonds, they go forth on holidays and pick them up on the seashore to hang on their children's coats and stick in their children's caps."

But, with greedy adventurers, came many hard-working, good, and kind people who, for many reasons, really sought a new homeland.

Some hoped to help "the red savages," as the Indians were known abroad. Inspired missionaries preceded the French. They carried the knowledge of the Christian religion to the Indians of Canada, who, unfortunately, never understood what the good missionaries sought to teach them; too often, thinking that "the black robes" came from hostile enemy tribes, they killed them.

To the English colonies came men and women who sought a place where they might worship God as they pleased.

In 1606, the attention of some rich merchants of England was directed toward America as a place to invest. In that year two wealthy corporations were formed to colonize the New World, the Virginia Company of London and the Virginia Company of Plymouth. To these companies, King James of England granted equal 100-square-mile tracts of land in Virginia.

"Virginia" did not mean to King James what it means to us. In those days, Virginia was all the land between Cape Hatteras, North Carolina, and the coast of Maine—everything, that is, that Spain and France had not already seized for themselves.

Immediately, the London Company organized an expedition to "South Virginia." Three ships—manned by some of

St. Augustine, Florida, is the oldest settlement in the United States.

the company's own members, a number of fashionable gentlemen, their servants, and enough laborers to build a settlement—set sail for the New World.

They landed on May 14, 1607, on a mosquito-infested swamp where, surely, no food would grow. There were no brooks or springs, only murky river waters to drink from. But, in the soggy earth, they spied bits of shiny yellow ore. Here—without land for crops or water to drink—they foolishly settled, thus condemning themselves to certain death.

SOLDIER OF FORTUNE

They were saved: by the 104th passenger to come ashore, a doer and fighter from early boyhood who, at only twenty-seven, had already prospected and adventured in many lands. The story of early Virginia is the story of Captain John Smith.

But for the watchfulness of Captain John Smith and the good will of the Indian maiden, Pocahontas, the settlement at Jamestown would have been utterly destroyed. Pocahontas, the daughter of the Indian chief, Powhatan, befriended the white people in many ways; and it is sad to think that after her friend, Captain Smith, had left the colony, the settlers repaid all her kindness by trying to kidnap the Indian girl so as to force provisions from her father. Powhatan was very angry, and threatened to wipe out the colony. Upon Pocahontas' request, Powhatan made a lasting peace with the white men. It is said that two Presidents of the United States, William Henry Harrison, and his grandson, Benjamin Harrison, are descended from Pocahontas and her English husband, John Rolfe.

Captain John Smith fell in love with America; he wrote and talked about it all the time. He showed his map of what he called New England to Prince Charles who dotted it all over with the names of well-known towns in England. Captain Smith told another English captain, Henry Hudson, about some of his ideas. In 1609, Captain Hudson, sailing in the service of Holland, recalled some of Captain Smith's words and located and explored the beautiful river that now bears his name, the Hudson.

Statue of Captain John Smith at Jamestown, Virginia, site of the first permanent English settlement in America. Captain Smith and his fellow settlers landed in three small ships on May 13, 1607.

A NEW AMSTERDAM . . . .

At the mouth of this river, in 1614, the Dutch built a settlement named New Amsterdam. The colonists were sent out by a rich corporation in Holland, the Dutch West India Company, formed, like the London and Plymouth companies, for the purpose of trade. They came to the Hudson River country to purchase furs from the Indians. This little trading post on Manhattan Island was the beginning of the giant city of New York.

. . . AND A NEW ENGLAND

Captain Smith's promising account of the New England coast, and those of other explorers who had sailed from Maine to Long Island Sound, turned attention in that direction. In 1620, the Pilgrims (driven first to Holland by reli-

This tower is all that is left standing of the old church at Jamestown. Here Pocahontas was baptized "Rebecca" and married to John Rolfe in 1614.

Pocahontas in Indian regalia.

gious persecution) sailed from Delft Haven in *The Mayflower*. On the twenty-second of December of that year, they stepped ashore onto the gray boulder now famous as Plymouth Rock, and there, in the bleak winter of 1620-21, founded the tiny settlement that was to burgeon into New England.

Within the next fifty years, other such settlements were made all along the Atlantic coast by emigrants from Europe —most of them from England—who desired homes in the New World. They were, for the most part, people who were not satisfied at home. They were, in many cases, sponsored by rich men who saw in the new land an opportunity to add to their fortunes, and, at the same time, help the poor or the persecuted.

AN INFANT NATION

The thirteen colonies—New Hampshire, Massachusetts, Rhode Island, Connecticut, New York, New Jersey, Pennsylvania, Delaware, Maryland, Virginia, North Carolina,

Below, a drawing of The Mayflower, and at right, the monument at Plymouth Rock, the spot where the Pilgrims first landed on the shores of their new country.

South Carolina, and Georgia—occupied but a narrow strip on the rugged sea-border of a vast and mysterious wilderness. Their pasts were full of disaster and disappointment; their futures were uncertain. Yet, these thirteen struggling settlements would one day be reckoned by England as the most important, although the most troublesome, of all her overseas possessions.

Try to picture the 3,000 miles of coastline from New Hampshire to Georgia of those early days, although it is hard to think of it other than as it exists today—a span of large cities, alive with busy throngs of men and women, boys and girls. In the old New England, the forests ran clear to the sea; beyond the white sands of the New Jersey and Carolina beaches, the land was dark with monstrous pines; and over all the land roamed the wolf, the bear, the deer, the elk, and all manner of wild beasts. Not a single horse or cow was to be found in all of North America; they were brought over later by the Europeans.

Scattered here and there throughout the land were Indian villages in which dwelled a people that no white man could trust, so strange were their ways. In the hunting and fishing seasons, bands of Indians came into the settlements to exchange their catch for some of the wonderful labor-

Exact reproduction of the Pilgrims' first fort and meeting house in Plymouth, Massachusetts.

saving tools the white man had brought with him; or to pry about, making man and wife nervous and uncomfortable.

All about the little settlements rose the uncleared forests; their depths and shadows harbored, in addition to the wild beasts and Indians, many lurking dangers. The woodman's ax had made but few openings as yet. Wooden blockhouses, clumsy forts, or picketed palisades were their only defense against unfriendly Indians, or the still more hostile soldiers of France and Spain.

No stores, supermarkets, warehouses, or factories existed for safekeeping of food or household stuffs; all who lacked had to go without, even starve until such time as the supply ship, braving storm and reef, finally came in.

The greatest threat to the struggling settlements lay in the colonists themselves. Here were people of all sorts and conditions: the poor and the proud, the sick and the well, the good and the bad, the weak and the strong, the wise and the foolish, the worker and the drone, the dissatisfied and the indifferent, the over-particular and the careless. Every class and every kind of mortal—driven by poverty, politics, religion, discontent, restlessness, greed, love, or ambition—had come across the sea for the advantages they had missed in the lands of their birth. Quarrels and jealousies over rights and privileges; distress from lack of human necessities; disease; sickness; death—all these ills of man visited each little settlement, hindering its growth at a time when it most needed healthy workers, happy spirits, and gentle influences.

Yet, despite all these drawbacks, the settlements slowly grew. In 1620, only 1,261 persons inhabited the various "plantations" of the Virginia Company; by 1634, the number of the Massachusetts colonists had more than doubled to between three and four thousand.

An example of the kind of armor which was often worn for defense in the early days of American colonization. Captain John Smith and other soldiers from England wore the type shown here.

TAMING THE WILDERNESS

There are few of us who do not enjoy getting away from civilization for a few days in the summer and "roughing it" in some out-of-the-way camp by river, lake, or sea. But, after a while, we weary of this "roughing it" and long for the comforts of home.

Life in the thirteen colonies in America was the hardest kind of "roughing it." Of conveniences, there were none; even necessities were few. Many of the new settlers simply could not stand the life. Some returned to the homes they had left across the sea. Some, unable to endure the privations they had to undergo, sickened and died in a strange land. But those who did survive—who could choke down the bitter homesickness, face the dangers, withstand the diseases—toughened under the hardship, grew stronger, sturdier, more independent.

The first houses were the roughest of shelters: holes dug in the ground and hastily roofed over. These were replaced by flimsy bark huts or rudely-made cabins. Finally, as wealthier people came to the settlements, more substantial houses of wood or stone were built. Sometimes, the finishing touches, the doors and windows, even the very bricks themselves of which the gable ends of the houses were built, were brought across the sea from England or Holland. Certain of these old landmarks, though grey with age and weather, still stand today.

Within the house, rooms were few; the kitchen with its huge fireplace, was dining and living room, too. It was the center of home life. Its crude, but sturdy, homemade furniture, its wooden dishes, and clumsy "kitchen-things" were real luxuries at the time.

There were, of course, finer houses built as the years went by and the people prospered, but even the finest mansions had but few of what we now call conveniences, and even the most highly-placed children of those early days endured privations that the boys and girls of our day would grumble at as absolutely unbearable.

Porridge for breakfast, mush or hasty-pudding for supper, with a dinner of vegetables and perhaps a little meat were their daily meals. As the settlements grew, and the fields expanded to yield more plentiful crops, larders were more bountifully stocked.

Except in the cities, such as Boston, New York, and Philadelphia, where English manners and English fashions characterized the wealthier families, the wardrobes of parents and children were scanty and plain. They were usually of homespun stuff; the whirring of the spinning-wheel could

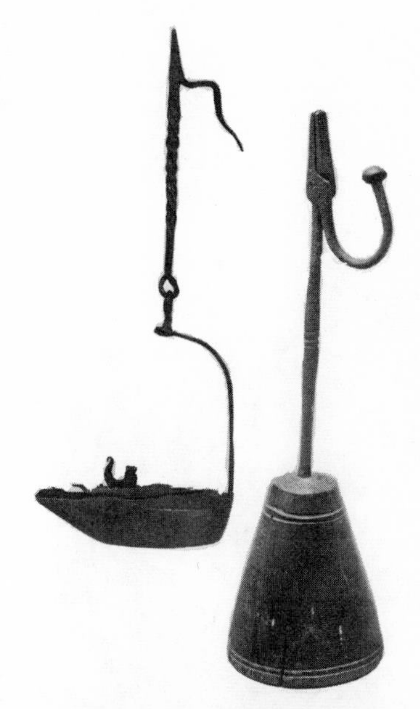

At left, the cheapest means of lighting in Colonial times, little iron dishes called Betty lamps which hung on the walls and were filled with whale oil. At right, a rush-light had a clamp at the top that held burning straws which were soaked in fat.

At left, typical furnishings of a seventeenth-century New England household.

be heard in every household. Leather breeches and homespun jackets were worn by father and son, but on Sunday, or at holiday time, there was a sudden brief display of lace ruffles and silver buckles.

The windmills ground the corn that the now fertile farms produced. The post-rider gallantly made his way from town to town with news and messages over the treacherous roads. The streets in the few towns were poorly paved and dimly lit.

A costumed "settler" holds a chicken — a delicacy in early Colonial times. This photograph is from the reconstruction of James Fort at Jamestown Festival Park, near Williamsburg.

Schools were rare. In the South, little was done toward educating the children, and many of the boys and girls in the early days grew up unable to write their names. But as time went on, this improved, too, and a little more attention, especially in the Northern colonies, was given to the children's instruction. The schooling was meager; "book-learning" was confined to a study of "the three R's" ("reading, 'ritin', and 'rithmetic"); the ferule and the birch rod were important tools of the schoolmaster's trade.

There were few wagons for hauling things, or carriages for riding. Later, pack horses would serve as land expresses. Boats and small sailing schooners carried heavy freights up and down the rivers.

Farming tools were clumsy and awkward, and it was a long time before the new farm-lands were cleared of stumps and rocks.

Many of the New England settlers were fishermen, and as the years went on, they built many vessels for use in the ocean fisheries. Shipbuilding, in fact, soon grew to an important industry along the Atlantic coast, and only six years after the settlement of New Amsterdam (New York), a "mighty ship" of 800 tons was built and christened the *Nieuw Netherlands*. But it proved so big and costly that it well-nigh ruined the enterprising Dutchmen who built it. Two hundred years passed before so great a vessel was again attempted in America.

There was so much work to be done that little time remained for rest or sport. People went early to bed and rose early in the morning. But, when they could find the time, the men and boys enjoyed themselves hunting and fishing; many of the youngsters grew up to be hunters and fishermen by occupation. Deer and wild turkeys abounded in the woods. Wild geese and fish swarmed in lake and river. Foxes, wolves, and bears were sometimes far too numerous for the farmer's comfort; a constant war was waged against them with trap, gun, and fire to frighten them away.

The boys and girls were strictly disciplined. The beadle and the tithing-man, the town-crier and the rattle-watch caught up with mischief-makers. In every village, in North and South alike, the stocks and pillory, the whipping-post, and the ducking-stool stood in plain view as a warning to all offenders. People became hardened to the sight of punishment. Boys and girls would even stand by and make funny faces while some poor "law-breaker" was trapped hand and foot in the pillory, or some woman who was guilty perhaps of no more than gossiping was doused and drenched on the ducking stool.

If unploughed land and unfelled forests had been the only obstacles with which the early colonists had to contend, if wolf and bear had been the only mortal enemies against which they had to defend themselves, then settlement of America would not have been so overwhelming a task.

Above, splitting fence rails at early Jamestown, and below, a seventeenth-century building is erected at James Fort.

THE WARS WITH THE INDIANS

Had Spaniards and Englishmen met the Indians in the spirit of friendship, much bloodshed and anguish might have been avoided. But the white man's insatiable greed made him careless of the Indian's rights. Understandably, the natural warmth of the Indian quickly turned to hatred and a desire for revenge of the wrongs imposed upon him.

When the Frenchmen returned to Florida, they found the pillar they had set up to display the arms of France garlanded with flowers and made an object of Indian reverence. When the Pilgrims huddled, half-famished, upon the Plymouth shore, the chief, Samoset, walked in among them with the greeting, "Welcome, Englishmen!" and brought back his tribesmen to help. When Chief Maquacomen helped the Maryland colonists of 1634 found homes, he said: "I love the English so well that if they should go about to kill me, if I had so much breath as to speak, I would command my people not to avenge my death, for I know that they would do no such a thing except it were through my own fault." At Jamestown, in Virginia, Chief Powhatan had asked Captain John Smith, "Why should you take by force from us that which you can obtain by love?" And he, too, like Samoset and Maquacomen, made the foreigners welcome.

Demonstration of the use of the stocks which were a means of punishing misdemeanors in the seventeenth century.

But, to the English, land was all-important. When they needed new acreage on which to plant their corn or tobacco, they simply took it from the Indians. This was especially true when tobacco became the chief cash crop of the settlers in Virginia. In both the North and the South, the Englishmen continued to extend their holdings deeper and deeper into the forest. They cut down trees, cleared great areas for plantations, killed game, so ruining the Indians' hunting grounds and means of existence.

The Indians were bewildered by this turn of events. At first they passively accepted it. Then, as was only natural, they began to resist by the only means they had—war!

The first mass Indian retaliation came in 1622. Chief Opechancanough, the younger brother of Powhatan who succeeded him as Sachem of Eastern Virginia, stealthily led a band of warriors out of the forest, struck the farms and plantations along a 140-mile front, and succeeded in killing 347 people. The settlers fought back. The war raged on and off for more than a decade, with hundreds of dead on the English side and thousands among the Indians. Finally, the Indians were overpowered. Opechancanough was killed, and the remaining Indians were put on reservations.

Many settlers lost their lives during the surprise attacks of the Indians.

This was the first in a long series of Indian retreats that would see the white man grind the proud Indian down into the dust of defeat and ultimately rule all of the New World from the Atlantic to the Pacific.

In 1637, only seventeen years after the landing of the Pilgrims, the Puritans in New England began a series of wars against the Pequot tribe, who inhabited parts of what are now Connecticut and Rhode Island. The Pequots' crime was the same as that of the Indians in Virginia. They wanted to keep their tribal hunting grounds.

The Puritan tactic was to take a Pequot village by surprise, burn it, and kill all the inhabitants. All but about fifty of these Indians were murdered. The few survivors were sold into slavery in Burmuda.

One of the bloodiest of the clashes between the Indians and the Whites in New England was King Philip's War. A young Indian named Metacomet was Chief of the Wampanoags, the tribe that had first befriended the Pilgrims. The

English called him King Philip. As his father had done before him, Philip made every effort to get along with his white neighbors.

But the leaders of Plymouth, which in fifty years had grown enormously in population, insisted that the Wampanoags place themselves under complete subjugation to the English. In addition, they demanded that the Indians pay a yearly tribute to the colony of 100 pounds. Philip decided to fight rather than submit.

A number of other New England tribes, including the powerful Narragansets, joined him in battle. In the spring of 1675, Philip began making systematic attacks on New England towns and villages. The young chief showed amazing ability as a commanding general. In a little more than a year, he had attacked and seriously damaged more than half the settlements in the Plymouth colony, and had completely wiped out at least a dozen of them.

The Puritan soldiers, in retaliation, attacked the Indian towns, slaughtering all the inhabitants to the last child. By 1678, the end was at hand for King Philip and his braves.

The outcome of this war, the most destructive in New England history, was predictable. By this time, the English colonists in New England outnumbered the Indian population by about four to one. Thus, as would happen in all the other Indian wars of our history, the Indians were overcome by the combined forces of man and gun.

King Philip was hunted down and killed; his wife and only son were taken to the West Indies and there sold as slaves.

QUARRELS . . . .

Foreign invasion was dreaded as much as the Indians. With France and Spain alike claiming the right of occupation, the English colonists could never rest in peace. The Dutch settlements in the New Netherlands (a section extending from the Connecticut to the Mohawk and from Lake George to Delaware Bay) were in constant fear of attack by England.

For the New Netherlands, this came at last when, in 1664, an English fleet sailed through the Narrows and dropped anchor before the little fort at New Amsterdam. "I would rather be carried out dead!" cried out Governor Peter Stuyvesant passionately. But resistance was useless. New Amsterdam lowered the flag of the Netherlands. The British colors waved above its ramparts and the New Netherlands became "the Province of New York."

Every war in Europe had its effect in America. In the Old World across the sea, France and England had always quarreled, ever since they had become France and England; in America, they quarreled just the same. France said that, by the right of discovery, all the land between the Alleghenies and the Rocky Mountains belonged to her. England asserted her claim extended beyond the Atlantic Seaboard, westward to the Pacific.

Most of all, France wanted to control the fisheries along the American east coast. But so did England! France was determined to monopolize the fur trade of North America; so was England.

The struggle between France and England really extended from the first capture of Quebec by the English on July 19, 1629, to its final capture on September 30, 1759—a span of 130 years. A treaty of peace between France and England, signed in 1763, gave England all the French possessions in America east of the Mississippi River.

Quite as hotly contested as the wars between the colonial empires were the religious quarrels within the Colonies. In these religious quarrels, the most earnest and most conscientious persons were also the most bigoted and vindictive, answering questions with persecution and arguments with banishment. Roger Williams, who challenged the religion of the Puritans of Boston, was so driven out of the city in 1635. But, undaunted, he and a few friends settled in the Rhode Island wilderness and eventually founded the city of Providence.

Quakers were whipped "at the cart's tail" by the Dutch rulers of New Amsterdam, and hanged on Boston Common by the Puritan rulers of Massachusetts Bay; "Papists," as the Roman Catholics were then called, were imprisoned in New York; Baptists were mobbed in Virginia. Puritans and Papists engaged in actual warfare in Maryland; "Dissenters" and "Churchmen" broke into fierce conflict in the Carolinas.

Roman Catholics in Maryland were forbidden to hold church services or even educate their children in the beliefs of their religion. Taxes collected from all the people were used to support the Anglican Church in Virginia to the anger of members of other faiths.

Statue of Roger Williams, clergyman and founder of the colony of Rhode Island, in the Statuary Hall of the United States Capitol.

. . . AND WITCHES

Superstition also bred cruelty. Our ancestors of two centuries ago were full of superstitions about good and bad luck. Their fathers had been so before them. They especially feared the influence of "witches." If anything went wrong, an evil spirit, they said, had "bewitched" things; at once, they hunted about—not to see why things had gone wrong, but to find the "witch" who had cast the evil spell.

So many things went wrong in the early Colonial days that the poor settlers began to think the "witches" had followed them across the sea. When one or two of their religious leaders said that they had, of course, everybody believed it and the witch-hunt began. It was a nightmare time. In almost all the Colonies, innocent people were persecuted, or put to death, as "witches" who had worked their evil spells upon people, cattle, crops, homes, the very weather.

Worst of all were the infamous Salem witchcraft trials in New England from 1688 to 1692. Twenty "witches" were put to death in Salem before people were made to see the truth and the horrible error of the course they had pursued.

And beside all these problems of mind and body that plagued the Colonies, there were others equally hard to bear. Pirates infested the coast; they robbed and killed, making any kind of travel perilous and business ventures risky. Wealthy and prominent colonists were partners-in-piracy with such freebooters as Bonnet and Worley in the Carolinas, Teach or 'Blackbeard" in Philadelphia, and Captain Kidd in New York.

But hard knocks often, it is said, "make a man" of the lad who sees the challenge through. And so it proved with the thirteen colonies of England in North America. The struggle against foes without, and foes within, made them at last strong, resolute, independent. Bigotry and persecution, jealousy and selfishness, in time, gave way to the more neighborly feeling that common needs and desires create. The wisdom of union became more apparent year after year as the Colonies more and more paralleled each other in achievements and aspirations.

Trial of a "witch" during the days of the Salem witch-hunts.

A.D. 1774 First Continental Congress, representing all Colonies except Georgia, convened at Philadelphia.

A.D. 1775 Battles of Lexington and Concord. English victorious at Bunker Hill.

A.D. 1776 Declaration of Independence.

A.D. 1777 Defeat of Washington at Germantown. Articles of Confederation drawn up.

A.D. 1781 Siege of Yorktown and surrender of Cornwallis; last battle of the Revolution.

A.D. 1783 England recognized independence of United States of America in peace treaty signed at Paris.

A.D. 1787 American Constitution. New York made Federal capital.

A.D. 1789 Washington, first President of United States; Destruction of Bastille in Paris start of French Revolution. Declaration of Rights of Man in France.

A.D. 1792 Austria and Prussia unite against France. Revolutionary massacres in Paris.
Monarchy abolished. Trial of Louis XVI.

A.D. 1793 Execution of Louis XVI. France declared war on Great Britain, Spain, Holland.

A.D. 1793-1794 Reign of Terror in France. Execution of Marie Antoinette. Worship of God abolished.

A.D. 1809-1825 Latin-American Wars of Independence (led by José de San Martín and Simón Bolívar). Columbia gained freedom for Spain (1813), followed by Uruguay (1814), Chile (1816), Peru (1831), Bolivia (1825).

A.D. 1840-1889 Progress of Brazil under leadership of Pedro II.

A.D. 1857-1862 Civil war in Mexico. Anti-clerical reforms.

A.D. 1863-1867 Mexico invaded by French forces. Empire under Maximilian.

A.D. 1889 First Pan-American Conference.

A.D. 1898 Spanish-American War.

The Age of Revolution

Think, for a moment, about our wanderings through man's history, about the current events of the present day, about your very own private life. Things hardly ever "just happen," do they? Certain singular men always push the world along the path of progress. Were it not for these men, we might still be living Stone-Age style.

Colonial America developed such heroes. The men who cleared forests to build their homes and farms developed an independence of spirit that made them resent being ruled from Europe. They began asking questions. What did those lawmakers on the other side of the Atlantic know about *real* American problems? Why should they be allowed to tell New England merchants where they could trade? Why should they make so much profit on the tobacco grown by Virginia planters? And, most important, why should they levy taxes on hard-working Americans who couldn't send representatives to the English Parliament?

THE NATION EMERGES

The first document of self-government in America was the Virginia Charter of 1618. This charter gave the Virginia colonists the privilege of dividing the lands they had settled into farms which individuals could own and work for themselves. It also gave them a voice in making their own laws by permitting them to name someone to speak for, or represent, them in the "General Assembly" of the colony. To us who have never known anything different, this does not seem like a great step forward. But it was, in the days of King James.

He was furious over what he called "the presumption of the people." So, in 1624, he took away all these rights and made the colony "a kingly province." But the ideals of personal liberty that the wise farmers of the Virginia Charter had implanted in that early paper endured and became, in later years, the inspiration for the Constitution and the Government of the United States of America.

The next advance toward liberty was a remarkable paper, or "compact," drawn up and signed in the cabin of *The Mayflower* by the Plymouth colonists. We call it remarkable because it was indeed a brave thing to do in those days when the people had so little to say about government.

As the little vessel lay off Cape Cod on November 11,

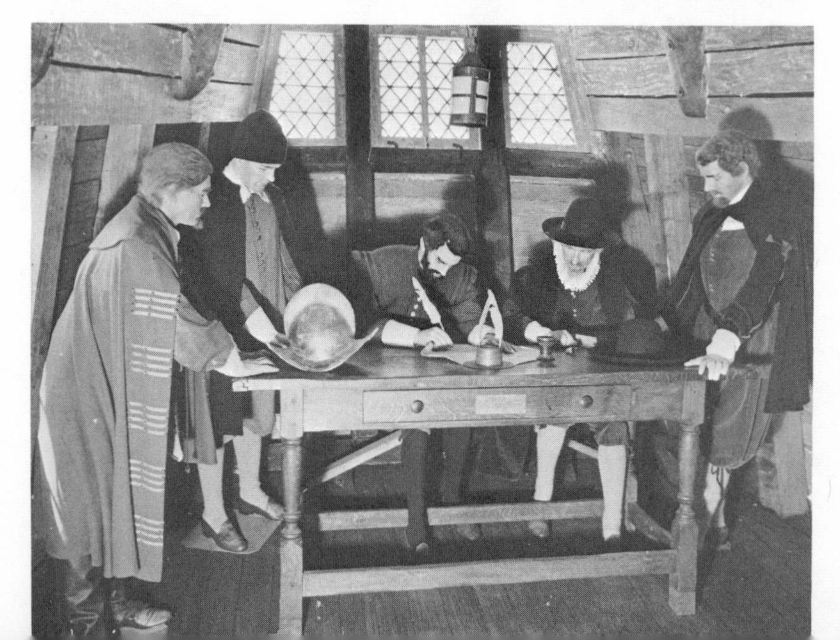

Signing of the Mayflower Compact.

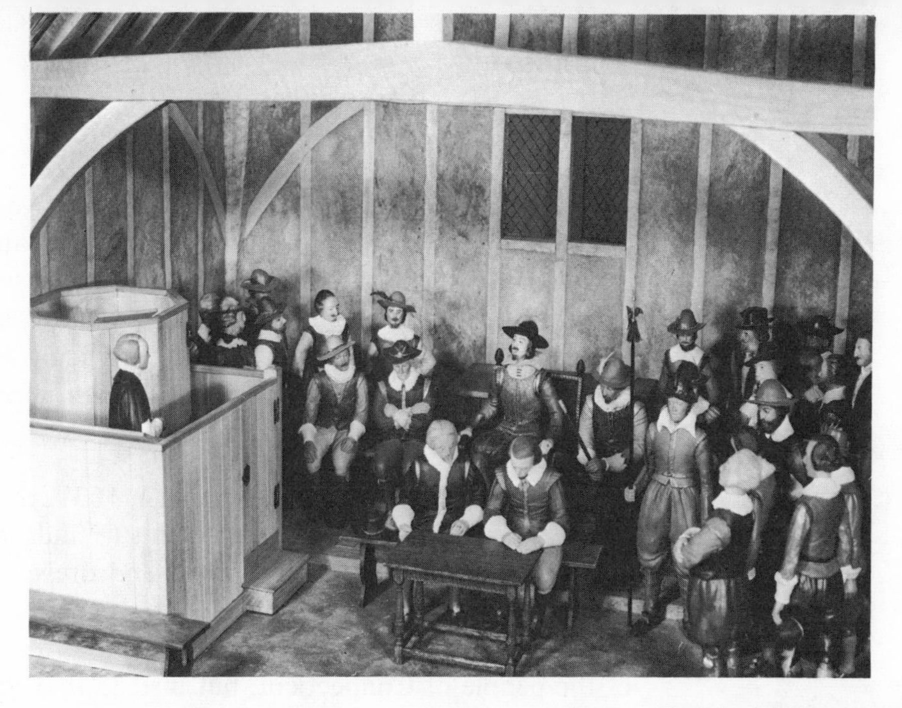

First legislative assembly in Virginia, held at Jamestown in 1619.

1620, the forty-one men who represented the different families united in that enterprise of colonization set their signatures to the following compact, "the first instrument of civil government ever subscribed to as the act of the whole people." Here it is in all its curious old-time wording, spelling, and punctuation:

> "*In ye Name of God, Amen.* We whose names are underwriten, the loyall subjects of our dread soveraigne Lord, King James, by ye Grace of God, of Great Britaine, France & Ireland King, Defender of ye Faith, etc. Having undertaken, for ye Glorie of God, and advancemente of ye Christian Faith and Honour of our King and countrie, a Voyage to plant ye first Colonie in ye Northerne part of Virginia, doe by these presents solemnly and mutually in ye Presence of God, and of one another, Covenant & Combine ourselves togeather into a Civill body Politick, for our better Ordering & Preservation & Furtherance of ye ends aforesaid; and by Vertue hearof to enact constitute and frame such just and equall lawes, ordinances, Acts, Constitutions & Offices, from Time to Time, as shall be thought most

meete & convenient for ye generall good of ye Colonie, unto which we promise all due submission and obedience. In witnes whereof we have hereunder subscribed our Names at Cap. Codd ye 11 of November, in ye year of ye Raigne of our Soveraigne Lord King James, of England, France & Ireland ye eighteenth, and of Scotland ye fiftie fourth, ano: Dom. 1620."

Monument erected at Jamestown by the Federal Government to commemorate the 300th anniversary of the 1607 founding of the first permanent settlement there.

Nineteen years later, on January 14, 1639, the "freemen" of the three river towns of Connecticut (Windsor, Hartford, and Wethersfield) met at Hartford and drew up "the first written constitution in the world." This paper did not recognize the right of any king or parliament to direct the actions of the people of Connecticut, but instead that the only persons who could share in the affairs of the colony were the "freemen." The people of Connecticut lived under the articles of this "constitution" for nearly 200 years.

The forms of government gradually adopted by the different colonies were an example to men everywhere to stand alone and act for themselves.

In Virginia, as we have seen, it was a General Assembly, or Houses of Burgesses, as it was more frequently called, elected by the people. . . .

In New England, it was a "township" government in which the people of the various towns taxed and governed themselves on a basis determined once a year by the adult men of the colonies in a coming-together called "the town-meeting." The town-meeting also elected to office representatives of a "general court" as the colonial legislature was called. A New England town-meeting would be very similar to the Assembly meeting we attended in ancient Athens. . . .

In South Carolina, a popular election in the several parishes of the colony selected representatives to the Colonial Assembly, as well as church officials. . . .

In Maryland and Delaware, the people of the different sections, or "hundreds," as they were called, assembled in "hundred-meetings," enacted by-laws, levied taxes, and appointed committees. . . .

In Pennsylvania, the officers of each local division, or "county," were elected by the people. . . .

In New York, the old system of village assemblies established by the early Dutch settlers was continued by their English successors. The direct vote of the people in a sort of town-meeting selected the governing body of the town for the coming year.

THE CLIMATE OF REVOLUTION

But, above all the people towered the ominous figure of the direct representative of the British king, the Royal Governor. He was generally a favorite of the king, and was sent over to tighten the yoke of a king three thousand miles away. The king and his governor were often at sword's points with the people, who knew their own needs better and were never slow to speak up for them. The Royal Governor was, in the opinion of colonists, forever interfering in matters which he could not understand. There was, therefore, a continual quarrel between the Royal Governor and the people he had been sent over the sea to control.

The thirteen colonies were prospering with each passing

Photograph of the Colonial Capitol at Williamsburg, Virginia.

year. Rich farmland was available to any man who would clear it. In New England, craftsmen were turning out fine furniture and cabinets, silverware, soap, candles, leather goods, guns, gunpowder, and sailing ships for the rapidly increasing trade with England. The big merchants were becoming wealthier.

In the South, the owners of great plantations, with the help of slave labor, were harvesting shipload after shipload of tobacco, cotton, rice, and indigo for transport to the mother country.

Cities sprang up: Boston, New York, and Philadelphia in the North; Williamsburg, Norfolk, and Charleston in the South. Schooners plied on regular schedules between the Colonies. Cleared roads replaced the blazed trails of earlier days. Inns and taverns began to dot the main highways, their swinging signs assuring travelers of a hot meal and a night's lodging. Guidebooks indicated the best routes between the larger towns.

Mail routes and stage lines were organized. A stagecoach called "the Flying Machine" made the trip between Philadelphia and New York in two days. The journey between Boston and New York required four or five days.

Every city had one or more newspapers, and these were distributed to outlying villages and towns. Most of the colonists of the upper and middle classes could read. Through the newspapers, the people of one colony could learn what was happening in other colonies. A sense of American nationalism began to develop.

The colonists realized that they were different from their English cousins in the old country—in their customs, their way of life, and even in their language. These Americans

The year is 1749; the harbor of New York was a busy one.

added their own words to the English language, such as fall (for autumn), skunk, hickory, coldsnap, swap, handy, and Yankee. But they still called themselves "Englishmen."

The seeds of revolution and independence were slowly being planted. There were grumblings in every colony. From time to time, there were open outbreaks. The governors themselves had anything but a pleasant time. As the years went on, the colonists grew more and more emphatic in their demand for self-government.

They saw that the land they lived in was destined to increase in importance, population, and riches, but they knew that unless they had their "say," this growth would be of no benefit to them. The English king and Parliament granted them few rights and looked down upon them as if they were inferiors. American craftsmen were not allowed to manufacture anything for their own use or for sale other than in England. The farmers were compelled to send their crops to England, and purchase their needs in English markets only.

A stagecoach called the "Flying Machine" made the trip between Philadelphia and New York in two days.

The merchants of England also did their share to cause the seeds of revolution to sprout. They felt that they owned the Colonies. After all, the people of America, as we have seen, could neither buy nor sell except through English traders. They could neither receive nor send away goods except in English vessels. The English manufacturers and traders held, in fact, what we call in these days a monopoly of the American trade; caring only for what money they could make, the English were unwilling to give the colonists any chance whatever for profit or trade. As a result, most American merchants and planters owed large sums of money to English businessmen and bankers.

The selfish spirit of the English businessmen naturally made the Americans very angry. As a result, certain of the colonists said that if England would not allow them to trade where they pleased, they would do it on the sly. This was smuggling, and England tried to punish the sailors and merchants who brought such goods into America unlawfully.

But America's coastline was full of little creeks and bays into which the smugglers could sail without being caught, and this "illicit trade," as it was called, rapidly increased and became very profitable.

"GIVE ME LIBERTY OR GIVE ME DEATH!"

To make matters worse, the cost of the wars with the French had tremendously drained the British treasury. It had more than doubled Great Britain's national debt. British taxpayers held that since these wars had been for the defense and benefit of the Colonies, America should pay the bill—or at least a certain proportion of it—and also the cost of governing and defending the Colonies in the future.

The Americans did not think this was just. The wars with France, they said, had been for the benefit and glory of England. The American Colonies were not given a voice in

In defiance of the Sugar Act, the New England colonists smuggled molasses into the country and unloaded the illegal cargo at night.

the British Parliament. "If we can be represented in the English Parliament," they said, "we are willing to be taxed for our support, but we do not propose to pay for what we do not get."

The British lawmakers, however, were determined. They would not yield to the desires of the colonists. They made new rules as to the commerce of the Colonies (the Navigation Acts) that were even harsher than the old ones. Then they ordered (the Writ of Assistance) that the Custom House officers in America should have the right to enter any house at any time to search for smuggled goods, and, if need be, to call upon the soldiers for help.

A penny stamp from 1765, the use of which was ordered in the hated Stamp Act.

CLIMAX

Yet, though they were enraged over this new British action, the colonists hesitated to act. England was the mother country, and resistance was rebellion. They were not yet ready to go that far. In the year 1765, however, on the eighth of March, King George and his councilors laid the last straw on the overloaded back of the Colonial camel. On that day, the English Parliament passed the measure now famous in history as the Stamp Act.

This celebrated act was particularly objectionable. It required that to all newspapers, almanacs, marriage certificates, pamphlets, and legal documents of every description must be affixed costly stamps furnished by the English Government. It was considered an "entering wedge" for other tyrannical acts. "If the king can tax our trade," the colonists said, "why not our lands?" And from the thirteen Colonies the cry arose, "No taxation without representation!"

When protest began to mount, the English Parliament passed the Quartering Act. This law, one of the most difficult laws for the colonists to accept, provided that Americans should pay the expenses of a British army of occupation in the Colonies. American citizens were obliged to take Redcoat soldiers into their own homes, and provide them with food and lodging. In Boston and in other cities, resentment against these unwelcome guests led directly to bloodshed.

On the evening of March 5, 1770, a crowd of Boston people were shouting insults at a squad of British soldiers. Small boys began to throw snowballs, and one sentry was struck by a club. Captain Preston, a British officer, brought several men to the sentry's assistance. Suddenly, the soldiers turned and fired their muskets into the crowd, killing four men and wounding several others. The country was horrified at what it called "the Boston Massacre."

On December 16, 1773, the next dramatic incident took place that led the outraged colonists one more step toward war. This was known as the Boston Tea Party. The Townshend Acts, unlike the Stamp and Quartering Acts, had levied a tax on imported goods. But after an American boycott, these Acts were repealed in 1770, except for the tax on tea. This enabled the English East India Company to sell tea in the Colonies more cheaply than American wholesalers could. The American merchants had been bypassed and were enraged.

In protest against British taxes on imported goods, including glass, the colonists refused to buy from abroad, and American-made glass like the above pitcher came into great demand.

When three English ships loaded with tea docked in Boston Harbor, a group of men disguised as Indians forced their way on board, tore open the hatches, and dumped the cargo of tea into the water. As they were doing this, thousands of people stood on the dock and cheered.

The British Government tried to punish the colonists for the tea incident by passing the "Intolerable Acts" in 1774; they closed the port of Boston—in effect cutting off most income and supplies for the people of Massachusetts. But these acts only served to unite the colonists. They met at the First Continental Congress in Philadelphia in 1774 to discuss their grievances. The movement for united action was under way; it was spurred on by Patrick Henry's famous cry: "I know not what course others may take; but as for me, give me liberty or give me death!"

In the months that followed, anti-British feeling in the

The "Boston Massacre" was the beginning of the Revolutionary War.

Colonies became more and more widespread. When the British ignored the pleas of the Congress, militia units were organized in every Massachusetts town. Volunteers in New England called themselves Minute Men, because they said they were ready to take up arms "at a minute's notice" to protect their freedom. These militia companies began to hide secret stores of guns and ammunition in various places in case they would have to fight.

". . . THE SHOT HEARD ROUND THE WORLD"

Early in April of 1775, General Thomas Gage, the British commander in Boston, learned from spies that such a store of war material had been hidden in the nearby town of Concord. He planned to march his army on a secret raid to capture the supplies early in the morning of April 19. But the Colonials, who had more spies in Boston than General Gage had throughout the countryside, quickly learned of his scheme. They planned that when the British Army began to march, church bells in all the surrounding towns would ring to summon the Minute Men to the defense of Concord.

Paul Revere, a Boston silversmith who had become famous as a Colonial dispatch rider, was chosen to ride and spread the alarm when the British began their march. Fearing that he might be captured before he left the closely guarded city, he made plans to send a signal to other riders across the river in Charlestown. If the British Army were marching by land across Boston Neck, Revere was to hang one lantern in the tower of the Old North Church. If they were going by water over the Charles River, he would hang two lanterns.

At about ten o'clock on the night of April 18, Revere received word that the British were going to leave Boston by the water route. Accordingly, he had a friend hang two lanterns in the church tower, and then he set out by boat for Charlestown. (In his famous poem, "The Midnight Ride of Paul Revere," Henry Wadsworth Longfellow confused the matter of the lantern signals, and so he has misled four generations of readers. Longfellow said that the lanterns were a signal to Revere. Actually, they were a signal from him.)

As an added precaution, Paul Revere sent another rider, a young man named William Dawes, to Concord by way of Boston Neck. Although they had narrow scrapes with British patrols, both riders made it as far as the town of Lexington, about ten miles from Concord. Here the two met, halted briefly to rest their horses, and refreshed themselves with a mug of hot buttered rum at Buckman's Tavern. At Buckman's, they picked up a third rider, young Doctor Sam Prescott, who volunteered to go the rest of the way with them. But, midway between Lexington and Concord, the three were ambushed by a British patrol. Revere and Dawes were captured, but Prescott made it to Concord with the warning. When the British Army marched into Lexington, they were met on the Village Green by a small force of Minute Men.

"Disperse, ye villains! Ye rebels, disperse! Lay down your arms! Why don't you lay down your arms and disperse?" called out Major Pitcairn, the leader of the British advance.

The Minute Men of Lexington were but a few against 800, but they stood their ground.

"Fire!" shouted Pitcairn, and under the deadly discharge of the hundreds of British muskets, eight of the "rebels" fell dead and nine were wounded. The British marched on to Concord.

At Concord, the Redcoats found that two cannons had been spiked in the tavern yard; sixty barrels of flour had been broken into pieces; 500 pounds of ball had been thrown into the mill pond; the liberty pole had been cut down; and some private houses had been broken into.

A hundred or more British soldiers were sent to guard the Concord Bridge. Several hundred Minute Men, led on by the schoolmaster, came down the hill to the bridge. The British soldiers, realizing that they were outnumbered by colonists, began to tear up the planks of the bridge. The Americans broke into a run. The British fired, and the schoolmaster fell dead. Major Buttrick, of Concord, cried out, "Fire, fellow soldiers!"

"Fire, fire, fire!" echoed his men. They fired—"the shot heard round the world." Two of the British fell.

Taken by surprise, it was the Britishers' turn to run. As they retreated down the narrow road back to Boston, the army was kept under fire every step of the way by Minute

Paul Revere's seventeenth-century house (above) still stands today in downtown Boston; Below, Paul Revere's ride, April 19, 1775.

Men who were shooting from behind trees, barns, rail fences, and stone walls. Had the Colonial Army been made up of frontiersmen with deadly accurate rifles, instead of farmers with clumsy old-fashioned muskets, it is doubtful that a single Redcoat would have survived.

The Redcoats sometimes halted to return the fire in volleys that were mostly wasted on empty air. They finally reached Boston in the evening; 273 Britishers had been lost in battle. Thus, the first battle of the Revolutionary War ended in a rousing victory for the Yankees.

The news of the fights at Lexington and Concord roused patriots in other parts of the land. Even people in the Southern colonies began to talk of freeing Boston from the harsh English rule. Yet, the leaders moved cautiously. They summoned another Congress to determine what they should do.

It would be an unequal contest. On one side was England with her power and advantages. On the other were the settlements, totally unprepared for large-scale war and strung along a vulnerable stretch of broken coastline—to the east, the deep sea, and to the west, only the trackless forests and their hordes of hostile Indians.

The Americans needed a leader. He was on the horizon. The North had opened the Revolution; the South would give it a real hero. On June 17, 1775, the Second Continental Congress, in session at Philadelphia, elected Colonel George Washington of Virginia as commander-in-chief. His army of 20,000? . . . all volunteers!

George Washington had been trained from early youth to lead. As a boy, he was captain of the company of small Virginians he drilled and marshaled. At sixteen, he was a sur-

Two famous paintings: Above, A. M. Willard's "Spirit of '76," and at right, E. Leutze's "Washington Crossing the Delaware."

An old lithograph shows General Washington and his wife Martha visiting camp at Valley Forge on Christmas Day, 1777.

veyor and "roughed it" in the Indian country. At twenty, he was a major in the king's service. At twenty-five, he was commander-in-chief of the Virginia forces. It was he who allegedly fired the first shot in the French wars of 1754, led the attack at Great Meadows, and by his valor, prevented the defeat of English General Braddock from becoming a massacre. He knew the weaknesses as well as the strengths, the endurance as well as the independence of the Colonial soldier. No man was better suited to lead the troops to victory; not one other general in the Revolutionary Army combined all the excellent qualities that make a great soldier as did George Washington.

On July 3, 1775, Washington assumed command of the New England Army, drawn up to receive him on Cambridge Village Green. He went at once to work to keep General Gage and his Redcoats so tightly locked up in Boston town that they were at last, on March 17, 1776, forced to flee the city by sea. Washington and the victorious Continental troops marched into the city; Boston's long enslavement was over!

Old engraving depicting the public reading of the Declaration of Independence in an American town.

On January 1, 1776, the new flag of the Revolution was raised over the American camp on Prospect Hill. On July 4, 1776, the Continental Congress, assembled in Independence Hall in the city of Philadelphia, declared the thirteen United Colonies "free and independent States." . . . "absolved from all allegiance to the British Crown, and that all politi-

John Trumbull's famous painting in the U.S. Capitol depicts the surrender of Cornwallis at Yorktown.

cal connection between them and the State of Great Britain is and ought to be totally dissolved." This was the Declaration of Independence written by Thomas Jefferson; ever since that memorable act, the fourth of July has been celebrated as the birthday of the United States of America.

The Declaration was but the first step toward independence. For nearly seven years, from April 19, 1775, to October 19, 1781—from the first conflict at Lexington to the last at Yorktown—the war raged.

The King of England, his councilors, and his people at last reluctantly gave up. They signed a treaty of peace with the new nation at Paris in November, 1782, and a year later, in December, 1783, the British soldiers sailed home from the city of New York. Liberty had triumphed.

"LET THEM EAT CAKE"

The French people watched the American rebellion. In France, the poor people were taxed so heavily that they had hardly anything left over for bread. The king and his nobles were getting richer, fatter, and more and more unmindful of the ordinary folks except when they needed service. The starving people ate black bread when they could get it, while the king and his court reveled in a constant round of gaiety and extravagance. If a poor man even whimpered a complaint, he was thrown into jail, and most likely, remained there—forgotten until he died and had to be removed.

The young king and queen had little idea of what was going on in France: Louis XVI was a shy, well-meaning man who liked to hunt better than to occupy himself with affairs of state. Marie Antoinette, his queen, was an Austrian princess who had come to the throne as a child. She loved pleasure so that her extravagances earned her the nickname of "Madame Deficit."

She became notorious, too, for saying, "Why don't they eat cake?" upon being told that the people lacked bread. Her remark was made in all innocence, really. In the midst of all the perfume, laughter, and dancing around her, she probably couldn't imagine anyone without cake, and other good things, to eat, or perhaps she thought the baker had made a mistake and had not baked enough bread to go around.

In the hovels of Paris, the hard-pressed people survived, just as stray dogs manage to exist. But, as their hunger grew, so did their hatred.

And the unruly mobs grew, too. One day, a black mass of ragged men and women appeared in the streets. They cursed and shook their fists. No one could stop that mob. The people's eyes flashed with a strange light, and their anger was terrible to behold.

"On to the Bastille!" someone shouted.

The Bastille was an old prison in the heart of Paris where

the poor prisoners lay forgotten. Those who had stolen a bit of bread to save the life of a loved one were kept there in filthy cells until they died. And many more—those who had offended nobles, or had been too sick to labor for the fancy folks—they, too, were in prison.

The people battered down the walls. They cut off the heads of the guards, stuck them on poles, and paraded through the streets with them. The people seemed to have gone mad: They jeered, laughed, screamed awful oaths of hatred. "Let Marie Antoinette not eat cake!" they yelled. "We shall stuff her pretty mouth with black bread!"

The French Revolution had really begun. This was on July 14, 1789. It was the French way of declaring independence from a king. Even Lafayette, a French general who had helped America win its independence, sent the key to the Bastille to George Washington as evidence that France, too, had become free.

The nobles were suddenly terrified; the rumblings and rumors from Paris were fearsome. They called for their

The storming of the Bastille in Paris gave the signal for the French Revolution.

fancy horses and gilded carriages. Off they went, toward the border, as fast as they could, leaving their king and queen entirely forsaken. The king and queen trembled in their palace at Versailles. They didn't know what to do.

A group of men, representing the people, met and drew up the Declaration of the Rights of Man. All men were born free and equal, it was declared. The people should make the laws; and the laws should be the same for everybody.

Still, the people, wild-eyed and armed with sticks and stones, marched the ten miles to Versailles. Into the beautiful palace which Louis XIV had built, the bedraggled mob rushed, screaming, "Bread! We want bread!"

Up the thickly carpeted staircase, they pushed and stumbled. No guard could stop them. Swords, armor, lances were useless against the onslaught. If one ragged figure fell, two others replaced him. There was an endless rush of people who were willing to die for their beliefs on the staircase—and others at the bottom of the stairs. They captured the king and queen.

Above, citizens of Paris wore red caps to show that they were for the Revolution and not against it. At left, a French nobleman is led to his execution on the guillotine, erected in the middle of the city for public viewing.

"On to Paris!" the crowd screamed, and brandished their sticks still more.

"Our king and beautiful queen will reign over the sewers of Paris! They shall have black bread to make glad their stomachs!" the people sang. Louis and Antoinette were kept prisoners in Paris. How different this was from the light-hearted pleasures and the sweet perfume of Versailles. Once, they tried to escape but as their carriage speeded through the night, soldiers of the people caught them.

"And leave your people? Would you abandon your subjects?" the captain mocked. His soldiers rocked with laughter. The king and queen knew that they were lost forever. When the National Assembly, the law-making body, drew up a Constitution with laws and regulations for France, Louis signed it. He was now king in name only, a puppet who shook before his master, the people.

"No king should live in France," some said.

"How many heads does he owe us?" another asked.

"Off with *his* head!" the people demanded.

There stood the guillotine, in the public square. A sharp blade suspended on a frame, it came down to neatly slice off an ill-fated head. The poor king, as pale as the white lace at his throat, mounted the platform. The knife descended. The king lay dead.

Still, the people rampaged through the streets, singing "The Marseillaise"; waving the famous emblem of the Revolution, the red, white, and blue tri-color; and calling out their motto, "Liberty, Equality, Fraternity!"

"Death to all nobles," some shouted, drunk with power. The hunt for more heads to feed to the guillotine was on. Beautiful Antoinette, who by now knew the difference between cake and black bread, died, too. It mattered not that some cringed to observe such cruelty from friends and neighbors who had once detested cruelty. If anyone so much as hinted that he felt sympathy toward those who were being executed, off he was rushed to the waiting guillotine without trial or hearing. One had only to point to another and whisper, "I think he favors the nobles," and that man stood convicted. If anyone disliked a neighbor, all he had to do was to accuse him of being against the people, and another head would roll. Everyone lived in fear as the timber of the guillotine rattled from morning to night. When the guillotine was busy, the doomed were lined up before great cannons. People were even thrown into the river to drown.

All France—for the frenzy had passed to the countryside and the peasants, too—seemed to have gone mad. The Reign of Terror had reached its peak.

THE LIBERATOR

Most of South America was ruled by Spain just as most of North America had been ruled by England. And the colonists of South America disliked being ruled from Europe just as much as had the colonists of North America. They watched with deep interest the overthrow of English rule by the American Revolution and the overthrow of the French monarch by the French Revolution.

• "George Washington!" they cried with joy. "We, too, must have our great leader." Secretly, behind closed shutters, the people spoke of freedom from Spanish rule. But it would be many years before Latin-Americans would rebel against the Spanish governors.

Meanwhile, the political pot bubbled. Unable to speak and meet in the open, the people of South America organized secret societies, met under cover of the night, aired their grievances by candlelight. And the name they most often whispered was, "Bolívar."

Simón Bolívar's parents were very wealthy. They owned many cattle ranches and hundreds of slaves. Simón had everything as he grew up: fine clothes, private tutors, good horses, many friends. Later, as a young man, he studied in Europe. There he became popular with princes and nobles; in fact, with all kinds of people. He was much admired for his good looks and sincere manner. But Simón was not an ordinary aristocrat. He wanted freedom for all his people. "I swear," he said, "that I shall never rest until my country is free from the Spanish king."

He came to the United States to observe first-hand the new freedom there. He talked with President Thomas Jefferson and other American leaders. Back in his own country, Simón Bolívar raised and trained an army. The example of George Washington shone in his mind and those of his followers as they fought many hard battles. Bolívar's soldiers marched over the Andes and across flooded rivers. Only the strongest survived.

At last, all the Spanish armies in greater Colombia were defeated. Bolívar returned to the capital of the country where he was born. There the people greeted him with great honor. He rode in a parade in a golden chariot pulled by twelve beautiful girls. Thousands cheered the great leader, flags waved, and bands played. He died in 1830. The same year, the Republic of Greater Colombia was divided into the present countries of Venezuela, Colombia, and Ecuador.

As Bolívar had fought in the north, another patriot fought the Spaniards in the south, Jose San Martín. He became South America's second greatest hero. After completing his education in Spain, he returned to his country, Argentina, and was made governor of his state.

Like Bolívar, San Martín was a man of the people, and like Bolívar, San Martín was greatly inspired by the success of the American Revolution. His band of followers grew by the day. When ready, they followed the path laid down by Bolívar; they crossed the Andes into Peru where they took the Spanish by surprise.

San Martín realized that South America would grow

strong if it would unite under only one great leader instead of many. He unselfishly turned over his government and armies to Bolívar.

One by one, the colonies of South America won freedom. Bolívar was hailed as "the Liberator of South America," and Bolivia, one of the new republics, was named after him.

On October 26, 1795, the great French revolutionary assembly had met for the last time. At two o'clock on that day, it had passed its last decree: "The National Convention declares its mission fulfilled and its sessions closed."

"What time is it?" a voice had demanded from the back of the room.

Across the benches had come a solemn reply, "The hour of Justice."

Justice has had many hours in history; for these, she wore a blood-stained cloak.

A.D. 1660 Formulation of Boyle's Law.

A.D. 1687 Newton's theory of gravitation.

A.D. 1738 Flying shuttle invented.

A.D. 1752 Franklin's experiment with kite.

A.D. 1759 Modern canals built in England.

A.D. 1764 Invention of spinning Jenny.

A.D. 1774 Priestley isolated ammonia; discovered oxygen.

A.D. 1776 Adam Smith's *Wealth of Nations (laissez-faire doctrine in economics).*

A.D. 1777 Lavoisier's theory of combustion, and his law of conservation of matter.

A.D. 1779 Invention of spinning mule.

A.D. 1784 Puddling process for refining ore.

A.D. 1785 Watt's steam engine used in industry. Power loom.

A.D. 1792 Cotton gin invented.

A.D. 1798 Safe vaccination against smallpox developed by Jenner.

A.D. 1800 Volta found way of generating flow of electricity.

A.D. 1815 Macadam roads introduced.

A.D. 1820 First railroad laid in England.

A.D. 1831 Invention of electric dynamo by Faraday.

A.D. 1844 Telegraph perfected by Morse.

A.D. 1847 First Law of Thermodynamics.

A.D. 1850 Smelting improved by Bessemer.

A.D. 1859 Second Law of Thermodynamics. Publication of *The Origin of Species* by Charles Darwin.

A.D. 1864 Pasteur explains germ theory.

A.D. 1869 Railroads across North America. Suez Canal completed.

A.D. 1876 Alexander Graham Bell invented telephone.

A.D. 1885 Pasteur cured rabies.

A.D. 1898 Pierre and Marie Curie isolated radium.

A.D. 1903 Wright brothers developed airplane.

A.D. 1905 Einstein's theory of relativity.

A.D. 1942 Nuclear-fission reactor developed by Enrico Fermi.

A.D. 1945 Atomic bomb on Hiroshima.

CHAPTER 14

A Peaceful Revolution

REVOLUTIONS do not always take place on battlefields, and heroes are not always soldiers. Men fight for things other than fame or glory.

Look around you: In your father's auto tool kit, let's say, the jack is only a perfected lever; the lever has been in use since primitive man first realized he could lift a stone up out of the ground with a stick. A Pullman car is a luxury wagon; the wagon, a super-cart; and the cart goes back to the time when some clever fellow invented the wheel, perhaps by cutting a round piece off the end of a log. Your television set, as simple as it is for you to operate, encompasses more than forty-eight separate discoveries by a multitude of men working either alone or together.

It is hard to believe that, as recently as 1800, none of these—nor any of the thousand and one other everyday comforts of invention, science, biology, and medicine—were available to mankind; that, a little more than 150 years ago, no European country had a postal system more rapid than that of the ancient Roman Empire; that even farming was still carried on much as it had been in Roman times.

Then, within the span of a century and a half (but the wink of an eye in man's history), there were so many un-

An artist's concept (on page 334) of the historic event that took place on March 10, 1876, in a Boston boarding house: the telephone transmits the first complete sentence. Bell is seen on the left; Watson, an assistant, on the right.

dreamed-of industrial, agricultural, and scientific inventions and discoveries that, in the late 1800's, it was proposed that the United States Patent Office should be closed because certainly everything possible must have been invented.

This is the new kind of revolution of which we speak, and the men who had these dreams and miraculously made them come to pass are our new heroes.

Even today, the sowing is still done manually on small farms, or in underdeveloped countries.

"THE SINGING PLOW"

Agriculture is the world's most important industry; it supplies most of man's food and the material he uses to make many products. At one time, most people were farmers, but science and machinery have made it possible for comparatively few people to raise enough food and other agricultural products for everyone.

One man who pioneered in bringing new crops to new soil was Jethro Tull, an English gentleman farmer who lived and worked around the turn of the eighteenth century in England.

Farmers were still sowing in the early Egyptian manner: The seeds were cast by hand over the fields. Only nine or ten pounds of seed were used on each acre of land, leaving as much as two-thirds of the ground unplanted. The remainder was so thick with seed that often the grain grew poorly.

Tull's invention – a drill that planted seeds! – did away with such waste and uncertainty. It enabled farmers to bore straight rows of holes across their land and then drop the proper number of seeds into the holes.

Tull made other important contributions, too, to the agricultural revolution when he developed a plow that dug more deeply into the soil, and found ways to banish weeds, which, in those days, were just as much of a plague to the farmers as those that had beset the ancient Egyptians in Joseph's time.

Across the Atlantic, the same questions had fired the creative imagination of a young village blacksmith. Westerners needed better plows for the heavy American prairie sod that seemed like "tar, mud, and molasses" to them. Wooden plows were back-breaking, and iron ones "poisoned" the ground, they said.

John Deere, of Grand Detour, Illinois, was going about his labors one day when he noticed how a discarded steel blade shone where it had been polished by friction. In his shop, he made a plow out of a circular blade. With this steel plow, he cut a dozen smooth, straight furrows in a neighbor's field. Onlookers, who had come to scoff, thought they were seeing things!

John Deere sold this first steel plow for ten dollars. This was in 1837. Within ten years, he was producing more than a thousand plows a year. A John Deere plow could be found in almost every wagon train making its way to the West. It became famous as "the singing plow" because the plowshare vibrated with a pretty humming sound.

But planting and cultivation are only the beginning of a farmer's work. The crop he has so hopefully set out must be harvested, too. And he has only so much time for this once man-killing job; if a crop is not cut down upon ripening, it is lost!

The only way early farmers reaped their grain was with a scythe. When grain is ripe, it must be harvested in about ten days. Otherwise, the dry husks around the kernels of grain open and the kernels fall to the ground and are lost. The scythe, with its long handle and sharp blade about three feet long, was very heavy and extremely tiring to use. Only a strong man could swing a scythe in the field all day. The

The McCormick reaper, above; the reaper in action, below.

early farmer desperately needed an easier way to harvest his crop.

In most early attempts to improve harvesting, the horse was used to pull the reaping machine, but it trampled down the grain before it could be cut. A man named Patrick Bell had a fantastic idea: put the horse behind the machine. How a poor horse could push a heavy reaper over ridges and furrows is difficult, and painful, to imagine.

The first real reaper was made in the United States by Cyrus H. McCormick in the middle of the nineteenth century. His first machine worked much like a hair clipper! A low platform, open at one side, was attached to the horse-drawn machine. This platform caught the stalks of grain as they fell from the cutting blades. A man, perched on one side of the reaper, raked the cut grain off the platform onto the ground.

McCormick's reaper was considered the most important single step towards the American mechanization of agriculture. It won him a first prize in a London exposition, membership in the French Legion of Honor, knighthood in several minor orders, and—many millions of dollars!

These new ways of farming were an advent everywhere, but especially in the United States, where—because of the abundance of land—farmers had hitherto simply moved on when the ground they had worked became "used up." Now—thanks to Tull, Deere, McCormick, and the many others who turned their genius to agriculture—men could plant the roots of society, too.

LIVING WITH MACHINES

While farmers were establishing homesteads, other kinds of societies were springing up and growing, too. Have you ever passed through an industrial district and, as you viewed the expanse of factories and flats, wondered why people would want to live in such ugly places? Well, the answer is

Spinning and weaving before the industrial revolution was a "home affair" (at left). Today, construction and equipment of the spinning frames guarantee smoother yarns and more even weaving (below).

that they never picked these homes; during the industrial revolution, the machines they depended on for their livelihood made the choice for them. Machines have even more power over men: they breed other machines, other industries.

The great clothing industry is an example. All early cloth was made by hand. In the 17th Century, cotton was taken from the pod, and the seeds were removed by hand. Wool was sheared from sheep, carefully washed, carded, and combed out, also by hand. Spinning wheels drew the cotton fibers into thread; the wool, into yarn. Cloth was then woven from this thread or yarn on hand looms. While a weaver's guild made sure that the workmanship was good, most of the cloth was made at the craftsman's home. He brought his finished cloth to a merchant or sold it at a fair. That's why cloth was so expensive in those days.

An accident changed all of this. One day, a housewife named Jenny Hargreaves tipped over her spinning wheel. The spindle, sticking straight up, kept right on turning and winding thread. Her husband watched. That night, he had an idea: Construct a row of vertical spindles to be turned by one wheel. The machine would produce as much thread as eight people at eight old spinning wheels. James Hargreaves called his new machine the "spinning jenny," in honor of his wife.

The spinning jenny started other men thinking about other types of spinning machines. In 1769, about five years later, an English barber, Richard Arkwright, devised a method of turning the wheels of the spinning machine by means of water power. His invention, called a water frame, was very successful, and spinning mills were built along the fast-moving rivers and streams of England. Workers no longer worked in their own homes; instead they hired out to the millowner and worked at his spinning machines. This was the beginning of factories.

With more thread ready for making into cloth, a need arose for a machine which would make cloth faster. In 1785, an English minister, Edmund Cartwright, invented the power loom. One man at Cartwright's power loom could produce as much cloth as a dozen weavers working at hand looms.

With spinning machines and power looms turning everywhere, there was a shortage of cotton fibers to feed them. Removing the seeds from cotton by hand was a slow process; even a very skilled worker could clean only four or five pounds of cotton a day. An American teacher, Eli Whitney, who, friends said, could "make anything," invented the cotton gin in 1793. This machine could separate the seed from the cotton very quickly, thereby matching the combined output of as many as fifty hand workers. It brought an avalanche of cotton that revolutionized the industry.

As time passed, larger spinning machines were built; other innovations made the thread smooth, tight, even. More machines cleaned and carded the wool for spinning. Silk and other fibers were spun by new machines. Looms improved, too. Presses printed patterns on the cloth as it left the loom. Soon, even the poor could cast aside their homespun garments for clothing sewn of factory-made cloth.

Then in 1846, an American, Elias Howe, perfected the sewing machine, said to have been invented three times over. This permitted mass-production of ready-to-wear clothing.

Whitney's cotton gin.

FEEDING THE MACHINES

At first, water power was used to run the new machines, but it had disadvantages. A factory had to be close to a swift-flowing river; there just were not enough rivers of this type in England, where the Industrial Revolution was then strongest. Also, many of the most desirable rivers for water power were often a great distance from the sources of raw materials and the markets for products. The wizards of the day turned to steam.

Howe's sewing machine.

By 1705, steam engines were pumping water out of English coal mines. These engines, designed by inventors such as Thomas Newcomen, Thomas Savery, and the Marquis of Worcester, were not very powerful. In the early 1760's, a Newcomen engine was sent to the Scottish instrument-maker, James Watt, for repair. Watt decided that the clumsy engine could be greatly improved. For the next few years, he worked on plans for perfecting it. By 1769, he presented a steam engine which worked better than any engine ever made before. Within a few years, it was running the vital machinery of many industries.

Watt's steam engine.

THE MACHINE EMPIRE

The old way of life—of living, and of making a living; of learning, and of gaining experience of life; of habits of thought and of conduct—were vanishing.

Workers could no longer live outside the towns. Spinning and weaving had once been family affairs in which everybody helped when not busy at other tasks. They worked when they felt like it. Perhaps a cousin was getting married,

Dr. Edward Jenner.

a time for celebration instead of work. Or the garden or animals—the pigs, chickens, cows, and horses—needed tending.

You can see how the old system kept the families together, and independent. Their farms provided enough to eat; their homes, warmth and companionship.

The factory system changed all this. Now spinner and weaver had to go where the power was; they had to leave their farms. And people were "steam-mill mad" because of the money to be made.

The people settled in the factory towns. These crowded and dirty places soon transformed them into a bitter lot. "Where there is muck, there is money," it was said.

The country villages had been places of tradition; there, a man meant something to his neighbors. In the cities, even the children worked as long as eighteen hours a day. Some of them were under eight years old! Many were pauper apprentices, bound to labor till twenty-one for their food and lodging—in effect, slaves. The steam engine was inhuman, and the greedy factory-owners were more so. Most of the factory-owners felt no humane obligation to care for their workers. The factory worker became another bit of machinery, laboring from early in the morning to late in the night. He breathed despair in the dank, dimly-lit factories as he worked faster, faster, and still faster to keep up with the machines.

The country-side was deserted, but in the towns, there weren't even enough houses for all the people. To shelter them, new towns had to be built quickly, and cheaply. Dreary hovels piled one upon the other, the first slums. Dread diseases swept through the garbage-littered alleys and streets, invaded the crowded tenements, and brought great suffering and loss to early factory workers. The people who lived during the time of Hippocrates had a better chance of recovery from illness than the factory workers of the early nineteenth century.

MIRACLE-WORKERS

Smallpox was one of the most perilous diseases in these factory-town slums. Toward the end of the eighteenth century, however, people began to notice the absence of smallpox in farmers who had come in contact with a similar disease in cattle called cowpox. Even if someone had had a mild case of cowpox disease, he was immune thereafter to further attacks.

These observations led the English physician, Dr. Edward Jenner, to conclude that people who had had cowpox would not get smallpox. He continued to experiment and, in 1778, he made the results of his tests public. He called his method of prevention of the disease vaccination, and it has virtually wiped out smallpox in every country that uses it.

Dr. Jenner opened up a whole new field of experiment and discovery, that of making the human body immune to disease by injecting into it a small dose of the very poison that causes the disease.

Dr. Joseph Lister.

Such diseases, it is now known, are caused by those pesky little creatures called "germs." They were first brought to man's attention by the French professor of chemistry, Louis Pasteur, who fermented beer and wine to convince non-believers.

Pasteur laid the foundations of modern bacteriology and of modern medical science for, if man knows the cause of a disease, he can take steps to avoid it. For example, typhoid fever, once known to every family, hardly exists any more in countries where it is law to kill the typhoid germs by pasteurization.

The British surgeon, Dr. Joseph Lister, hastened to apply Pasteur's germ theory to surgery. Surgery was crude and painful. If the patient survived the hack-work, it was just luck if he did not die of an infection in the wound. Lister tried carbolic acid to cleanse the wound of bacteria. It stung —but it worked! Later, he demonstrated that everything that touched the wound—hands, knife, cotton, bandages, even the very air that the surgeon breathed down upon it—had to be sterile, too.

Men went on to learn more about the nature of these germs that were killing seventy-five per cent of the children under five and thousands who had survived to youth or middle age. In 1876, a German physician, Robert Koch, obtained a pure culture of a germ—specifically, that of anthrax disease. He produced the germ in his laboratory, studied it, experimented with it. He miraculously happened upon a way to kill that special germ.

Here was a new method of fighting disease: the antitoxin. Since then, many specific antitoxins have been discovered for specific diseases of man. Diphtheria is a striking example of a disease that can be cured by antitoxin. Doctors are constantly working on antitoxins for tuberculosis, meningitis, influenza, and many other plagues of man.

The pages of medical history are filled with the names of such heroes of civilization. Together, they have freed the Western World from the terrible scourges of typhus, smallpox, diphtheria, yellow fever, and a host of other killers. They have lowered the death-rate and greatly increased the number of people in the world.

It is a good thing to be free of fear. Whether it is a good thing to have more people in the world depends on whether they can live decently and comfortably.

Such hope was offered workers from two sources: humane laws and the organization of unions. The British Factory Act of 1833 was a landmark of social reform, even though

after it cut the working-day of children under eighteen, they still had to work twelve hours a day. A long line of protective legislation followed.

English trade-unionism dates from 1825, but it did not become effective for many years. The first unions were secret organizations, bitterly fought by employers and the government.

The year 1840 opened a decade of great hardship and starvation. It was followed by a prosperity that greatly improved the lot of the British worker. Hours were shortened and, since 1830, wages had doubled. Henceforth, the increase in wealth brought about by machinery would gradually be shared by labor.

CLIPPER SHIPS

In this age of speed, America was setting some new standards for the world: American clipper ships held most of the world's records. In Chinese ports, crack British ships would lie at anchor day after day, waiting to be loaded. American clippers would sail into port, hurriedly take aboard what they had come for, and then dash off again for a 10,000-mile cruise to London, maintaining an hour-after-hour average of ten or more knots!

The peak of perfection in the sailing ship was reached by the American, or Yankee, Clipper. She first appeared in the 1840's and was used principally on the long voyages to the West Coast, India, and China, often, when favored by the winds, sailing faster than many cargo ships today. A few

The S.S. SAVANNAH

small clippers were built after 1862. But almost five thousand years of sailing ships ended about 1900; Clipper ships were doomed by the coming of the steamship.

In the closing years of the eighteenth century, many experimented with the steam propulsion of boats. Robert Fulton, an American inventor, did *not* invent the steamship. No one actually invented the steamship; rather, it evolved. Fulton built *The Clermont,* whose sensational run up to Albany and back on August 17, 1807, popularized their general use.

The SS Savannah, a wooden-hulled paddle-wheeler like *The Clermont,* left Savannah, Georgia, on May 22, 1819, and arrived at Liverpool, England on June 20. She was a small sailing ship but her engine was used about 105 hours in the thirty-day trip. Because *The SS Savannah* used her sails for most of her journey, she cannot entirely be called the first steamship to make a transatlantic voyage.

Various other sailing ships were fitted with steam engines and paddle-wheels, but not until 1858 did a vessel cross the Atlantic Ocean under steam power alone. That year, two British companies decided to compete in North Atlantic travel. Their rival ships left England within a few hours of each other in a race for New York. *The SS Sirius* was the first to arrive in New York Harbor; six hours later, *The SS Great Western* came up the Narrows in New York harbor—both ships throwing off great clouds of black smoke. On shore, cannons saluted, church bells tolled, and thousands of people shouted and waved. The age of steam had begun!

Meanwhile, an equally important revolution in construction was under way. The early steamships were built of wood. Experiments in the use of iron for the hulls of ships had been made even before the end of the eighteenth century, but most shipbuildrs had been afraid to use iron; they feared that iron, being heavier than water, would impair the ship's capacity to float.

The British *Vulcan,* built in 1818, was the first all-iron sailing vessel. Between 1845 and 1880, iron gradually replaced wood in the hulls of large steamships. In 1881, the British *SS Servia* was the first all-steel ship to cross an ocean. All modern ships are of steel construction.

IRON HORSES

Many men were dreaming of opening America with a steam-engine railroad. With the development of a high-pressure steam engine light enough and small enough to pull its own weight, the steam carriage became a taunting possibility. More wizards went to work around the clock. In no time, steam-engine railroading burst on America with a loud roar.

An English-built seven-ton locomotive, *The Stourbridge Lion,* was brought to America in 1829 by Horatio Allen, a young civil engineer. A two-mile trial run on a coal track in Pennsylvania made it the first steam engine to move on a railroad in this country. Too heavy and too stiff for American roads, the *Lion* was honorably retired. The ride must have been quite an experience for Mr. Allen because he said, fifty years later, "I had never run a locomotive nor any other machine before and I have never run one since."

America had to develop its own locomotives to fit its own conditions. In 1825, the first such locomotive was built by Colonel John Stevens of New Jersey. He operated it on a circular track on his estate, never using it commercially.

The Tom Thumb, built by Peter Cooper, another young civil engineer, in 1830, was the first engine to pull a load of passengers in America. People lined the tracks in Baltimore to catch the wonderful sight of an iron horse going at the unheard-of speed of eighteen miles an hour.

This pint-sized engine, weighing only about one ton, once ran a race with a fast stagecoach horse. It was an exciting event; the puffing of the horse matched the puffing of *The Tom Thumb*. At first, the locomotive drew ahead. Then, at the last minute, *The Tom Thumb* had a minor mechanical failure. The horse won the race!

The day was August 25, 1830. The spirited race between a horse-drawn carriage and Peter Cooper's locomotive,* The Tom Thumb, *was won by the horse.

Horatio Allen had meanwhile joined the newly formed South Carolina Canal and Railway Company (now the Southern Railway System), which became the first railroad to use steam power for its regular service. The locomotive, *The Best Friend of Charleston,* designed by Allen, pulled forty passengers in four cars over their rails at twenty-one miles an hour. A year later, this railroad began carrying United States mail. In 1833, the Southern line was extended to 136 miles, making it the longest railroad in the world at that time.

Let's take an imaginary trip behind the famous *De Witt Clinton.* This was the third locomotive built in America; it was put into service between Albany and Schenectady in New York on August 9, 1831. The entire train consisted of: a four-wheeled engine; a tender containing water and firewood; two passenger cars made from the bodies of stagecoaches fastened onto the rails. The cars were connected with a three-link chain about a yard in length. The engine, eleven and one-half feet long, had a towering smokestack. One man operated the engine. Tickets for the trip were sold at hotels and other public places.

We, along with the other passengers, climb into the carriages and take our seats. The conductor, after collecting our tickets, mounts a little seat on the tender and blows a horn. This is the signal for the engineer to start the train. As the train starts to move, there is a terrific jerk that sends us and the other coach passengers sprawling all over each other. But, once we get settled again in our seats, the engine moves along smoothly.

Then, as the fire in the boiler gets hotter, more and more sparks, cinders, and smoke beat down upon us, the passengers of *The De Witt Clinton*. Finally, we have to stand to beat the flames from our burning clothes.

When the train makes a stop, the engineer pushes a lever that is designed to apply brakes to the wheels and slow the train. The device works well: The engine is abruptly checked; the tender bumps into the locomotive; the first passenger car crashes against the tender; and the second coach rams the first. We who are sitting in the coaches are once again sent sprawling, now forward from our seats, instead of backward, as we had been when the train first started.

Train schedules were somewhat irregular in these days. When it rained, trains could not run because they had no way to keep from slipping on the wet tracks. They could not run at night because there were no lights on the trains. There were many delays in the service, too; often, the train ran out of firewood, and the passengers had to help gather more wood so that the journey of the iron horse could continue to their destinations.

Railroads had many problems in the early days. Some people were strongly opposed to all railroads and even held mass meetings against them. Others claimed that the cattle would be injured, or that it was not healthful to travel at the dangerous speed of fifteen miles an hour. Some predicted that trains and their passengers would just blow up! Unfortunately, there was some evidence to support these claims, but the railroads did what they could to make travel safe.

To protect cattle and engines, a small truck (a set of wheels) was put ahead of it. One model of truck had two iron spears attached. Later, a crossbar was substituted, and in time, this became the V-shaped cowcatcher, or pilot.

The Stourbridge Lion *(1829)*.

The Best Friend *(1830)*.

The John Bull *(1831)*.

Henry Ford seated in his first car, built in 1896.

A 1901 Oldsmobile.

Most of the early locomotives had simple brakes, or no brakes at all! When a train puffed into its destination, a group of citizens ran out, grabbed the train wherever they could, and pulled it to a stop! After these pioneer trains had been operated for a while using this trial-and-error method, the brakes were improved until the present air brakes evolved. These automatic brakes, worked by compressed air and controlled from the locomotive, can be applied throughout a long train in just a few seconds.

As time went on, night operations became increasingly necessary, and inventive minds devised ways of illuminating the track ahead of the train. The first practical step in this direction was taken by Horatio Allen when he attached a small flatcar to the front of the locomotive, and covered the floor of the car with a heavy layer of sand, on which he kept a bonfire of pine knots. Soon, though, reflectors and oil lamps came into use. Today, all our locomotives are equipped with electric headlights.

HORSELESS CARRIAGES

Just as the steamboat developed the river-sides and the railroads opened up the lands, the automobile shaped the faces of countries. Networks of highways connected new cities, towns, farmlands, mines, entire industries everywhere.

Today's modern automobile traces its ancestry back to the 1860's. Its grandfathers: Austrian Gottlieb Daimler, German Nicholaus Otto and Karl Benz, French Alphonse Beau de Rochas, Pierre Emile Lavasseur, Jean Lenoir, and others of that era. After Lenoir built the first practical gasoline combustion engine in 1860, several vehicles were attempted. Daimler and Benz built their first cars in 1885. The French carriage-building firm, Panhard & Levasseur, produced the first self-powered vehicle to approach today's concept of the automobile.

The first successful American car propelled by an internal-combustion engine was "the buggyaut," a motorized carriage assembled by Charles E. and J. Frank Duryea in their Springfield, Massachusetts, machine shop. The Duryea brothers' claim to this distinction has been challenged by many people. Some insist that Elwood Haynes or the Apperson brothers, Elmer and Edgar, should have the greater glory for America's first car.

About the same time—the early 1890's—Ransom E. Olds, Alexander Winston, and Henry Ford were working on vehicles that eventually would lead to the creation of large companies. The basic test of a "successful" auto was whether it could be produced for commercial sale. Hundreds of early vehicles never made it. Many of the forgotten pioneers built only one model and gave up. Generally, these experimenters and their achievements were ignored by the giants who built the industry. In the modern concept of automobiles, it seemed far-fetched to count Napoleon's Captain Cugnot's three-wheeled gun tractor as a contribution.

A 1904 Studebaker-Garford (16-horsepower).

A 1907 Ford.

FLYING MACHINES

For centuries men had envisioned human flight, but they had looked upon it as a sort of acrobatic feat.

In the latter part of the nineteenth century, Otto Lilienthal, a German scientist, and Samuel P. Langley, an American astronomer, experimented with gliders. Their work had great impact on the Wright brothers, Wilbur and Orville. They were critical readers who separated the right, the wrong, and the questionable in the reports of Lilenthal and Langley.

As the Wright brothers studied and tinkered, they decided that, if men were ever to fly successfully, they must learn how to build wings, how to power the machine through the air, and how to control the machine up in the air. The first two problems had been worked on considerably. The third needed the most attention; that was the area in which the Wright brothers decided to concentrate.

A Cadillac model from 1908.

On December 14, 1903, the Wright brothers had their

airplane ready for its first trial. They were to take turns at flying it. The wind was only five miles per hour, and so the first attempt at flight, by Wilbur, did not last long enough to count. But, three days later, with Orville at the controls, the machine rose into the air in a twenty-seven-mile-an-hour wind and flew for twelve seconds. They flew three more times that day. The longest flight—852 feet in fifty-nine seconds—was made by Wilbur. Thus, Orville and Wilbur Wright accomplished the first successful flight in a heavier-than-air craft, at Kitty Hawk, North Carolina, on the memorable date of December 17, 1903.

Since then, thousands have improved the airplane. Today, air travel, steadily gaining in safety and speed, has made the world very small, indeed.

This is how Leonardo da Vinci saw the possibility of flight.

MORE MAGIC

Many other inventions and discoveries have changed our way of life. The electric dynamo developed by the Englishman, Michael Faraday, around 1830 deserves honorable mention. The dynamo was really a small electric machine by itself. It changed the power created by the steam engine, or the water wheel, into an electric current. The ability to move an electric current along wires made possible many of the electrical inventions that now brighten the world.

For instance, an American, Samuel F. B. Morse, *interrupted* the flow of an electric current to send messages. Morse worked on his telegraph for over five years. The United

With Orville Wright at the controls, the first powered flight took place on December 17, 1903, at Kitty Hawk, North Carolina.

States Congress, in 1843, acknowledged its success by passing a bill that permitted the construction of a telegraph line from Baltimore to Washington. People excitedly watched the tall poles and wires go up, the first telegraph line. Morse tapped out the first message, a series of dots and dashes, from Washington to Baltimore: "What hath God wrought?"

"Lightning wires," as they came to be known, were strung up all over the United States, and far into Canada. Cables were laid under the ocean; the telegraph was welcomed throughout Europe. A network of wires soon encircled the globe. Along these wires flashed messages telling what was happening in nearly every part of the world. In those days, and for a long time, every message began with "Dear Sir" and ended "Respectfully yours."

Photograph of the original telegraph apparatus that Morse built in the winter of 1835-36.

The same principle was used to transmit human voices. In 1876, an American, Dr. Alexander Graham Bell, invented the telephone. He called it "the talking telegraph." Messages may now be sent to any country in the world by cable, or long-distance telephone.

Electric current lights up homes, streets, factories, innumerable places, thanks to Thomas Alva Edison, who made other history by starting the business of "inventions to order." Electric current passing along wires is used in thousands of ways.

Men later found that electric waves would pass through the air without wires to carry them. The first experimenter to achieve this was an Italian, Guglielmo Marconi. On December 2, 1901, he sent the letter "S," using the Morse Code, across the Atlantic Ocean from England to Newfoundland.

Building on the foundations laid by Marconi, an American, Lee De Forest, and others, discovered how to transmit the human voice via radio. Television has the same background of genius.

Dreamers, wizards, and tinkerers: all heroes of civilization; their victories, the greatest. Their acts of creation transformed a wilderness into our wondrous world.

A.D. 1795 Paris riots. Napoleon Bonaparte placed in charge of troops.

A.D. 1796 Napoleon drove Austrians out of Italy.

A.D. 1798-1799 Napoleon's expedition to Egypt. Establishment of dictatorship.

A.D. 1812 French invasion of Russia. Burning of Moscow. Retreat from Moscow.

A.D. 1814 Abdication of Napoleon; restoration of French monarchy. The "Hundred Days."

A.D. 1815 Napoleon returned to Paris. Battle of Waterloo. Second abdication. St. Helena exile.

A.D. 1860 Abraham Lincoln elected 16th President of United States.

A.D. 1861 Outbreak of American Civil War.

A.D. 1861-1862 Joint naval and military forces blockade southern coasts. Engagement of *The Monitor* with *The Merrimac.*

A.D. 1863 Decisive battle of Gettysburg. Battle of Chattanooga drove Confederates from Tennessee and opened road into Georgia. Sherman's campaign.

A.D. 1865 General Lee capitulated at Appomattox. Last Confederate army surrendered at Shreveport, Louisiana. Lincoln assassinated.

A.D. 1914-1918 World War I.

A.D. 1917 Beginning of Russian Revolution.

A.D. 1918 World War I Armistice signed.

A.D. 1919 League of Nations organized.

A.D. 1928 War renounced in Kellogg-Briand Pact.

A.D. 1933 Hitler became Chancellor of Germany.

A.D. 1936 Ethiopia conquered by Mussolini-Rome-Berlin Axis.

A.D. 1937 Italy allied with Germany and Japan.

A.D. 1938 Hitler coup against Austria.

A.D. 1939 Non-aggression pact signed by Russia and Germany. World War II began with German invasion of Poland.

A.D. 1941 Japan attacked United States at Pearl Harbor; United States enters war.

A.D. 1945 Death of Roosevelt. Nazi Germany surrendered. Dropping of atomic bomb on Hiroshima and Nagasaki and surrender of Japan. Hitler and Mussolini met violent deaths.

A.D. 1946 United Nations held first assembly in London.

A.D. 1947 Truman doctrine. Aid for Greece and Turkey.

A.D. 1948 Republic of Korea formed. Israel became a state.

A.D. 1949 North Atlantic Treaty.

A.D. 1950 South Korea invaded.

A.D. 1951 U.N. forces in Korea attacked by Chinese Communists.

A.D. 1952 First hydrogen bomb tested by United States.

A.D. 1953 Stalin died.

A.D. 1954 Racial segregation in schools outlawed by U.S. Supreme Court decision.

A.D. 1955 West Germany admitted to NATO.

A.D. 1956 Suez Canal seized by Egypt.

A.D. 1957 Beginning of Space Age with firing of Soviet Sputnik.

A.D. 1960 First around-the-world trip by United States nuclear-powered submarine.

A.D. 1961 Erection of Berlin Wall by East Germany.

A.D. 1962 Confrontation of Russia and United States over Russian missiles based in Cuba.

A.D. 1963 President John F. Kennedy assassinated.

A.D. 1965 Death of Winston Churchill.

A.D. 1965 United States Mariner IV photographs Mars.

A.D. 1965 8-day orbital flight of United States manned spacecraft *Gemini 5.*

"... A Parenthesis in Eternity"

FOR centuries, the kings and emperors of Europe sat upon their thrones ordering their subjects to do this and to do that, secure in the belief that they had a "divine right" to rule. They believed, and so did most of the people, that God had intended them to give the orders and that it was the duty of everyone else to obey.

But the beheading of the French king and the cries of the French people for liberty and equality aroused the fears of all the European monarchs. If the French were allowed to get away with treating their king this way, who knows, maybe *their* subjects might begin to get the same kind of peculiar ideas.

So the kings and emperors put their crowned heads together and decided to teach the French a lesson. They all went to war against France, determined to put a French king back on the throne—and, of course, while they were doing it, they might just as well nibble off some pieces of French territory or some French colonies here and there throughout the world.

THE NAPOLEONIC PERIOD

Napoleon Bonaparte.

But the rulers of Europe were not to get their way as easily as they thought. An ambitious little man—he was only five feet tall—called Napoleon Bonaparte saw to that.

Born in the year 1769, at Ajaccio on the Mediterranean island of Corsica, Napoleon was a natural-born soldier. He joined the French Army as a boy, swiftly rose through the ranks from private to corporal to sergeant, and by the time he was sixteen, he was a lieutenant. He joined enthusiastically in the French Revolution, fought successfully against the English at Toulon, and at twenty-six, became a brigadier general.

Six years after the French Revolution began, most of the French people were becoming weary of the bloodshed, the foreign wars, and the disorderly rule of their elected representatives. Many of them, forgetting the hunger that had driven them to rebel, began to long for the good old days of the monarchy. So, on October 5, 1795, a huge mob—30,000 strong—marched on the building where the leaders of the French Republic were meeting. The government leaders asked Napoleon to protect them.

The fearless Napoleon stepped in front of the crowd and gave a command: "No one shall go one step farther." To enforce his order, he pointed his cannons down the street and cleared away the mob "with a whiff of grapeshot." From that moment, the rioting ceased.

During the next few years, Napoleon led French armies to victories against the Austrians in Italy. He went on to fight English and Turkish forces in Egypt, Palestine, and Syria.

When news reached him that things were not going so well at home, he returned to Paris in 1799. Taking a leaf from the pages of the history of the Roman general, Julius Caesar, whom we met on our travels sometime ago, he had himself declared First Consul, or dictator, of France. A few years later, in 1804, he crowned himself Emperor.

Within the next few years, Napoleon's armies conquered much of Europe, and he placed his brothers and favorite generals on the thrones of many of the European countries. He made grandiose plans to invade England, but the powerful British fleet forced him to give up that idea. Like most greedy generals and dictators, Napoleon overreached himself finally by attacking Russia in 1812. He captured Moscow, but the fierce cold of the Russian winter, and the stubborn resistance of the Russian peasants who burned their homes and food, rather than let them fall into the hands of Napoleon, destroyed the French Army.

The next year, Napoleon met defeat again at the Battle of Leipzig against the combined forces of England, Prussia, Russia, Spain, and Sweden. And, in 1814, he was forced to give up the throne of France to Louis XVIII, while he went into exile on the tiny Mediterranean island of Elba. Europe heaved a huge sigh of relief.

But the little man with the big ambition to rule the world soon came roaring back out of exile. He returned to Paris in 1815, drove out Louis XVIII, and again took command of the French Army, which hailed him as a hero. His rule this time, however, was destined to last only a hundred days.

England, Prussia, and all of Napoleon's old enemies swiftly sent their armies marching against him again. On June 18, 1815, the English Duke of Wellington defeated Napoleon for the last time at the little Belgian village of Waterloo. Napoleon was bundled off under English guard to the remote island of St. Helena near the west coast of Africa. He died there a few years later, still trying to figure out what went wrong in his plans.

The Nelson Monument in Trafalgar Square in London, England, commemorates the victory of the British fleet, under the command of Lord Horatio Nelson, over Napoleon's fleet.

THE CHANGING MAP OF EUROPE

With Napoleon's departure from the scene, Europe had one of its longest periods of peace—more than forty years. At the Congress of Vienna in 1815, England, Austria, Prussia, and Russia carved up Europe to suit themselves, so they had no reason to quarrel among themselves for the next few years. But this does not mean that all the nations that were gobbled up were happy.

The efforts of Giuseppe Garibaldi in the 1860's helped weld together Italy into a unified nation for the first time since the decline of the Roman Empire. The Austrians were driven out of northern Italy, and Victor Emmanuel became king of the new nation in 1861.

Ten years later, through the efforts of Prince Otto von Bismarck, the dozens of little feudal states of Germany were brought together for the first time with King Wilhelm I of Prussia proclaiming himself the first Emperor of Germany. The unification came about largely as the result of a war that Bismarck had waged against France from 1870 to 1871.

COLONIALISM IN ASIA AND AFRICA

The successful revolutions by the colonists in North and South America had forced the European monarchs to give up the idea of expanding their empires in the Western Hemisphere. So, in the 1800's, they turned their attention to Asia and Africa as sources of wealth and power.

The capture of French guns by the British "Union Brigade" at Waterloo, 1815.

Although we remember that the Portuguese explorers reached India first by rounding the southern tip of Africa, the British decided that they needed this part of the world for their own empire. By the mid-1800's, the British had taken most of the Indian sub-continent, and suddenly, on the north, they found themselves face-to-face with Russia, which was trying to expand southward.

In 1854, on the shores of the Black Sea, the Crimean War began between Russia and the Ottoman Empire, which had taken over the lands once held by the eastern Roman Empire and the Byzantine Empire and which was now ruled by Moslem Turks. France and England joined the war to help the Turks prevent Russia from expanding its borders to the Mediterranean Sea.

Florence Nightingale nurses the wounded in the primitive hospital in the Crimea.

The Russians were stopped, but a more important—and unexpected—result of the Crimean War was the development of the modern profession of nursing. A good-hearted Englishwoman by the name of Florence Nightingale became worried by reports that soldiers were dying by the thousands on the battlefields from lack of medical care. So, for the first time in history, a group of women, led by Florence Nightingale, went to the battlefields to tend the wounded. She and her helpers saved the lives of many soldiers who otherwise would have died. From that time on, nursing became a respected profession for women. Florence Nightingale's name will always be remembered, while the names of the generals who fought the bloody Crimean battles have long since been forgotten.

Elsewhere in Asia, the French took Indochina on the southeastern tip of the continent, the Dutch took the East Indies, the Spanish held the Philippines, and the British expanded into Burma and the island of Ceylon. The important ports of China were captured by the various European powers, but no one had enough manpower to try to take over that entire vast country. The Japanese also withstood European efforts to take their islands.

Likewise, the European powers divided Africa among

themselves, without regard for the rights or wishes of the peoples who had lived there for thousands of years. England and France took the largest shares of this southern continent, while Italy, Germany, Spain, Portugal, Belgium and The Netherlands had to content themselves with smaller portions of this colonial feast.

Having learned the lesson in America that giving some degree of self-government to colonies could only lead to desires for even more liberty, the European empires were now more careful to rule the Asian and African colonies with "an iron hand." They kept all the powers of government in their own fists and maintained military forces large enough to prevent any local uprisings. Thus, they were able to exploit the resources of their colonies without too much fear of some new George Washington or Thomas Jefferson spoiling their profits.

WESTWARD EXPANSION OF THE UNITED STATES

The Constitution of the United States that was written in 1787 and that went into effect in 1789, with George Washington as the first President, gave the new nation a unique federal form of government. Some powers were reserved for the states, and other powers were delegated to the national government. A Bill of Rights insured that the powerful national government would never be able to take away the rights of individual citizens–the right to speak their minds, the right to print and publish what they chose, the right to belong to watever religion they wished or even follow no religion at all, and many other rights and freedoms, including the right to a trial by jury. As the years rolled by, other nations saw that the Constitution provided such a stable form of representative government that they often used it as a model in changing their own governments.

The young nation grew and grew during the nineteenth century. Millions and millions of refugees came from Europe, seeking liberty, seeking peace from the turmoil of

Europe's wars, seeking religious freedom, and most of all, seeking an opportunity to achieve success.

A constant stream of pioneers flowed westward toward the American frontier. Some walked. Some rode on horseback. Some rode trains. Some went on canal boats. Some went by covered wagon. Free land, cheap land, beckoned the farmers. The discovery of gold and silver lured the miners.

And the frontier itself constantly moved westward, too. Under President Thomas Jefferson, the territorial size of the United States doubled in 1803 with the Louisiana Purchase. Jefferson bought this great expanse of land from Napoleon, who needed $15,000,000 to fight his wars more than he needed the land that now stretches across thirteen states from Louisiana to Montana.

American efforts for expansion had a setback under James Madison when "the war hawks" wanted to add Canada to the United States by the War of 1812. But the war with England ended in a stalemate with no land changing hands, and the Capitol and White House in flaming ruins. Only Andrew Jackson profited by this war when he won national fame by whipping a British army in the Battle of New Orleans.

The land of sunshine and oranges, Florida, became part of the United States under President James Monroe when it was purchased from Spain in 1821 for $5,000,000—an amount that could be collected today by getting only $1 from each person living in the state.

The huge western area of Texas declared itself independent of Mexico in 1836, adding an unforgettable page to American history with the Battle of the Alamo in which both James Bowie and Davy Crockett died for freedom. Nine years later, Texas joined the Union as the twenty-eighth state.

The United States grew again in 1846 when a treaty with Great Britain straightened out the boundary in the Northwest, giving the Union new territory that eventually became the states of Oregon, Washington, and Idaho.

A dispute between the United States and Mexico about the proper location of the southern boundary of Texas led to the Mexican War. And by the time the fighting was over in 1848, Mexico was willing to sell for $15,000,000 the land that became California, Nevada, Utah, and parts of Colorado, Arizona, and New Mexico. Some motion pictures produced in Hollywood cost more than that today, and without this purchase, there would have been no Hollywood at all. A few years after the Mexican War, in 1853, the United States paid Mexico another $10,000,000 in the Gadsen Purchase for the southern parts of Arizona and New Mexico.

Andrew Johnson was President in 1867 when American diplomats talked Russia into another real-estate bargain, buying all of Alaska for only $7,200,000. The Russians thought of Alaska only as a good place to catch seals—they didn't know that less than thirty years later, gold would be discovered "in them thar hills."

The island republic of Hawaii was annexed to the United States in 1898. That same year, the Spanish-American War brought the United States control of Guam, Puerto Rico, and the Philippine Islands in return for payment to Spain of $20,000,000. Many years later, after World War II, the United States granted the Philippines their freedom.

American Civil War drum from about 1860.

"WITH MALICE TOWARD NONE— WITH CHARITY FOR ALL"

But all was not such smooth sailing for the United States as it might seem. Almost from the beginning of the new nation's history, there were quarrels between the Northern States and the Southern States. The two sections of the country had vastly different interests. The South favored a weak national government with most powers being held by the states; the North believed in a strong national government with fewer powers being left to the states. The South was mainly interested in farming—in growing cotton and tobacco; the North was more involved in manufacturing, busi-

Above, a scene from the Battle of Gettysburg, which lasted from July 1 to July 3, 1863. The battle is often called the turning-point of the Civil War. Below, Charleston, South Carolina, ruined by the war.

ness, and banking. The issue, however, on which there was absolute and complete disagreement was *slavery*.

Most Northerners felt that a nation that had been started with a declaration that "all men are created equal" should not permit slavery to continue—particularly after Great Britain abolished slavery throughout its colonies in 1833. But the Southerners contended that, without slaves, they would be unable to continue to plant and harvest the cotton and tobacco crops upon which their economy depended.

This is one of the few photographic portraits for which Abraham Lincoln posed.

Although Abraham Lincoln himself had moderate views on slavery and did not openly advocate abolishing it, he was supported in the national election of 1860 by those who wanted to do away with slavery at once. The Southern States threatened to leave the Union if Lincoln were elected President, and when he was, they made good their threat. South Carolina, Mississippi, Florida, Alabama, Louisiana, Georgia, and Texas joined to form the Confederate States of America a month before Lincoln took office.

In his inaugural address in March, 1861, Lincoln appealed to the people to save the Union. But a month later, Confederate troops attacked a Federal military post, Fort Sumter, in South Carolina. The bloody Civil War had begun.

Families were divided as brother fought against brother. More than 600,000 men, from both North and South, died in the four-year struggle—more than all the American losses in the two later great wars, World War I and World War II. But when the fighting ended on April 9, 1865, with the surrender of Confederate General Robert E. Lee, the Union had been preserved.

Midway in the Civil War, on January 1, 1863, Lincoln issued the Emancipation Proclamation freeing all the slaves in the Confederate States. But slavery was not outlawed throughout the land until Amendment 13 to the Constitution became effective three years later.

Although the Civil War had ended on the battlefield, the hatreds it aroused did not end so quickly. Lincoln himself was killed by a Southern sympathizer only five days after Lee's surrender. And the problems of caring for and educating the nearly 4,000,000 Negro slaves who had been freed continued to plague the nation for many years while the South tried to rebuild its war-shattered economy.

The Shrinking World

THE world of the second half of the twentieth century in which we live is so vastly different from the world of the last century that it is difficult to believe that all the changes have taken place within the average lifetime of a man. Back in 1900, it took about four days to travel from New York to San Francisco by the fastest train, but today, an astronaut in a spaceship can circle the earth sixty times in that same number of days. At the beginning of the century, there were no airplanes, no radios, no television, and only a few automobiles and telephones. All the modern devices of transportation and communication have made the world seem much smaller.

At the beginning of the 1900's, the presidents, kings, emperors, and prime ministers of the world were remote beings. The public only saw them occasionally, and then at special ceremonies. But today, these world leaders come into your living room to talk directly to you through your television set. The greater speed and ease of transportation and communication have made everyone become more interested in what is happening throughout the world, because events

Below, the leaders of the Central Powers (the Triple Alliance):

Emperor William II.

Emperor Francis Joseph.

King Victor Emmanuel III.

even on the other side of the earth can quickly affect the lives of every one of us.

When this century began, England, France, and Germany were still considered the greatest powers in the world. Since then, there have been World War I, a Great Depression, World War II, and a Cold War. And now, the United States and Russia have grown to rival each other as the most powerful nations of the earth.

Let's climb into our magical time-machine again and go back to the early 1900's to see how things came to be the way they are.

THE WAR TO END ALL WARS

In the early 1900's, the nations of Europe had divided themselves into two opposing military alliances: the Triple Alliance and the Triple Entente. The nations of the Triple Alliance included Germany, Italy, and Austria-Hungary (the remains of the old Holy Roman Empire). The Triple Entente was made up of Great Britain, France, and Russia. Each group of nations feared the other. The nations of the Triple Alliance resented the fact that England and France had staked out a king-sized share of colonies throughout Asia and Africa; the nations of the Triple Entente were worried that someone might try to take their colonies away from them. Both built larger and larger armies and navies.

All that was needed was some minor incident to trigger off a major conflict. This incident took place on June 28, 1914, in the little Balkan town of Sarajevo where a nineteen-year-old Serbian, Gavrilo Princip, shot and killed Austrian Archduke Franz Ferdinand and his wife Sophie. In retaliation, Austria invaded Serbia (now part of Yugoslavia) on July 28, 1914. Within a few days, Germany declared war on Russia and France and then invaded Belgium. In turn, Great Britain declared war on Germany. Italy remained aloof from the war for almost a year, then

The assassination of the Austrian crown prince, which triggered the first World War.

Below, the leaders of the Allied Powers (the Triple Entente):

King George V.

turned on its former partners, declaring war on Austria-Hungary.

World War I raged for more than four years — the bloodiest conflict man had ever known up to that time. More and more nations were dragged into the war as the fighting spilled outside Europe into Asia and Africa. The United States, which had tried to maintain neutrality, finally became so angered by German submarine attacks on unarmed ships that it entered the war on the side of Great Britain and France on April 6, 1917. By that time, Germany, France, and Great Britain were exhausted by the fighting that had raged on the Western Front. The new supplies and fresh troops from the United States tipped the balance of the war against Germany. And the last shot of the war was fired on November 11, 1918, when an armistice (a surrender by Germany) went into effect at 11 A.M.

American President Woodrow Wilson, who had urged American soldiers into action to make "the world safe for democracy," went to France to help write the peace treaty

Czar Nicholas II.

President Raymond Poincare.

Los Angeles Examiner

CHARACTER · QUALITY · ENTERPRISE · ACCURACY

AN AMERICAN PAPER FOR THE AMERICAN PEOPLE · THE GREAT NEWSPAPER OF THE GREAT SOUTHWEST

VOL. XIV—NO. 113 | Official Forecast—Cloudy | TUESDAY | LOS ANGELES, APRIL 3, 1917. | PRICE TWO CENTS | TELEPHONES—MAIN 8300, HOME 10195

WAR! SAYS WILSON; BIG ARMY WANTED

FIRST OF U.S. ARMED SHIPS IS 'U' VICTIM

Steamer Aztec, Carrying Guns Manned by American Sailors, Torpedoed Without Warning Off Coast of France; 11 Missing

New War Horror Reported as

LATEST EARLY MORNING NEWS

(By International News Service)

PASSAIC, N. J., April 2.—A Jewish volunteer regiment of 1000 members is being recruited here. They are preparing to offer their services to the President at the first call for volunteers.

* * *

(By International News Service)

PANAMA CITY, April 3.—Officials here have received a report of a German mobilization at Tampico on the east coast of Mexico.

* * *

(By International News Service)

CHICAGO, April —The nation's food supply received a blow from an unlooked for source today when it was reported that an alarming shortage has developed in the tin plate industry. There are no tin cans in the country and little material from which to manufacture them. As a re-

500,000 MEN NEEDED AT ONCE; AID TO ALLIES WITHOUT LIMIT

President Calls on Congress to Throw All Nation's Resources Against German Autocracy

(BY INTERNATIONAL NEWS SERVICE)

WASHINGTON, April 2.—The address of the President follows:

"Gentlemen of the Congress:

"I have called the Congress into extraordinary session because there are serious, very serious choices of policy to be made, and made immediately, which it was neither right nor constitutionally permissible that I should assume the responsibility of making.

"On the third of February last I officially laid before you the extraordinary announcement of the Imperial German government that on and after the first day of February it was its purpose to put aside all restraints of law or of humanity and use its submarines to sink every vessel that

Here Is American Congress War Declaration Resolution

(BY ASSOCIATED PRESS)

WASHINGTON, April 2.—Immediately after the President left the Capitol, the Senate and House reconvened and an identic joint resolution was introduced in both Houses declaring the existence of a state of war. The resolution follows:

"Joint resolution declaring that a state of war exists between the Imperial German Government and the Government and people of the United States, and making provision to prosecute the same;

"Whereas, the recent acts of the Imperial German Government are acts of war against the Government and people of the United States;

"Resolved, By the Senate and House of Representatives of the United States of America in

CONGRESS RALLIES TO STIRRING PLEA OF NATION'S CHIEF

Amid Scenes of Wild Enthusiasm President Advises 'State of War' Declaration and Men, Ships and Money to Crush 'Foe of Liberty'

(BY ASSOCIATED PRESS)

WASHINGTON, April 2.—Senate administration leaders planned to have the Foreign Relations Committee promptly report the war resolution at tomorrow morning's meeting, if possible, and bring

Typical headline from an American newspaper of April, 1917.

after the war, hoping to reach an idealistic settlement that would prevent all future wars. But he was soon disillusioned by the diplomats of Europe who were much more interested in taking revenge on their former enemies. The United States, as a result, did not approve the Versailles peace treaty. At that time, the American people were tired of war and the world's problems—they only wanted to be left alone to "return to normalcy." So, even though President Wilson had promoted the idea of a League of Nations to help preserve world peace, the United States refused to join the organization when it was formed.

THE RUSSIAN REVOLUTION AND COMMUNISM

During World War I, an event occurred in Russia that has had a great influence on the world even to the present time. A revolution overthrew the Czar (emperor) of Russia. The revolutionaries imprisoned the Czar and his family and eventually executed them. At first glance, this revolution does not seem too unlike the one that took place in

France over a hundred years earlier, but its outcome was far different.

The revolutionary government was taken over by a group called the Bolsheviks who believed in a political and economic philosophy called Communism. This idea of Communism had begun to be promoted some years earlier by a German writer named Karl Marx. He believed that, until governments took over ownership of all property, the workers would never receive enough money in wages because of the profits kept by the private owners of businesses. Marx urged the world's workers to revolt and to turn all businesses over to a government that the workers in turn would run as a democracy. Although the Bolsheviks said they believed this, their government in Russia never quite worked out this way.

A former lawyer called Lenin led the Bolsheviks in taking over the revolutionary government of Russia in 1917. He soon set himself up as a dictator—claiming that this was just "temporary" until a democracy could be formed. Factories were taken over by the government, and the workers were organized into groups called *soviets,* meaning "councils," presumably to run the factories and the government. But the way that it worked out was that the *soviets* mostly just took orders from the dictator. Five years after the revolution, Russia changed its name to the Union of Soviet Socialist Republics, but it continued to be run as a one-man dictatorship. Eventually Lenin died (in 1924) and

"Over the top!" was the command that began the daily charges when the war had bogged down into trench warfare.

November 7, 1917: Soldiers, sailors, and workers storm the winter palace of the czar in Petrograd, once Petersburg, at the start of the Russian Bolshevik Revolution.

was succeeded by another dictator called Stalin. In turn, Stalin died (in 1953) and was followed by another dictator. And so on and on, with one dictator following another —always on a "temporary" basis.

The Russian dictators ran their country with "an iron hand"—even more so than Napoleon. They abolished all political parties except the Communist party. And anyone who dared oppose the government was swiftly thrown in jail, then executed, or sent to distant Siberia.

By the late 1920's, the government had taken over the ownership of all businesses and all farms. From that time on, the government planned what the factories should make and what the farms should produce in a program of Five-Year Plans.

The other countries of the world feared Russia, not so much because of what was going on inside the country, but because the Russian Communists began urging workers in all the other countries of the world to revolt and set up Communist governments. Communist parties were organized in almost every country of the world. These groups met in secrecy—making plans to overthrow governments, sending back spy reports to Russia, and trying to cause as much trouble as possible in order to help along what they called "the world revolutionary movement."

BETWEEN THE WORLD WARS

Although Italy was one of the victors in World War I, it suffered such great losses that the whole country was in bad shape. There were many strikes by the workers, and there were some fears that the Communists might cause a revolution like that in Russia. A former newspaper editor by the name of Benito Mussolini saw a chance to make himself another Julius Caesar. He formed an organization called the Fascists, organized a private army called the Black Shirts, and, in 1922, made himself dictator of Italy. He allowed King Victor Emmanuel III to keep his throne, but took away all his power. Mussolini told the people he was saving them from Communism, and that he would restore the glory of ancient Rome. Later, he tried to make good on his boasts by invading the African kingdom of Ethiopia in 1935. The barefoot Ethiopians were no match for the Italian tanks and bombing planes, so Ethiopia became an Italian colony and Mussolini felt satisfied that he was well on the way to establishing a modern Roman Empire.

North of Italy, on the other side of the Alps, the country of Germany was in even worse shape after World War I. The German Kaiser (meaning "emperor") had been forced to give up his throne and a republic had been formed. But, as in Italy, the country had many strikes and much unemployment, and here, too, it was feared that the Communists might take over the government. A war veteran by the name of Adolf Hitler organized a political party called the

Nazis with a private army called, in this case, the Brown Shirts. He told the people he would save them from Communism and restore Germany to greatness. In 1933, he became dictator of Germany. He began building a huge army with which he planned to conquer the whole world.

On the other side of the world, another country, Japan, also was making plans for world conquest. Earlier, it had become the strongest nation in Asia, winning wars against China (in 1894-1895) and against Russia (in 1904-1905). During World War I, it had seized German colonies in China and in the Pacific islands. In the 1930's, it again went to war with China, taking over the northern part of that country, Manchuria, which the Japanese renamed Manchukuo.

The United States, meanwhile, was paying little attention to what was going on in the rest of the world. During the "Roaring Twenties," most Americans had better incomes than ever before. Mass-produced automobiles—"tin lizzies"—became the commonest means of transportation, and the movies and radio broadcasting boomed as great entertainment and advertising industries.

Then, after the stock-market crash of 1929, the Great Depression descended on the United States, bringing with it much unemployment and hunger. Under President Franklin D. Roosevelt, who came into office in 1933, the national Government took over many services that previously had been left to the states and to private persons. The Government tried to create new jobs for the unemployed, and a social security system was set up to try to protect the aged from the misfortunes of unemployment.

WORLD WAR II

On September 1, 1939, Adolf Hitler decided that the time was ripe to start his campaign to conquer the world. On that day, he sent his armies and dive bombers into

Hitler (at left) and Mussolini (at right) inspect a German Nazi honor guard in Munich, Germany, during a visit the dictator of Italy made to the dictator of Germany in 1937.

action against the unprepared country of Poland. Great Britain and France immediately declared war on Germany. Three months later, Russia, which had its own plans for world conquest, attacked the neighboring country of Finland.

In the spring of 1940, German armies conquered Denmark, Norway, Belgium, Luxembourg, The Netherlands, and even France! Italy joined the war, attacking France from the rear, marching into the African colony of British Somaliland, and invading Greece.

Hitler, like Napoleon, made preparations to cross the English Channel and conquer Great Britain. But the heroic fliers of the British Royal Air Force, aided by the new invention of radar, smashed the German Air Force.

Turning his attention to the east, Hitler—again like Napoleon—made the fatal mistake of invading Russia in 1941. Although the German armies successfully marched deeper and deeper into Russia, winter cold and "the scorched earth" destruction of food and shelter by the Russians stalled Hitler's forces.

D-Day, June 6, 1944: The allied invasion of Europe has begun.

Throughout all this fighting, the United States tried to avoid becoming involved. However, when Great Britain was left alone to fight against the combined forces of Germany and Italy, the United States began shipping large amounts of supplies to aid the British.

Then, the empire-hungry Japanese, determined to be masters of the entire Pacific Ocean, made a sneak air attack on the Pearl Harbor naval base in Hawaii, destroying most of the American Pacific Fleet, on December 7, 1941. At the same time, they attacked United States bases in the Philippines. The next day, Congress declared war on Japan. Three days later, Germany and Italy declared war on the United States.

Becoming "the arsenal of democracy," the United States turned its huge factories to the production of guns, tanks, and airplanes. Hundreds of new warships were built. Millions of young men were trained as soldiers, sailors, and airplane pilots.

The tide of war soon turned against Germany, Italy, and Japan. American and British forces invaded Italy in 1943, and the Italian Government soon surrendered. On June 6, 1944, Allied armies under General Dwight D. Eisenhower, landed on the Normandy coast of France. German strongholds fell one by one. Then, on V-E Day (Victory-in-Europe Day), May 7, 1945, the last German armies surrendered, ending the war in Europe. Hitler killed himself; Mussolini's own people shot him and hung his body up by the heels as a token of disrespect.

In the Pacific, the rebuilt American Navy carried marines and soldiers on an "island-hopping" campaign that captured one island group after another from the Japanese, slowly tightening a noose on Japan itself.

Then, just as an invasion of Japan itself was about to be launched, the United States unveiled the biggest surprise in the history of warfare. It was the deadliest weapon ever designed–the atomic bomb. In an effort to bring about a quicker Japanese surrender and save the lives of untold thousands of American servicemen and Japanese civilians, President Harry S. Truman ordered the bomb dropped on the Japanese city of Hiroshima on August 6, 1945. Three days later, a second atomic bomb was dropped on the city of Nagasaki.

Stunned by the awful destruction of the atomic bombs, which devastated both cities, the Japanese surrendered. On V-J Day (Victory-in-Japan Day), August 14, 1945, World War II came to an end.

Mushroom cloud of an atomic explosion.

THE COLD WAR

Even before World War II was over, representatives of the United States, Russia, Great Britain, France, and China agreed on the need to set up a world organization to preserve peace. This new organization, the United Nations, came into being on June 26, 1945, with fifty-one member

The United Nations headquarters in New York, as seen from the Long Island side of the East River.

nations. At its headquarters in New York City, representatives of the nations of the world meet to talk over world problems and try to solve them.

But the world soon learned it was not to enjoy prolonged peace. Russian troops occupied most of the countries of Eastern Europe, and Communist governments were organized in Albania, Bulgaria, Czechoslovakia, East Germany, Hungary, Poland, Romania, and Yugoslavia. Russia annexed to itself the formerly independent countries of Latvia, Estonia, and Lithuania, and parts of the territory of Czechoslovakia, Finland, Poland, and Romania. The Russian dictator, Stalin, warned that wars would go on until all nations in the world adopted Communism.

England, France, and the other countries of Western Europe lay in ruins at the end of World War II. To help them and to prevent Communists from taking over their governments, the United States gave them large amounts of money and supplies to make them strong again.

As the European nations struggled to rebuild at home, one by one, their colonies in the other parts of the world won their freedom. In the period of fifteen years after World War II, fourteen Asian countries won their independence, including Burma, Cambodia, Ceylon, Cyprus, India, Indonesia, Israel, Jordan, Korea, Laos, Malaysia, Pakistan, the Philippines, and Vietnam. During the same period, more than thirty countries in Africa freed themselves from colonialism.

Russian spies stole the secret of the atomic bomb from the United States. So, by 1949, Russia tested its first A-bomb, and soon it boasted that it had built as many of these fearful weapons as had the United States. The threat of awesome destruction hung over the world. The United States and Russia might go to war with each other, using these weapons and the new missiles that could carry bombs accurately to targets thousands of miles away. Both Russia and the United States spent billions of dollars each year, preparing for a World War III that everyone hoped would never come.

At the end of World War II, Russian troops had occupied the northern part of China and Korea. They supported Chinese Communist forces that conquered that huge country and drove the ruler of China, Chiang Kai-shek, and his army to the island of Formosa.

On June 25, 1950, Communist armies from North Korea attacked South Korea. President Truman ordered American military forces to go to the defense of the South Koreans, and they were joined by troops of sixteen other

Companies of the American 35th Infantry Division enter the walled city of Sumon in Korea during the Korean conflict.

members of the United Nations. Chinese and Russian Communists supported the North Koreans. The first war in which jet airplanes were used extensively, the Korean conflict dragged on for three years, and finally ended in a stalemate with the same boundary between North and South Korea as when the war began.

Fidel Castro overthrew the Government of Cuba in 1959 and established a Communist government less than a hundred miles off the tip of Florida. When it was discovered in 1962 that Russia was building missile bases in Cuba, President John F. Kennedy ordered a naval blockade of the island and demanded that the Russians remove the missiles. The world waited breathlessly, fearing that atomic warfare between the United States and Russia might break out at any moment. But Russia gave in to President Kennedy's demands, and the threat of war eased.

Russia, the United States, and Great Britain took a first step toward international control of atomic weapons in 1963. They signed a treaty banning the testing of atomic weapons in the earth's atmosphere, under water, or in outer space. But, just as the world hoped that the tensions of the Cold War were beginning to relax, President Kennedy was

May 5, 1961: President and Mrs. Kennedy, with Vice President Johnson (who became President when Kennedy was assassinated), watch, like so many other Americans, the take-off and space flight of Astronaut Alan Shepard.

shot to death on November 22, 1963, by an assassin as he rode through the streets of Dallas, Texas.

During the Administration of President Lyndon Johnson, who succeeded Kennedy, American military forces in large numbers aided the Government of South Vietnam in its war with the Communists of North Vietnam. The Chinese Communists, who, in 1964, had tested their first atomic bomb and now considered themselves a world power equal to the United States and Russia, supported the forces of North Vietnam. Communist China's dictator, Mao Tse-Tung, threatened that Communists would conquer the world.

THE SPACE AGE

While the forces of Communism and the forces of democracy competed with each other throughout the world in the Cold War, a new, and more peaceful, race developed between Russia and the United States to see which could go first and farthest in exploring the immensity of the universe. The Russians officially opened the Space Age on October 4, 1957, by sending *Sputnik,* the first man-made moon, or artificial satellite, into orbit around the earth. Over three months later, the United States sent its first satellite, *Explorer,* into orbit. The Russians sent a rocket to the moon in 1959.

Then, on April 12, 1961, the first man in space, Russian cosmonaut Yuri Gagarin, sped around the earth in a spacecraft in the breath-taking time of one hour and forty-eight minutes. (Remember when it took Magellan's fleet thirty-six months to sail around the world?) Later in 1961, American astronauts made their first short journeys into space, and on February 20, 1962, John H. Glenn, Jr., became the first American to orbit the earth.

Russian and American spacecraft were used in the 1960's to obtain close-up pictures of the surface of the moon. And in 1965, an American spacecraft sent back pictures of the the surface of Mars that indicated no intelligent beings live on that distant planet.

The eight-day orbit of *Gemini 5* in late 1965 proved that man can live and work in space for the amount of time it would take to journey to the moon and back.

LOOKING BACK AND LOOKING FORWARD

As we climb out of our imaginary time-machine and return to the world of today, we know that, by having visited the peoples, places, and events of the past, we now have a better understanding of today's shrinking world. (We can read of today's events of history in our daily newspapers or weekly news magazines. We can listen to history-in-the-making on radio. Or we can turn on our television set and actually *see* history as it occurs—some television programs are relayed from any part of the world by space satellites, letting us "travel" around the world even faster than an astronaut.)

Even more important, we realize that, although we saw many important persons during our imaginary journey, kings and emperors, dictators and presidents, millions and millions of other people made important contributions to the events—soldiers and statesmen, farmers and factory workers. In fact, most persons in their lifetimes make some contributions to history; sometimes the contribution is great, and sometimes it is small.

We also realize that no one can tell what is going to happen next in history. The Egyptians who built the pyramids were sure they had reached the height of civilization, and in their wildest dreams, they could never have imagined the skyscrapers of New York City. The unknown inventor of the wheel could never have guessed that someday it would be used on self-propelled automobiles whizzing down super-highways. That great explorer, Christopher Columbus, would have thought anyone was crazy who said that a man could travel around the entire earth in less than two hours. So it is interesting to wonder what unimaginable things are going to happen next. What will the world be like ten, or a hundred, or a thousand, years from now? What will have happened that no one can even guess?

Things to come: This is an artist's concept of a landing on the moon in a lunar landing research vehicle, designed to investigate the problems of lunar landing.

Index

Numerals in italics refer to pictures

The New York Times.

"All the News That's Fit to Print."

NEW YORK, SUNDAY, MAY 22, 1927.

LINDBERGH DOES IT! TO PARIS IN 33½ HOURS; FLIES 1,000 MILES THROUGH SNOW AND SLEET; CHEERING FRENCH CARRY HIM OFF FIELD

COULD HAVE GONE 500 MILES FARTHER

Gasoline for at Least That Much More—Flew at Times From 10 Feet to 10,000 Feet Above Water

ATE ONLY ONE AND A HALF OF HIS FIVE SANDWICHES

Fell Asleep at Times but Quickly Awoke—Glimpses of His Adventure in Brief Interview at the Embassy.

LINDBERGH'S OWN STORY TOMORROW.

CROWD ROARS THUNDEROUS WELCOME

Breaks Through Lines of Soldiers and Police and Surging to Plane Lifts Weary Flier from His Cockpit

---

12 SPORTS THE NEW YORK TIMES, SATURDAY

Home Run Record Falls as Ruth Hits 60th

RUTH CRASHES 60TH TO SET NEW RECORD

Babe Makes It a Real Field Day by Accounting for All Runs in 4-2 Victory.

1921 MARK OF 59 BEATEN

Fans Go Wild as Ruth Pounds Ball Into Stands With One On, Breaking 2-2 Tie.

CONNECTS LAST TIME UP

GIANT DEFEAT ENDS THEIR GALLANT RACE

MAJOR LEAGUE BAS

REDS HALT PIRATES

The New York Times.

"All the News That's Fit to Print."

LATE CITY EDITION

NEW YORK, MONDAY, DECEMBER 8, 1941.

JAPAN WARS ON U. S. AND BRITAIN; MAKES SUDDEN ATTACK ON HAWAII; HEAVY FIGHTING AT SEA REPORTED

CONGRESS DECIDED

Roosevelt Will Address It Today and Find It Ready to Vote War

CONFERENCE IS HELD

TOKYO ACTS FIRST

Declaration Follows Air and Sea Attacks on U. S. and Britain

TOGO CALLS ENVOYS

"All the News That's Fit to Print."

EDWARD VIII ... YORK WILL ... PARLIAME...

CODE FOR INDUSTRY VOTED HERE TO BACK AIMS OF NEW DEAL

Association of Manufacturers Pledges Cooperation for Era of Good Feeling.

ASKS FOR CENSUS OF IDLE

4,336,000,000 Francs Set As French Budget Deficit

The New York Tim...

"All the News That's Fit to Print"

NEW YORK, TUESDAY, AUGUST 7, 1945.

FIRST ATOMIC BOMB DROPPE... MISSILE IS EQUAL TO 20,000 T... TRUMAN WARNS FOE OF A 'R...

HIRAM W. JOHNSON, REPUBLICAN DEAN IN THE SENATE, DIES

Isolationist Helped Prevent U. S. Entry Into League—Opposed World Charter

Jet Plane Explosion Kills Major Bong, Top U. S. Ace

Flier Who Downed 40 Japanese Craft, Sent Home to Be 'Safe,' Was Flying New 'Shooting Star' as a Test Pilot

KYUSHU CITY RAZED

Kenney's Planes Blast Tarumizu in Record Blow From Okinawa

REPORT BY BRITAIN

'By God's Mercy' We Beat Nazis to Bomb, Churchill Says

The New York Times.

"All the News That's Fit to Print"

LATE CITY EDITION

NEW YORK, WEDNESDAY, JUNE 28, 1950.

TRUMAN ORDERS U. S. AIR, NAVY UNITS TO FIGHT IN AID OF KOREA; U. N. COUNCIL SUPPORTS HIM; OUR FLIERS IN ACTION; FLEET GUARDS FORMOSA

114 RESCUED HERE AS LINER GROUNDS AFTER COLLISION

Excalibur, With Hole 15 Feet Wide in Side, Settles on Mud Flat Off Brooklyn

FIRES START ON FREIGHTER

One Person Slightly Injured—Responsibility for the Crash Still to Be Decided

SANCTIONS VOTED

Council Adopts Plan of U. S. for Armed Force in Korea, 7 to 1

THE SOVIET IS ABSENT

Yugoslavia Casts Lone Dissent—Egypt and India Abstain

President Takes Chief Role In Determining U. S. Course

Truman's Leadership for Forceful Policy to Meet Threat to World Peace Draws Together Advisers on Vital Move

U. S. FORCE FIGHTING

MacArthur Installs an Advanced Echelon in Southern Korea

Statement on Korea

BID MADE TO RUSSIA

President Asks Moscow to Act to Terminate Fighting in Korea

MAINLAND ATTACKS ENDED BY FORMOSA

Chinese Nationalists Halt Air, Navy Forays in Accordance With Request by Truman

HOUSE VOTES TO PROLONG

The New York Times.

"All the News That's Fit to Print"

LATE CITY EDITION

NEW YORK, SATURDAY, NOVEMBER 23, 1963. TEN CENTS

KENNEDY IS KILLED BY SNIPER AS HE RIDES IN CAR IN DALLAS; JOHNSON SWORN IN ON PLANE

Gov. Connally Shot; Mrs. Kennedy Safe

President Is Struck Down by a Rifle Shot From Building on Motorcade Route—Johnson, Riding Behind, Is Unhurt

By TOM WICKER

DALLAS, Nov. 22—President John Fitzgerald Kennedy was shot and killed by an assassin today.

He died of a wound in the brain caused by a rifle bullet that was fired at him as he was

LEFTIST ACCUSED

...in a Pro-Castro ... Is Charged—...iceman Slain

"All the News That's Fit to Print"

Mayor Still Weighs Dismissal of Board

AID DEBATE IN HOUSE T... STIFF FIGH...

100 CADETS LINKED TO CHEATING RING AT AIR ACADEMY

The New York Times.

LATE CITY EDITION

NEW YORK, THURSDAY, JULY 15, 1965. TEN CENTS

U.S. Jets Strike a Target 40 Miles From Red China

Raid Is Called Farthest North in Vietnam—2 Marines Killed

JOHNSON ORDERS PANEL TO ASSESS WATER SHORTAGE

Calls for Udall to Report in Week on Problem Along the Eastern Seaboard

DEMOCRATS MAKE NEW BID TO STAY ELECTION IN FALL

Legislative Leaders File 2d Petition With Harlan Despite U.S. Ruling

ADLAI STEVENSON DIES IN LONDON STREET AT 65; JOHNSON LEADS TRIBUTE

ENVOY ON STROLL

Mrs. Tree, With Him, Gets Help but Fails in Revival Effort

By ANTHONY LEWIS

ADLAI E. STEVENSON

Right Man, Wrong Time

MARINER 4 MAKES FLIGHT PAST MARS

Finds No Significant Field of Magnetism—Malfunction in Picture-Taking Feared

Martinis Jurors, Closer to Verdict, Locked Up Again

The New York ...

"All the News That's Fit to Print"

NEW YORK, FRIDAY, JULY 16, 1965.

HARRIMAN MEETS KOSYGIN IN SOVIET; TALK 'SIGNIFICANT'

Conference, Arranged After Moscow Rebuffs, Deals With Vietnam Issues

BID BY HANOI REPORTED

Nkrumah, Member of Peace Group, Said to Be Asked to Northern Capital

Johnson Policy Next Year Will Seek to Prolong Boom

Administration Commits Itself to Spur Economy by Tax Cut or New Spending—Course of Action Still Uncertain

SENATE APPROVES HOUSING MEASURE WITH RENT SUBSIDY

Administration Forces Beat a Republican-Led Effort to Kill 'Rentcare'

FIRST MA... MARINE... LACKS...

C.A.B. to End Limit